Please return item by last date shown,
or renew either by phone
T: 01563 554300 or online at:
http://libcatalogue.east-ayrshire.gov.uk

ALSO BY NIGELLA LAWSON

HOW TO EAT
The Pleasures and Principles of Good Food

HOW TO BE A DOMESTIC GODDESS
Baking and the Art of Comfort Cooking

NIGELLA BITES

FOREVER SUMMER

FEAST
Food that Celebrates Life

NIGELLA EXPRESS
Good Food Fast

NIGELLA CHRISTMAS

KITCHEN
Recipes from the Heart of the Home

NIGELLISSIMA

INSTANT ITALIAN INSPIRATION

NIGELLA LAWSON

PHOTOGRAPHS BY PETRINA TINSLAY

Chatto & Windus

LONDON

Published by Chatto & Windus 2012

2 4 6 8 10 9 7 5 3 1

First published in Great Britain in 2012 by
Chatto & Windus
Random House, 20 Vauxhall Bridge Road,
London SW1V 2SA
www.rbooks.co.uk

Addresses for companies within The Random House Group Limited can be found at:
www.randomhouse.co.uk/offices.htm

The Random House Group Limited Reg. No. 954009

By arrangement with the BBC.
The BBC word mark (and logo) is a trademark of the British Broadcasting Corporation and is used under licence
BBC Logo © BBC 1996

A CIP catalogue record for this book
is available from the British Library

ISBN 9780701187330

Design and Art Direction: Caz Hildebrand
Cookery Assistant: Hettie Potter
Editorial Assistant: Zoe Wales
Home Economics Adviser: Caroline Stearns
Props: Lucy Attwater
Layout/Typesetting: Julie Martin
Index: Vicki Robinson

The Random House Group Limited supports The Forest Stewardship Council (FSC®), the
leading international forest certification organization. Our books carrying the FSC label are
printed on FSC® certified paper. FSC is the only forest certification scheme endorsed by
the leading environmental organizations, including Greenpeace. Our paper procurement
policy can be found at www.randomhouse.co.uk/environment

Printed and bound by FIRMENGRUPPE APPL, aprinta druck, Wemding, Germany

CONTENTS

INTRODUCTION

IT WAS WHEN I WAS SIXTEEN or seventeen that I decided to be Italian. Not that it was a conscious decision; nor was it even part of the teenage armoury of pretension – the battered Penguin Modern Classic stuffed conspicuously into a basket, the Anello & Davide tap shoes, the cult of the Rotring pen filled with dark brown ink – of the time. No: I simply felt drawn to it, to Italy. While doing other A-Levels I did a crash course in Italian and, before I knew it, I'd applied to read Italian at university. I sat an entrance exam in French and German – in the olden days you still sometimes had to do this – with a plea to swap French for Italian. Certain universities then, and I would guess still now, took a slightly condescending view towards the Romance languages: at Oxford, the authorities saw no reason why Spanish, Italian or Portuguese couldn't be studied at degree level from scratch; if you knew Latin and French, they blithely assumed you were pretty well there, anyway.

At my interview, I talked of spending my gap year in Italy, and it came to pass that I did. I think I may have implied that my destination was along the lines of a stint at the British Council in Florence. And Florence was, indeed, where I went – at first – not as a student of culture, but as a chambermaid. I'd sworn to do anything to earn a living except clean lavatories, so of course that's what I ended up doing. But I did learn Italian – after a fashion. A year or so on, in a translation class at university – we had been given the task of rendering, orally, a piece of the *History of Western Philosophy*, or some such – my tutor said to me: "That's fine grammatically, Nigella, but I'm sure Bertrand Russell wouldn't have sounded like a Florentine greengrocer!"

I wish I sounded like a Florentine greengrocer now; I am afraid my Italian these days has the halted stammer of any smitten British tourist. But if I don't spend as much time in Italy as I'd like, I bring as much of Italy as I can into my kitchen. And that is what this book is about.

I fear I never write the introduction to a book without claiming that I had the germ of an idea for it way, way back. It's how I work, though: the books I really want to write are the ones I put off for longest. I will be charitable to myself here, and claim that it must be because I need to let them filter through and become part of me first. It is true that the book I have now written is not quite the one I originally intended. That's how it should be if the process of writing has any meaning. I had thought that one day I would write my "Italian book" and that it would concentrate on food as it is cooked in Italy. As someone who, since putting the project on the back-burner, has bought a whole wallfull of Italian cookery titles (about 500 titles at the most recent count), I no longer felt so driven to write it. I also had a sense of embarrassment about my original idea; without the fearlessness (or arrogance) of youth, I blushed at the presumption of an English person's finger-wagging on the subject of authentic

Italy – for all that I derive much pleasure as well as instruction from many Anglophone Italian cookbooks. And yet still I felt that Italian food was so central to me, and to how I cook, that I couldn't drop the project altogether.

In that family-run *pensione* in Florence, where I worked as a chambermaid, I spent a lot of time with *Nonna* – the paternal grandmother, straight from Central Casting – in the kitchen. She didn't teach me to cook, but I learnt from her. Actually, I cooked already but, being a child of the time in general, and of my Francophile parents in particular, my way in the kitchen was profoundly influenced by France and its cuisine. In that tiny little kitchen in Florence, I learnt about pasta and how the sauce that dresses it mustn't swamp; I learnt to cook meat on the hob, and to make the simplest, scantest gravies with de-glazed pan juices; I learnt about *verdura*, cooked soft and served at room temperature, so unlike the crunchy vegetables that were strictly *comme il faut* in France-festishizing Britain at the time. I learnt a lot more besides. I had very little money (chambermaiding is hardly lucrative, and a schoolfriend and I were sharing the position and hence also the accommodation and the wages) so eating out was limited. I mean, we did eat out a lot, but that mostly involved stretching a carafe of wine, a basket of that unsalted Tuscan bread, and a bowl of tortellini *in brodo* over an entire evening; luckily, when you're nineteen and female in Italy, you can pretty well get away with anything. When we ate in the evenings in our room with a view (squished together on a window ledge overlooking the Duomo) we could just afford a bottle of wine, a loaf of bread, a kilo of tomatoes and some olive oil between us. And when our wages didn't stretch to wine, we drank the vodka and gin we'd bought duty-free on the way over, spritzed with the Aspro-Clear from our medicine bag; mixers, costing more than wine, were beyond our budget.

So, of course, it made sense to be in the kitchen, eating with Nonna. This was strictly prohibited by her son, but he and his wife – Ugo and Gabriella – were often at their farm in the country, and her grandson, Leonardo, was at school, so Nonna would invite me in for company, unaware that she was teaching me how to cook. She taught by example and involvement, the only way any of us really learn anything important. Thus, she drew me in, and from then on, I never wanted to be anywhere else.

But the recipes that follow are not those that issued from Nonna's kitchen: they are what I cook and, more importantly, how I cook, in mine. I've often joked that I pretend to myself that I'm Italian, but actually it is just that, a joke – against myself, more than anything – and I feel strongly that it is essential for me, in or out of the kitchen, to be authentic. What I am is an Englishwoman who has lived in Italy, who loves Italian food and has been inspired and influenced by that: my food and the way I cook demonstrate as much.

So, no I don't claim that these recipes are authentically Italian, but authentic they are nonetheless. Food, like language, is a living entity: how we speak, what we cook, changes over time, historically and personally, too. As I've said elsewhere in these pages: usage dictates form. It has to. Quite apart from there being something hopelessly reductive about endless discussion of whether some recipe may be considered authentically Italian or not, it doesn't make real sense. Not only has "Italy" existed for a relatively short time (since 1861 to be precise) but customs change and, while tradition is to be cherished, the way we cook must evolve. In fact, one of the aspects that is most admirable about Italians and their food is that they manage to safeguard their culinary traditions – with all their anarchic variety – while remaining constantly interested in the new. (Not that this kind of culinary cultural embrace will surprise any Roman Empire obsessives.)

This quality, however, is entirely unregistered by many people, since it doesn't fit with our romantic idea of Italians or their cooking. Our picture of authentic Italian food is conveyed by an image of some glorified peasant past, when food was simple and good, and was enjoyed by large families around a kitchen table. The reality is that the peasant class did not own kitchen tables, often did not have kitchens, and frequently didn't have food. What we outside Italy tend to think of as Italian food is, most commonly, food from the Italian diaspora. In some very real sense it was the Italians who left who furnished the table for those who stayed behind. Their hankering after the produce of home created a huge industry, the vast Italian export business, which fed Italians abroad and enabled those in Italy to afford to eat similarly. And when émigré Italians who'd got used to the spoils of the soil from the Land of Plenty returned to their homeland, they brought new habits and newly indulgent ways of cooking back with them. At the same time, a worldwide market for Italian food was created. Italy (post Rome) has never had much of an empire, but its culinary colonization of the entire world is now almost complete.

What is happening today in Italy is riveting. Where once was a country of regions with often little in common, and where culinary tradition was everything, for no other reason (we are not talking about France here) than that there was nothing else on offer, or nothing they had come across, now Italians are turning a greedy gaze outward. It is true that they still respect their traditions but – as mooted above – Italians are suddenly learning and wanting to learn about other ways of cooking. Not least, this is due to the internet and to global markets in television programmes which mean that Italians, like the rest of us, see people on TV cooking cupcakes and muffins, or fiery Thai curries, in a way that wouldn't have been within the comprehension of earlier generations. I've gone a little further into this blossoming of non-Italian cooking in Italy (and specifically from the Anglo-American culinary canon), where relevant, at the beginning of certain recipes; and I do find it remarkable that one of my most interested audiences is Italian (at time of writing this, the highest number of non-Anglophone followers of my Twitter account come from Italy). Personally this is deeply gratifying, but I find it objectively interesting, too. What I admire about this new-found curiosity is that it doesn't come at the expense of the old. You are welcome to cook, for example, a dish of pasta with aubergines and tomatoes and feta (where "authentically" in Italy ricotta salata would be used) and no one will ridicule you for doing so; they may well try it themselves – provided you don't call it "Pasta alla Norma". (And, by the way, you can find my own shamelessly inauthentic version on my website, should you want to.) In other words, innovation is not viewed with suspicion so long as there is no misappropriation going on. It is for that reason – among others – that I have tried to avoid giving recipes here Italian names. I am not attempting to pass recipes off as Italian. In most cases, it is the inspiration for, not the identity of, the recipe that comes, authentically, from Italy.

You could say that this book is just part of my long love affair with Italy and Italians, one that started as a heady teen romance and has weathered the ensuing years intact. But (compared with some of my others) this is a fairly slim book, and my passion is huge. I am aware, too, of the irony that the number of Italian recipes in all my other books combined, exceeds the number of recipes in this, my "Italian" book.

I was, indeed, tempted to include some old favourites, but forbade myself: all the recipes that follow are newly published in book form, although three of the recipes included have been printed in *Stylist* magazine, another is adapted from a piece for the *Guardian*, and a further one has appeared on my website. It pained me, initially, not to present my Spaghetti Carbonara again, until I realized that, since it is freely available on my website, I could allow myself to move forward, as they say in that splendid foreign repository of Italianness, America.

But before I do, I should acknowledge that my version of this classic is not, in any case, authentic: I use pancetta, not *guanciale*, and I add cream. Also, I add wine (or, more usually, vermouth) and remain unapologetic (for all that I broke the rule by giving my recipe its Italian name). I have made many conquests with this recipe, all of them culinary, I hasten to add, and a lot of them Italian. What is accessible to me to cook with is both more limited and less limited (according to ingredient) than might traditionally have been the case. That's how cooking evolves. After all, we think of tomatoes as being an essential ingredient of Italian cooking and yet they are not originally Italian at all but from South America, and were introduced to Italy only in the sixteenth century.

Similarly, Italians, like all of us, now have access to ingredients that have never been part of their culinary traditions thus far and they cook with them; just as we cook with ingredients that would have been unknown to our ancestors. And, for me, it is in the acceptance not denial of this, that authenticity actually lies.

●●●

Now, all this harrumphing may be heartfelt, but "*a tavola!*" as they say in Italy: time to eat! And, although I am the last person to want to come between a person and their food, I have to keep you from the table for just a little while longer. It's time for practicalities. So that all the recipes that ensue will make sense fully, I must discuss the contents of my kitchen cupboards with you. Don't worry, I am not going to tell you to store canned tomatoes and pasta or the other essentials that anyone who steps into a kitchen has already, but I do want to tell you what I need in order to make my daily (Italian-inspired) cooking life easier.

VERMOUTH

The first thing I have to say to you is **vermouth**. I have, in earlier books, written about my enthusiasm for **dry white vermouth**: it costs no more than wine, it comes with a screw-top and can be kept for as long as needed in a cupboard; thus, you can, in effect, create wine flavour in food without having to uncork a new bottle. I have now expanded this enthusiasm and my supplies, and rely all too readily on **dry red vermouth** (which is rubily mellow, and doesn't require the long cooking time that red wine needs to fuse itself with other ingredients); and I am ecstatic about my latest discovery, rosé or rather **rosato vermouth** (I have found only Italian variants so far) which is sensational in cooking, bringing a blossom-fresh fruitiness to anything and everything, but is also pretty damn good, as it is, to drink, and makes for fine cocktails, too. Highly recommended.

MARSALA So, too, is **Marsala**, as many faithful readers will already know. This Sicilian fortified wine lends its distinct but flexible flavour to many a recipe that follows; please note that "Marsala" in any ingredients list generally means dry – not the sweeter "*all'uovo*", though when the recipe is for a dessert and not savoury dish, you can of course use sweet Marsala; for my part, however, I find it less cupboard-cluttering and more cost-effective to use dry throughout.

SHALLOTS When you start reading the recipes in this book, you will notice that there is much evidence of what I have always known as a **banana shallot**, but which is these days often sold in the UK as an **echalion shallot**. I mentioned these most useful of alliums in *How to Eat* (1998) but I am newly enamoured of them. The point is this: when you're strapped for time or energy, peeling, chopping and cooking an onion can seem burdensome (even if it is embarrassing to admit). In *Nigella Express* (2007) I presented the labour- and time-saving properties of the spring onion; now I want to urge you towards the banana shallot. I won't linger, but you do need to know that a banana shallot is much easier than an onion to peel (you just cut off each end, more or less, and the skin falls away) then you chop it, much as you would a spring onion. And because it is sweet and tender, it cooks much faster than a regular onion. I find all the above things gratifying, but on top of all this there is the fact that the taste of a shallot is transformational, providing richness and depth, but delicately.

ANCHOVIES I feel I should hover around the subject of **anchovies** here, if only because so many favoured recipes of mine start with a rich base of these, melting in a warm pan of **garlic oil** (another essential for me, even though it is not widely considered a creditable ingredient); and I do want to urge even those who think they don't like anchovies to try them once, cooked just to create a base of intense, rounded saltiness, and to give them a fair go. But I, too, wish to play fair and so, wherever I think that another ingredient could be used, or the anchovy be disregarded, I have said so in the introduction to the respective recipe.

The only recipe for which I have not offered an anchovy-opt-out clause is the Spelt Spaghetti with Olives & Anchovies (see **p.26**). I'm not saying you *couldn't* make this without anchovies, but it wouldn't be anything like this recipe. Not that I want to sound unduly proscriptive (here or anywhere else), for I firmly believe that cooking is what we do while in the kitchen rather than while obeying a cookery book – this is not to discredit what I do, but to remind you that a recipe is always just a starting point.

Still, the mention of pasta prompts me to tell you what *my* starting point is, portionwise, at least. I reckon on 100g dried weight of **pasta** per person, on average; there are variables of course, appetite and age chief among them. Other factors that come into play, when it comes to weighing out pasta, are what – if anything – else is being eaten and which kind of sauce partners it. Now, you will notice that the book is not divided into Antipasti (though some of these can be found in the chapter entitled An Italian-Inspired Christmas), First Courses, Second Courses and so on: this is because I don't eat like that. When I make my supper, I make my supper, and it tends to comprise one course, whether that course be pasta or meat or, indeed, vegetables. I concede that many of the vegetable dishes are designed as accompaniments, but not all. Most of the recipes in the vegetable chapter are vegetarian, though not exclusively.

On the whole, I've tried to place the recipes here in the way that most clearly echoes how I cook and eat them at home. This is my way of explaining why not all pasta or pasta-related

PORTIONS & COURSES

recipes are, in fact, included in the pasta chapter; though you'll find a list of other pasta recipes or suggestions on **p. 48** at the end of the pasta chapter.

ORZO   What I haven't done in the pasta chapter, however, is to give full rein to my enthusiasm for **pastina** (small, soup pasta) in general and **orzo** (the one that looks like rice, or more accurately, barley) in particular; all the other names for this type of pasta are listed on **p.43**. I often make this as an effortless potato substitute, if that makes sense, and here's how. You cook the orzo, about 50–75g per head as an accompanying starch, according to packet instructions but check a couple of minutes before the pasta's meant to be ready. Before draining, reserve some pasta-cooking water and when the orzo is draining, melt a little butter in the saucepan, and whisk in a little of the starchy cooking water to help make an emulsion. Add salt and pepper to taste, tip in the drained pasta and beat in a sprinkling of grated Parmesan to taste and as much of the pasta-cooking water as you need to make sure the pasta grains are just coated with a lightly flavoursome gleam of sauce.

PASTA-COOKING TIPS   With this easy orzo, the pasta water comprises most of the sauce, but elsewhere in the book, you will find this technique of holding back some **pasta-cooking water** to help bind a sauce to the pasta – and it is a particularly Italian technique. Please, promise me that you will get into the habit of doing this every time you cook pasta. Indeed, you should make yourself incapable of draining pasta without first lowering a small cup into the cooking water to remove and reserve some for the sauce.

If it makes your life easier (not too much bubbling away on the stove), when you're feeding a lot of people, you can follow a pasta-cooking tip from Anna Del Conte: the Vincenzo Agnesi method, which reduces the risk of overcooking and is as follows. Bring your water to the boil, add salt, then tip in the pasta, stirring well to make sure it's all in and not clumped together. Once the water comes back to the boil, let the pasta cook for 2 minutes, then turn off the heat, cover the pan with a clean, thin tea towel (not a waffled-textured one) and clamp on a tight-fitting lid. Let the pasta stand like this for as long as the packet tells you to cook it normally. When the time is up, drain the pasta, remembering to remove a small cupful of cooking water before doing so.

My only remaining word of wisdom on this subject is also from Anna Del Conte and it is that the water you cook pasta in should be as salty as the Mediterranean. Contemporary dietary mores could not run more counter to such a recommendation; you, of course, are free to act on my advice or ignore it, as you see fit.

BLACK RICE   The only time that I am in accordance with the anti-salt brigade is when I cook rice, apart from when it's in a risotto. What I have mentioned within the book's pages (see **p.80**), but not given a recipe for, however, is a non-risotto rice, the **black Venere rice** from Italy that adds glamour, to be sure, but more importantly, is easy to cook and has a gloriously comforting aromatic flavour. I haven't offered a recipe, because you don't need one, but it would be helpful to have a method. So here goes. For 2–4 people (it will stretch to 4, but I love it left over to make for a very unItalian rice salad, so I cook no less if there are two of us eating) you need 1 cup of black rice to 1½ cups of cold water; I find volume the best way of cooking rice, but if you want weights and measures, 1 official cup will give you 200g of rice and 1½ cups filled with water will give you 375ml. Put both in a pan (salting if you wish) and when the contents of the pan come to the boil, clamp on a tightly fitting lid, turn the heat down to very, very low and cook for 30 minutes. If, by that time, all the water is not absorbed, then turn off the heat, remove the lid, drape with a clean tea towel, clamp the lid back on and leave to stand for 5–10 minutes. And you can leave it standing for up to half an hour.

● ● ●

Before I finally let you into the kitchen, there are a few things I am either honour or (disagreeably) duty bound to tell you, namely:

Always be sure to read a recipe right through before starting to cook.

The Ⓝ symbol above the list of ingredients in a recipe indicates that you'll find information in the Notes on **pp.264–267** about preparing ahead, freezing or keeping.

I often use ready-grated Parmesan, even if it is shaming to admit it out loud. If you want to adopt this bad habit of mine, then do, but please be sure the cheese is fresh Parmigiano Reggiano or Gran Padano from Italy and comes in a resealable tub to be kept in the fridge.

When you have people coming for supper, make sure you get any ovens heated or pans of water filled and hot well in advance. I often do this quite a long time before. Once the pasta or vegetable water has come to the boil, I turn off the heat, but leave it with a lid on to keep warm. When it's time to eat, you can bring the water to boil again, salting and proceeding with the recipe, without making everyone wait for 40 minutes to eat. (But see also tips for pasta cooking, opposite, **p.xii**.)

All eggs used in these recipes are large, organic, though sometimes, where mentioned, I use pasteurized egg white from a carton. Dishes containing raw or partially cooked eggs should not be served to those with weak or compromised immune systems, such as pregnant women, young children or the elderly, unless you are using pasteurized egg which can be bought in frozen, liquid or powder form (and do check the carton to make sure they are indeed pasteurized).

When deep-frying, please regulate the temperature of the oil as instructed and keep a careful watch on your pan at all times: you must always be alert and vigilant.

All olive oil listed is regular (not extra-virgin), unless otherwise stated.

All milk for these recipes is full-fat.

Meat should, for preference, be organic.

For garlic, I use a fine-grade Microplane grater and generally grate the peeled garlic straight into the dish I'm cooking – no crushing or chopping required – but you can mince finely by hand and add it as usual, if you prefer.

If you don't have a cake tester, I suggest you do as the Italians and use an uncooked stick of spaghetti.

For Stockists of specialist items, see my website **www.nigella.com**

PASTA

I HAVE COME ACROSS MORE THAN ONE VERSION of "pesto Trapanese", the Sicilian pasta sauce from Trapani that differs from the more popularly known Genoese variety in a number of ways. Chief of these is that almonds, not pine nuts, are ground into the mix – a divergence whose origins (in common with a lot of Sicilian food) owe much to Arabic cooking.

Giorgio Locatelli, the London-based Italian chef and restaurateur, uses mint as his herb of choice for this; others go, as they more usually do up north, for basil; some use nothing more than tomatoes, garlic and olive oil. The recipe below is rather more baroque in its sweep, which seems entirely right for a dish that is inspired by Sicily.

Throughout Italy, eaters do not grate Parmesan over pasta sauces that contain fish (or are very garlicky), so you should consider cheese here doubly ill-advised, unless you wish to substitute 4 tablespoons grated pecorino for the anchovies.

I like to use fusilli lunghi, which are like long golden ringlets (or, less poetically, telephone cords – and you can see them in their raw state on **p.49**) but, if you can't find them, simply substitute regulation-size fusilli (or indeed any pasta of your choice).

Since the sauce is unheated, it would be wise to warm the serving bowl first but, having said that, I absolutely adore eating this Sicilian pasta cold, should any be left over. It is so easy to make and, being both simple and spectacular, is first on my list for a pasta dish to serve when you have people round.

SICILIAN PASTA WITH TOMATOES, GARLIC & ALMONDS

SERVES 6 Ⓝ

500G FUSILLI LUNGHI OR OTHER
  PASTA OF YOUR CHOICE
SALT FOR PASTA WATER, TO
  TASTE
250G CHERRY TOMATOES
6 ANCHOVY FILLETS
25G GOLDEN SULTANAS
2 CLOVES GARLIC, PEELED
2 X 15ML TABLESPOONS CAPERS,
  DRAINED
50G BLANCHED ALMONDS
60ML EXTRA-VIRGIN OLIVE OIL
LEAVES FROM SMALL BUNCH
  BASIL (APPROX. 20G), TO SERVE

Put abundant water on to boil for the pasta, waiting for it to come to the boil before salting it. Add the pasta and cook according to packet instructions, though start checking it a good 2 minutes before it's meant to be ready.

While the pasta is cooking, make the sauce by putting all the remaining ingredients, bar the basil, into a processor and blitzing until you have a nubbly-textured sauce.

Just before draining the pasta, remove a cupful of pasta-cooking water and add 2 tablespoonfuls of it down the funnel of the processor, pulsing as you go.

Tip the drained pasta into your warmed serving bowl. Pour and scrape the sauce on top, tossing to coat (add a little more pasta-cooking water if you need it) and strew with basil leaves. ∎

THIS IS ONE OF MY FAVOURITE PASTAS, but I must start with a warning: it isn't as easy on the eye as on the palate; this is a dish made for pleasure not a photo-op. In order for the courgettes to acquire the sweet, braised flavour they imbue the pasta with here, they are cooked to a squashy khaki.

I feel somewhat self-conscious using the French word, courgettes, here, but I would feel even more so were I to dub them (outside of Italy or North America) zucchini. Whatever they're called, this is how I prepare them: before dicing them, I peel away strips of skin, which gives them a striped look, and see the photo on **p.22**. This habit is a maternal legacy that I don't expect you to inherit, too. So peel or don't peel, wholly or in stripes, as you see fit.

I like casarecce pasta, which for all that it means "homemade", is produced by most good pasta manufacturers and indeed is so common that I find it at my local supermarket. Casarecce are small, loosely rolled tubes with a gap – where the roll doesn't quite meet up along the side – which catches every bit of flavoursome sauce. The more colourfully named strozzapreti ("priest-stranglers") work in much the same way. Please don't be put off making this should either of these shapes elude you. My Italian friends blithely suggest, as an alternative, either penne or farfalle.

PASTA WITH COURGETTES

Put a pan of water on for the pasta, salting generously (or to taste) when it comes to the boil, then add the casarecce – cooking as per packet instructions, though tasting a couple of minutes before they're meant to be ready – and get on with the sauce.

Put the garlic oil and chopped spring onions in a heavy-based pan (that comes with a lid) on medium heat and cook, stirring, for 1 minute.

Add the diced courgettes and cook for 5 minutes, stirring every now and again.

Add the wine or vermouth, letting it bubble up, followed by 2 tablespoons of the chopped parsley, salt to taste, then lower the heat, cover with the lid and cook for a further 5 minutes, by which time the courgettes should be gorgeously tender.

Before draining the pasta, remove a cupful of starchy cooking water.

Tip the drained pasta back into its pan, add the braised courgettes, or add the pasta to the pan of courgettes, along with 3 tablespoons grated Parmesan and 4 tablespoons of pasta-cooking liquid. Combine thoroughly and taste to see if you wish to add more cheese or salt or pepper or, indeed, cooking liquid, then stir in the butter and most of the remaining parsley and divide between 2 warmed bowls, sprinkling with the rest of the parsley, and more Parmesan if wished, on serving. ■

SERVES 2
200G CASARECCE PASTA
SALT FOR PASTA WATER, TO
   TASTE
2 X 15ML TABLESPOONS
   GARLIC OIL
4 SPRING ONIONS, FINELY SLICED
500G COURGETTES (PREFERABLY
   ORGANIC), FINELY DICED
60ML DRY WHITE WINE OR
   VERMOUTH
SMALL BUNCH FRESH PARSLEY,
   CHOPPED
3 X 15ML TABLESPOONS GRATED
   PARMESAN, PLUS MORE
   (OPTIONAL) FOR SPRINKLING
SALT AND PEPPER, TO TASTE
2 TEASPOONS (10G) UNSALTED
   BUTTER

ALTHOUGH THIS RECIPE DOES NOT ITSELF issue from Italy, the inspiration is entirely Italian. One of my favourite things to eat is a risotto Milanese, sometimes called "risotto giallo" – or yellow risotto – and it occurred to me that pasta cooked similarly, or at least cooked to taste similar, would be perfect, and very easy. So here it is: spaghetti in an eggy, saffron-tinted, lightly cheesed and creamy sauce: it is a bowlful of golden heaven. And see Note to the Reader on **p.xiii** about eggs before you start.

YELLOW SPAGHETTI

SERVES 2

¼ TEASPOON SAFFRON STRANDS
3 X 15ML TABLESPOONS MARSALA
200G SPAGHETTI
SALT FOR PASTA WATER, TO TASTE
2 EGGS
4 X 15ML TABLESPOONS GRATED PARMESAN, PLUS MORE TO SERVE
2 X 15ML TABLESPOONS DOUBLE CREAM
SALT AND PEPPER, TO TASTE
1 X 15ML TABLESPOON (15G) SOFT UNSALTED BUTTER

Put plentiful water on for the pasta and at the same time put the saffron and Marsala into the littlest saucepan you have – such as one you'd melt butter in – and when the Marsala starts bubbling, take it off the heat and leave to steep.

When the pasta water comes to the boil, salt generously, then add the spaghetti and cook according to packet instructions, though start testing 2 minutes early. You want to make sure it's al dente, as it will swell a little in the sauce later.

While the spaghetti is cooking, get on with the creamy sauce, by whisking together the eggs, cheese and cream in a small bowl, adding a sprinkling of salt and a grinding of pepper.

Just before draining the spaghetti, remove a cupful of the starchy cooking liquid, then return the loosely drained pasta to its pan along with the butter and toss it over a low heat. Add 2 tablespoons of the pasta-cooking liquid to the saffron and Marsala in the little pan before pouring it over the pasta. Toss straightaway, working the sauce through the spaghetti, and watch the pale yellow of the spaghetti strands take on the deeper tint of the saffron; then remove the pan from the heat.

Now throw the egg, cheese and cream mixture over the pasta, and toss to combine gently but thoroughly, before checking for seasoning and dividing between 2 warmed bowls or plates. Serve with more grated Parmesan on the side. ∎

"RAGOÛT" IS FRENCH, "RAGÙ" ITALIAN and this meat sauce recipe is certainly inspired by the Sicilian combination of sweet lamb, dried wild mint and crushed chilli flakes, though I've added an Anglo note with a little redcurrant jelly (as well as the dash of Worcestershire sauce). If you were to have more time, then the sauce would benefit from being cooked at a lower heat for longer, but note I do not say "improved". This is perfect as it is, and is one of my go-to week-night suppers.

I do love pappardelle, wide egg-rich ribbons, here, but mafaldine, these Neapolitan curly-edged pasta – like pappardelle with a party dress on – really make my heart sing.

CURLY-EDGED PASTA WITH LAMB RAGÙ

Put a large pan of water on to boil for the pasta; then warm the garlic oil in a small, heavy-based pan (with a lid), and cook the shallots, stirring, for 2 minutes.

Sprinkle in the herbs and chilli, stirring again in the hot pan before adding the meat and cooking for a couple of minutes, stirring to break it up with a wooden spatula or spoon, until it loses a bit of its pinkness.

Add the tomatoes, redcurrant jelly, Worcestershire sauce, pinch of salt and some grindings of pepper, give a good stir, and bring to a bubble, then partially cover with the lid and simmer for 20 minutes.

Check the instructions on the pasta packet and at the appropriate time, salt the boiling water and cook your pappardelle, making sure to check for readiness a couple of minutes before it's supposed to be done. Once cooked and not-too efficiently drained, return the pasta to the pan and dress it with the lamb ragù. Sprinkle a little fresh mint, should you have some, onto each warmed bowl as you serve. ∎

SERVES 2

1½ X 15ML TABLESPOONS
   GARLIC OIL
1 ECHALION OR BANANA
   SHALLOT, CHOPPED
1 TEASPOON DRIED MINT
1 TEASPOON DRIED OREGANO
¼ TEASPOON DRIED CHILLI
   FLAKES
250G MINCED LAMB
1 X 400G CAN CHOPPED
   TOMATOES
2 TEASPOONS REDCURRANT
   JELLY
1½ TEASPOONS
   WORCESTERSHIRE SAUCE
PINCH SALT, PLUS MORE FOR
   PASTA WATER
FRESHLY GROUND PEPPER
200G MAFALDINE OR
   PAPPARDELLE
FRESH MINT, TO SERVE
   (OPTIONAL)

I KNOW THIS SOUNDS LIKE A DR SEUSS recipe (only without the elastic scansion) but it is, as the Italians say, "sul serio", no joke. The green factor is not crucial, but since this came about because I happened upon some spinach-dyed stubby coils of trottole – the pasta shape named after its supposed resemblance (I don't see it) to a spinning top – it feels right to me. Serendipity is only part of the story: I have also always had a thing about pasta and blue cheese, both separately and in conjunction. This recipe is in many ways an evolution of the Pasta with Gorgonzola, Rocket & Pine Nuts in my *Quick Collection* app, and indeed you could make any sort of mishmash of the two. The major developments here are that I felt the need – or rather a fancy – to sprinkle the deep green of the pasta with the paler pistachios, and I add no crème fraîche or mascarpone (as I used to) since a little pasta-cooking water, whisked into the cheese, makes it as creamy as you could wish for. This is not a dietary stance, but because the starchy water doesn't mute the palate-rasping piquancy of the Gorgonzola.

If you can't find trottole or, indeed, radiatori, which have a similarly corrugated form, do not despair. While I love the way the scant but fierce sauce cleaves to the shape, you do get some of that effect with the curl of fusilli.

GREEN PASTA WITH BLUE CHEESE

SERVES 2 HUNGRY PEOPLE
250G TROTTOLE VERDE OR ANY
    CURLED PASTA OF CHOICE (SEE
    ABOVE)
SALT FOR PASTA WATER, TO
    TASTE
125G GORGONZOLA PICCANTE,
    CRUMBLED OR CHOPPED
100G BABY OR SALAD SPINACH
    LEAVES
FRESHLY GROUND PEPPER,
    SLIGHTLY COARSER THAN
    REGULAR IF POSSIBLE
3 X 15ML TABLESPOONS
    CHOPPED PISTACHIO NUTS

Heat water in a pan for the pasta, salting it when it comes to the boil, then add the pasta and cook according to packet instructions, but checking 3 minutes before it's meant to be done. This needs to be really al dente because it will carry on cooking as you make the sauce.

Before draining the pasta, remove a cupful of pasta-cooking liquid, then tip the drained pasta back in the hot pan with 2 tablespoonfuls of the liquid, the crumbled cheese and the baby spinach, and give a good grinding of coarse black pepper. Put the lid on the pan – off the heat, though back on the stove – and leave to stand for 2 minutes.

Remove the lid, turn the heat back on low, and stir the pasta, cheese and spinach together, along with as much of the cupful of cooking liquid as you need – I find 100ml total is about right – until the cheese is melted into a light sauce and the spinach wilted.

Take off the heat, toss with about two-thirds of the chopped pistachios and divide between 2 warmed bowls, sprinkling each bowl with the remaining nuts. Serve immediately. ∎

SOMETIMES I YEARN FOR OLD-FASHIONED PASTA, that's to say, the sort that comes in a creamy sauce, soft and slippery. Comfort is key here, but this doesn't mean I want blandness, and I exult in the husky depth and mellowness provided by the Marsala-soaked porcini. What's more, there's pasta, Parmesan, porcini, mascarpone (which has a long fridge life) and Marsala always to hand in my kitchen, so I know I'm always under 15 minutes away from a glorious and reassuring supper.

I do realize that 250g of fettuccine is an inelegantly large amount for 2 people, given the egginess of the pasta and richness of the sauce, but it tends to come in 250g packets and, frankly, it seems silly to leave 50g in the packet.

By the way, if you're not using egg pasta (which cooks more quickly) you should get the pasta on first and then cook the sauce while the pasta is bubbling away rather than as below.

FETTUCCINE WITH MUSHROOMS, MARSALA & MASCARPONE

SERVES 2
15G DRIED PORCINI
60ML MARSALA
60ML WATER
125G MASCARPONE
FRESHLY GRATED NUTMEG
GROUND PEPPER
2 X 15ML TABLESPOONS
   CHOPPED FRESH PARSLEY, PLUS
   MORE (OPTIONAL) TO SERVE
SALT FOR PASTA WATER, TO
   TASTE
250G EGG FETTUCCINE OR
   TAGLIATELLE
1 X 15ML TABLESPOON (15G)
   UNSALTED BUTTER
SMALL CLOVE GARLIC, PEELED
4 X 15ML TABLESPOONS GRATED
   PARMESAN

Measure the porcini into a tiny pan, such as one you'd melt butter in, then cover with the Marsala and water, put on the heat and bring to the boil. As soon as it starts boiling, turn off the heat and leave to stand for at least 10 minutes. Put the water on for the pasta.

Measure the mascarpone into a bowl, adding a good grating of fresh nutmeg and ground pepper, and when the porcini have had their soaking, strain the contents of the mushroom pan into the bowl, letting the mushroom-Marsala liquid trickle over the mascarpone. Whisk or fork this together to combine.

Squeeze the porcini out over the bowl, then remove them to a chopping board, top with the parsley and chop both together with a mezzaluna.

The pasta water should be boiling by now, so salt it and add the fettuccine, then move swiftly on with the sauce.

In a wok or similarly capacious pan, warm the butter and grate in (or mince and add) the garlic, stirring it over the heat for about 30 seconds, then mix in the chopped porcini and parsley and cook for a couple of minutes. Whisk in the contents of the mascarpone bowl and stir till it comes to a bubble, which should be a scant minute. Turn the heat off.

Reserve a small cup of the pasta-cooking water, then drain the pasta and tip it from the colander into the pan of mushroom-mascarpone sauce and toss to coat, adding a little pasta water to loosen the sauce should you want to.

Now add the Parmesan and toss again; you may want to add 2 spoonfuls at first, then the remaining 2 only to taste. Obviously, check seasoning, too.

Divide between 2 warmed bowls, scattering some more parsley over, if you would like. ■

MACARONI CHEESE IS THE QUINTESSENTIAL comfort-food supper; this version, while even simpler to make than the nursery staple, is altogether more elevated. The cheese sauce is almost instant: no roux at its base, just grated cheese mixed with a little cornflour whisked into wine-lightened chicken stock. For this method, I have the maestro Heston Blumenthal to thank. The stock base stops the sauce – with its three cheeses and truffle butter or oil – from becoming unmanageably rich; the portion size helps too. My decision to bake the pasta in little ramekins was originally made to speed up cooking time, certainly not to be chichi. Indeed, I usually avoid the individual portion approach, feeling it not suited to eating at home. Here it works: cute meets cosy and becomes chic. Of course, it's partly the pennette that make it – think enchanting little pixie penne – but if you can't find them, use the small bulging crescents that are chifferi, or indeed regular macaroni, instead.

MINI MACARONI CHEESE ALL'ITALIANA

Preheat the oven to 200°C/gas mark 6, or heat the grill. Butter the 6 ramekins, and put a pan of water on to heat for the pasta. While you're waiting for the water to come to the boil, toss the grated Gruyère with the cornflour in a bowl, and chop the mozzarella and let it stand somewhere to lose any excess liquid.

Salt the water once it's boiling, and cook the pennette until on the firm side of al dente: read packet instructions and start checking 3 minutes before the pasta's meant to be ready.

Meanwhile, heat the vermouth (or wine) in a saucepan big enough to hold the pasta later, and let it come to the boil before adding the chicken stock. Let it come to a bubble again, then take it off the heat and whisk in the cornflour-tossed Gruyère. The cheese will melt into a mass of gooey cheese strings.

Add the mascarpone to the pan and whisk again, then add the truffle butter/paste or oil – go slowly and taste – stirring it into the sauce.

Tip the cooked, drained pasta into the sauce and stir to coat. Then tumble in the chopped mozzarella, and stir again so that it is distributed throughout.

Ladle the cheesy pasta into the ramekins, trying to get an even amount of pasta and sauce in each. The sauce will seem very liquid but don't panic, as the pasta sucks it up in the oven. Sprinkle the Parmesan on top, dividing it equally between the 6 ramekins, and give a good grinding of white pepper to each one. Don't worry if black pepper is all you've got. It's more a matter of aesthetics (mine) than taste.

Bake for 10 minutes in the hot oven, or grill until golden on top, and let stand for 5 minutes, at least, before eating. ■

MAKES 6 (8.5CM DIAMETER) RAMEKINS Ⓝ

SOFT BUTTER FOR RAMEKINS
100G GRUYÈRE, GRATED
1 X 15ML TABLESPOON CORNFLOUR
1 X 125G BALL (DRAINED WEIGHT) MOZZARELLA (NOT BUFFALO), CHOPPED
200G PENNETTE, OR USE CHIFFERI OR MACARONI
SALT FOR PASTA WATER, TO TASTE
60ML DRY WHITE VERMOUTH OR WINE
300ML CHICKEN STOCK
50G MASCARPONE
1 TEASPOON TRUFFLE BUTTER/ PASTE OR FEW DROPS TRUFFLE OIL
3 X 15ML TABLESPOONS GRATED PARMESAN
FRESHLY GROUND WHITE PEPPER, TO TASTE

I DO REALIZE THAT A DISH that needs an hour in the oven, might not, at first glance, seem to qualify for the epithet "quick", but I'm not trying to pull a fast one. All things are relative, and what makes this recipe feel so speedy is that there is no white sauce – with its roux and patient stirring – involved, the meat sauce takes around 5 minutes, and the lasagne sheets are used straight from the packet (no pre-boiling) and cook in the exaggeratedly liquid meat and tomato sauce. The recipe comes courtesy of an Italian informant of mine from Calabria, where sliced cooked ham and hard-boiled eggs are part of the local lasagne, and is known in Casa Mia as Lisa's Lasagne.

True, this is not as meltingly light a dish as it would be if you made the pasta yourself and rolled it out so thin you could read a newspaper through it, but it is reassuringly homespun and feels like cosy, safe-making food. The high carb content – you really can taste all the pasta layers wodged together – means it's a firm family favourite in my house: a tableful of teenagers make alarmingly light work of it. For the same reason, it is very good party food: I can't think of anything better to absorb excess alcohol. (It's also wonderful cold the next day as a hangover cure.) Should you wish to provide a vegetarian version, boost the number of hard-boiled eggs to 6, the mozzarella balls to 4 and dispense with the meat, stirring a couple of canfuls of chopped tomatoes into the passata instead. Without the meat to bulk up the non-pasta part, it is certainly on the stodgy side, though that is not necessarily unwelcome. But you could certainly increase the cheese content – perhaps adding a stronger-tasting cheese, too. Don't be tempted to use buffalo mozzarella: not only would it be a waste of money, but the less expensive regular mozzarella seems to melt less stringily.

QUICK CALABRIAN LASAGNE

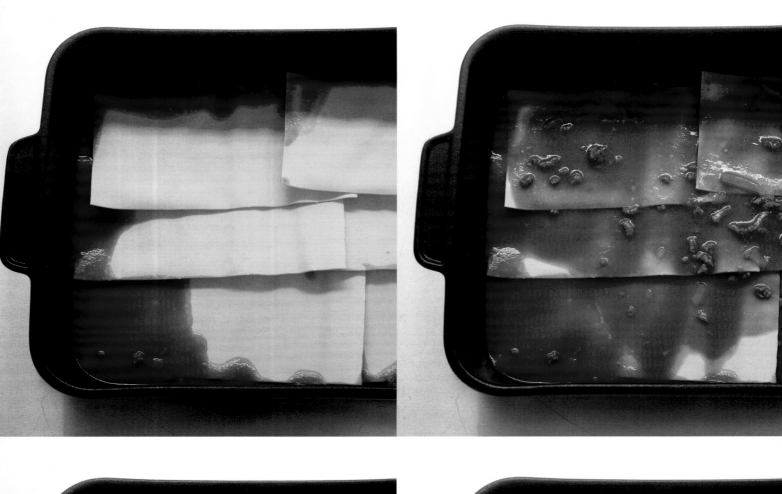

Preheat the oven to 200°C/gas mark 6. Put the eggs into a pan of water, bring to the boil and let it boil for 7 minutes, then pour off the water and sit the pan under an abundantly flowing cold tap; turn it off and leave the pan filled with cold water in the sink until the eggs are cool enough to peel.

Warm the oil in a large, heavy-based pan (that comes with a lid), then add the onion, sprinkle with salt, and let it cook for a few minutes until it begins to soften.

Add the meat and turn it in the pan just long enough for the raw red colour to turn brown.

Add the wine or vermouth, then the passata, pouring the water into the empty passata bottle or carton and swilling it out into the pan. Bring to a bubble, then put the lid on the pan and cook at a robust simmer for 5 minutes.

Peel and finely slice the eggs (which will crumble into a mess), and finely slice the mozzarella; then put a deep, greased lasagne dish, measuring approx 34 x 23 x 6cm, onto a baking sheet and get ready for the grand assembly.

First, put a ladleful or so of very runny meat sauce into the bottom of the lasagne dish, to line the base, then arrange a layer of lasagne sheets – using about a quarter of them – on top, to cover the sauce – don't worry about a bit of overlapping.

Add another ladleful of sauce, just to wet the sheets, then add a layer of ham slices, using up a third of them, before dotting with a third of the egg and of the mozzarella slices.

Now add a second layer of lasagne sheets, then a couple of ladlefuls of sauce, followed again by a third of the ham, then egg, then mozzarella slices.

Repeat with a further layer of lasagne sheets, another 2 ladlefuls of meat sauce, then the remaining ham, egg and mozzarella slices, before topping with a final layer of lasagne sheets.

Pour the remaining sauce over the top, sprinkle with the Parmesan and cover with foil – making sure the edges are sealed – and put in the oven still on the baking sheet, for 1 hour.

When the hour is up, remove the foil, to reveal the top layer runkled like a Shar Pei made of pasta, and push a knife point through the lasagne to check it is soft – if not, re-cover it and return to the oven for about 10 minutes – then let it stand uncovered, out of the oven, for 15–20 minutes (although I love this barely above room temperature if I can bear, or have time, to wait – for up to 2 hours) before slicing into hearty slabs and serving. ◼

SERVES 6–8

4 EGGS

2 X 15ML TABLESPOONS OLIVE OIL, PLUS MORE FOR GREASING

1 SMALL ONION, PEELED AND CHOPPED

1 TEASPOON SEA SALT FLAKES OR ½ TEASPOON POURING SALT, OR TO TASTE

500G MINCED BEEF

60ML RED WINE OR VERMOUTH

1 LITRE TOMATO PASSATA, PLUS 1 LITRE WATER

2 X 125G BALLS (DRAINED WEIGHT) MOZZARELLA (NOT BUFFALO)

500G LASAGNE SHEETS (DRIED NOT FRESH)

350G COOKED HAM, THINLY SLICED

4 X 15ML TABLESPOONS GRATED PARMESAN

IN THE SOUTH OF ITALY, savoury fried or toasted breadcrumbs are often known as "*il Parmigiano dei poveri*", the Parmesan of the poor. These days, many high-toned restaurants think up ways to flavour breadcrumbs and scatter them over costly dishes of pasta, but this doesn't detract from the time-hallowed peasant traditions behind this dish. And I always relish an opportunity to use up ingredients that would otherwise go in the bin. I am not saying you must not buy breadcrumbs (as long as they are not the ultra-sandy, excessively orange ones that come in tubs) but the idea of going out and buying breadcrumbs for a recipe that is about scraping by with leftovers does make me feel a little queasy, even though I have been known to do it.

The thing to do is make breadcrumbs with stale bread whenever it's to hand. Stash the breadcrumbs in airtight bags in the deep freeze and use whenever needed, without thawing first. I am not totally old-school, though: I don't grate my stale bread to make breadcrumbs, but blitz it in the food processor. As a final note on the breadcrumbs, may I suggest you measure in volume not weight? Every batch of breadcrumbs seems to differ in density so much that when I cook with them I go by cup measures, but I have given the weight as well for those who feel reassured by that. How much or little you use here doesn't matter enormously, though. It's just not that kind of recipe.

SPAGHETTINI WITH LEMON & GARLIC BREADCRUMBS

Bring water to the boil for your pasta, salting generously when it starts bubbling. Add the spaghettini, stir with a pasta fork or your equivalent and let the pasta cook according to packet instructions, tasting a couple of minutes before it's meant to be ready.

Warm the 1 tablespoon regular olive oil in a non-stick frying pan and add the lemon zest; it will sizzle fragrantly. Now add the breadcrumbs and toast by stirring them in the warm pan until they turn a deep gold. Remove immediately to a cold dish.

Important step: before draining the pasta, remove a cupful of the starchy water. I often mention it, nearly always in fact, but here it is crucial.

Tip the drained pasta back into its own cooking pan, then add the extra-virgin olive oil and half the lemon juice and toss to combine in the hot pan until a lot of the liquid is absorbed. Add the dried chilli flakes and salt (to taste) and grate in (or mince and add) the garlic, and toss again, adding some pasta-cooking liquid to help it amalgamate into a sparse but gleaming sauce. Season to taste and to check whether you want to add the remaining lemon juice.

Mix the chopped parsley into the toasted breadcrumbs and add most of the breadcrumb-parsley mix to the pasta, tossing well.

Divide between 2 warmed bowls and sprinkle the remaining lemony, parsley-flecked breadcrumbs over each. ■

SERVES 2

200G SPAGHETTINI

SALT FOR PASTA WATER, PLUS 1 TEASPOON SEA SALT FLAKES OR ½ TEASPOON POURING SALT, OR TO TASTE

1 X 15ML TABLESPOON REGULAR OLIVE OIL

ZEST AND JUICE 1 UNWAXED LEMON

½ CUP (APPROX. 50G) BREADCRUMBS

2 X 15ML TABLESPOONS EXTRA-VIRGIN OLIVE OIL

¼ TEASPOON DRIED CHILLI FLAKES

SMALL CLOVE GARLIC, PEELED

PEPPER, TO TASTE

SMALL BUNCH PARSLEY (APPROX. 20G), CHOPPED

THERE IS NO TYPE OF MINESTRONE I don't like, but a green minestrone – one unsullied by tomatoes – is my favourite. The recipe that follows is a remarkably low-effort version with a generous yield: a minor episode of chopping is the prelude to a warming and sustaining meal for many.

I've got a couple of notes before gambolling to the recipe. I specify that the courgettes should be half-peeled, by which I mean taking a vegetable peeler and shaving the skin off in strips, so that you end up with dark- and light-green striped courgettes (see photo below). As I've mentioned before, you do not have to do likewise, but it's how my mother always peeled hers and I cannot do otherwise. As for the rest of the veg, you can really use any you want, and do treat what's below as a guide, in which case work on a ratio – give or take – of 1.5 litres of water per 1 kilo of vegetables.

For normal week-nights, when you may have less of a crowd to feed, you might prefer to halve quantities, though you can still use the whole potato; leaving half a potato palely loitering in your fridge is pointless. But don't rush to downsize: I love this a day or two on, when the pasta's cooled in the soup and you're left with a thick vegetable stew stuffed with billowing soft pasta parcels to be reheated gently, but thoroughly.

TORTELLONI MINESTRONE

SERVES 8 Ⓝ

3 X 15ML TABLESPOONS
GARLIC OIL

LEAVES FROM A FEW SPRIGS
FRESH THYME OR 1 TEASPOON
DRIED THYME

400G FROZEN PETITS POIS

2 LEEKS (200G TOTAL), HALVED
LENGTHWAYS AND FINELY
SLICED

1 BAKING POTATO (APPROX.
250G), PEELED AND FINELY
DICED

1 STICK CELERY, FINELY DICED

2 LARGE COURGETTES (425G
TOTAL), HALF-PEELED AND
FINELY DICED

200G GREEN BEANS, TRIMMED
AND CUT INTO SHORT
LENGTHS

2 LITRES COLD WATER

2 TEASPOONS SEA SALT FLAKES
OR 1 TEASPOON POURING SALT,
OR TO TASTE

2 X 400G CANS CANNELLINI OR
FLAGEOLET BEANS, DRAINED
AND RINSED

500G SPINACH-AND-RICOTTA
TORTELLONI (FROM CHILL
CABINET)

LEAVES FROM SMALL BUNCH
BASIL (APPROX. 20G)

2 X 15ML TABLESPOONS GRATED
PARMESAN

Warm the oil in a large, heavy-based pan (that has a lid), stirring in the thyme.

Add the peas and turn them in the garlic oil, then tip in the prepared leeks, potato, celery, courgettes and green beans and stir in the heat of the pan.

Pour in the water, add the salt, put the lid on the pan and leave to come to the boil, then – you will have to keep an eye, or certainly an ear, on it to tell when – remove the lid and let everything bubble cheerfully for 10–15 minutes or until the vegetables – check the potato particularly – are tender. You could leave the soup to stand at this stage; if I'm planning to press forward within an hour or so, I put the lid on to keep in the heat, otherwise it is better to let it cool swiftly before reheating.

Remove 3 ladlefuls of soup mixture, trying to scoop up more vegetables and less liquid, and tip into a blender goblet (or a large bowl if you're using a stick blender) and set this aside.

Add the drained, rinsed cannellini or flageolet beans to the pan and bring back to a boil, then add the tortelloni and bring it all up to the boil again. Turn off the heat.

Add the basil and Parmesan to the reserved vegetables in your blender or bowl and whizz to a vibrant green purée, then scrape this back into the pan, stirring it into the soup. Let it stand for 10–15 minutes before eating. ■

TRADITIONALLY IN ITALY, THERE IS ONLY one authentic wholewheat pasta dish, which is the Venetian *bigoli in salsa*: rough-hewn, buff-coloured spaghetti dressed in an earthy onion and anchovy sauce. And I see now that the recipe below, while consciously inspired by a Sicilian pesto, similar to the sauce on **p.2**, only without the tomatoes, has much in common with the Venetian original. While this makes my concoction a rather unorthodox marriage between north and south (though historically Venice and Sicily share some notable qualities, not least the Moorish influence evident in both recipes) it is a convincing union. And I've since been delighted to see that La Loren herself created a similar recipe – the eponymous *Linguine con salsa Sophia* – in her book *Recipes and Memories*.

Here I use spelt spaghetti, as it's called on the label – though I use Italian spaghetti *di farro* interchangeably – and find its textured earthiness perfect with the pungency of the olive-sharp anchovies. And, in fact, it has a smoky, subtle strength that doesn't overwhelm less feisty sauces, either. Some regular wholegrain pastas work well, here at least, but choose a high-quality Italian brand, unless you are in pursuit of claggy, heavy indigestibility.

The amount of pesto-like sauce you're making is so scant that you really do need a stick blender, a relatively inexpensive and (for me) indispensable piece of gadgetry, unless you have a processor that comes with a small bowl to fit into it. Of course, to make this in the trad manner, you'd need a pestle and mortar, and should you have one and want to use it, ignore my recommendations on the machinery front and enjoy the elbow grease and authenticity.

There may seem to be an awful lot of anchovies in this. Indeed there are. But for those of us who love anchovies, there is nothing to complain about, and those who feel viscerally opposed to them would recoil at even half this amount.

I must say, finally, that the spelt spag – much like soba noodles – is also good cold, so any leftovers make for a perfect packed lunch. It'll keep for 2 days in the frigo.

SPELT SPAGHETTI WITH OLIVES & ANCHOVIES

SERVES 2

200G SPELT SPAGHETTI (OR *DI FARRO*)

SALT FOR PASTA WATER, TO TASTE

10 PITTED GREEN OLIVES

10 ANCHOVY FILLETS (FROM CAN OR JAR), DRAINED

1 CLOVE GARLIC, PEELED AND ROUGHLY CHOPPED

▶

Put a pan of water on to boil for the pasta. When the pan comes to the boil, salt the water generously, or to taste, and add the pasta; my spelt spaghetti needs 8–9 minutes, so I set the timer for 7 and start testing for doneness then.

To make the sauce, put the olives, anchovies, garlic, pine nuts, parsley, lemon zest and juice and olive oil in a small bowl and blitz with a stick blender (or in your mini processor bowl). Don't worry about the odd unmashed pine nut (or olive); indeed, they are rather appealing.

Just before draining the pasta, remove a cupful of starchy cooking water and immediately add 2 tablespoons of it to the bowl of sauce, then give another brief blitz to combine those last ingredients.

Tip the drained pasta back into its pan, then pour and scrape the sauce on top and toss to mix, adding more of the cooking liquid if you feel you need the sauce to be looser.

Season to taste – you may want pepper or more lemon juice, but I can't see salt being necessary – then toss again and turn out onto a warm serving dish or divide between 2 plates or bowls. ■

2 X 15ML TABLESPOONS PINE NUTS

LEAVES FROM SMALL BUNCH (APPROX. 20G) PARSLEY

ZEST AND JUICE OF ½ UNWAXED LEMON

60ML OLIVE OIL

PEPPER (OPTIONAL)

THOSE UNUSED TO THE DARK CHARMS of spaghetti al nero should be warned, straight off the bat, that this is no first-date food: the sauce is the very devil's ink and I would rather not be observed, by any but the already committed, eating it. There is no absolute need to use black spaghetti, the sort that comes in malevolent Hallowe'en bundles, as the sauce will tint any spaghetti it coats, but I found some black tonnarelli (like spaghetti, only square-cut rather than round) at one of my favourite Italian delis, and thought there could be nothing wrong in intensifying this desirable darkness.

I concede that 4 sachets of squid ink (found at fishmongers or online) is an exuberant quantity, but I need flavour as well as colour. And heat freaks can up the chilli flakes at will. I find using canned San Marzano tomatoes – I bulk-buy them online and hoard them greedily – is the clincher here. They are always preferable, but for this sauce I would be tempted to insist upon them. The acidity of regular canned tomatoes can drown out the subtle sea-scent of the squid ink.

All in all, this has to be quite the easiest, most exotic storecupboard standby: a handful of spaghetti, a can of tomatoes, some sachets of squid ink, garlic, a throaty glug of red vermouth and a sprinkling of dried chilli flakes – if you're fresh out of parsley, don't worry – is all you need to make a fierce but exquisite supper.

BACK-TO-BLACK SPAGHETTI

SERVES 2

200G SQUID INK (OR REGULAR)
  SPAGHETTI
SALT FOR PASTA WATER, TO
  TASTE
1 X 15ML TABLESPOON OLIVE OIL
¼ TEASPOON DRIED CHILLI
  FLAKES, OR TO TASTE
1 CLOVE GARLIC, PEELED
2 X 15ML TABLESPOONS
  CHOPPED FRESH PARSLEY
1 X 400G CAN WHOLE PEELED
  SAN MARZANO TOMATOES,
  DRAINED AND CHOPPED
60ML DRY RED VERMOUTH
4 SACHETS SQUID INK
SALT AND PEPPER, TO TASTE
1 FRESH RED CHILLI, FINELY
  CHOPPED (OPTIONAL)

Put water on for the pasta and, when boiling, salt to taste. Add the spaghetti, stir with a pasta fork or similar and cook according to packet instructions, though do make sure to test 2 minutes before they're supposed to be ready.

The sauce can safely be made while the pasta's cooking. Put the oil in a medium–sized pan along with the chilli flakes and grate in (or mince and add) the garlic, then set it on a medium heat – stirring – till beginning to sizzle. Now stir in the chopped parsley.

Tip in the drained, roughly chopped tomatoes and give a good stir in the heat of the pan. Add the dry red vermouth, stir and bring to a bubble, then let it simmer robustly for 3 minutes; it will reduce a little.

Turn off the heat and – I wear disposable vinyl gloves, CSI-style, for this – squeeze in the gloopy contents of 4 squid ink sachets until you have a darkly, delectably menacing sauce in front of you.

Before draining the spaghetti, remove and reserve a cupful of water, then tip the drained pasta into the pan of black sauce, tossing to combine, and adding a spoonful or two of pasta-cooking water if you need the sauce to be more liquid. Divide between 2 warmed plates or bowls and sprinkle with some finely chopped red chilli – for a devilish finish – or just scatter a little more parsley over them. ■

I HAVE ALWAYS BEEN EMPHATICALLY ANTI-TOMATO when it comes to seafood sauces, liking my spaghetti alle vongole and any similarly conceived dish strictly *in bianco*. (I should, at this point, refer you back to the Quick Calamari Pasta in *Kitchen*, where the sauce is, give or take, just squid rings sautéed in garlic and chilli and splashed up with white wine.) I don't renounce my previous preferences, but find I am now an enthusiastic consumer of the more southerly and less elegant red sauces, too. I certainly love the gutsiness of this fiery, tomatoey squid pasta. Rather like the Sausages with Beans & Peppers on **p.76**, it has all the swagger and gusto of old-fashioned gangster food, which is all the more astonishing since the recipe comes via the coolly northern and irreproachably chic Anna Del Conte.

SQUID SPAGHETTI

Put a large pan of water on to boil for the pasta.

Heat the oil in a heavy-based pan that can take the spaghetti later, then add the chopped shallot and a sprinkling of salt. Cook, stirring, for a few minutes over a medium heat.

Turn the heat down a little, then grate in (or mince and add) the garlic, sprinkle in the 3 tablespoons chopped parsley and the chilli flakes, stirring for 30 seconds or so before adding the can of tomatoes.

Tip in the wine or vermouth, bring the sauce to a bubble, then leave to cook at a robust simmer for 10 minutes until slightly thickened.

At this point, you could salt the pasta water and cook your spaghetti, or you could stop here and reheat the sauce when needed.

Cook the spaghetti according to packet instructions, though checking 2 minutes before it's due to be ready and remembering to remove a cupful of pasta-cooking water before draining.

When the sauce has had its 10 minutes, stir the prepared squid into it, and by the time the sauce comes back to a simmer the squid should be tender and just cooked through, but do check.

Add a couple of tablespoons of reserved pasta water to the sauce, then tip the drained spaghetti into the squid sauce, adding more of the cooking liquid if you feel the sauce needs help to cling to the spaghetti strands. Sprinkle with some more parsley (but no cheese) on serving. ∎

SERVES 4 Ⓝ

3 X 15ML TABLESPOONS OLIVE OIL

1 ECHALION OR BANANA SHALLOT, PEELED AND FINELY CHOPPED

SALT, TO TASTE

1 CLOVE GARLIC, PEELED

APPROX. 3 X 15ML TABLESPOONS CHOPPED FRESH PARSLEY, PLUS MORE TO SERVE

½ TEASPOON DRIED CHILLI FLAKES

1 X 400G CAN CHOPPED TOMATOES

125ML DRY WHITE WINE OR VERMOUTH

300G SPAGHETTI

450G CLEANED SQUID, TUBES CUT INTO SHORT STRIPS AND TENTACLES INTO BITE-SIZED PIECES

THIS IS A REAL HYBRID OF A RECIPE; I'm afraid it might even, in Anna Del Conte's disapproving parlance, be called "Britalian". But I defend it, because I strongly believe that its honest evolution needs no apology. The inspiration lies in the fabulous pasta *con le sarde*, the traditional Sicilian pasta with sardines, capers and currants or sultanas (these, their Moorish legacy) and wild fennel. I wanted to make a faster version that came from our larder rather than the Mediterranean. Canned sardines just don't work for me, at least not in this context, but the English larder stalwart, smoked mackerel, begged to be tried, and – as not always with cooking – in this instance fortune truly did favour the brave. Dill, a herb that I feel is enormously underused (outside of Scandinavia) stands in for the almost-irreplaceable wild fennel.

What this emphatically is not is pasta *con le sarde*, to be sure. But in and of itself it works. More than that, it delights. And it happens to be an incredibly useful storecupboard standby; I can never have too many of those.

By all means use fresh mackerel fillets, if you have a patient fishmonger ready to remove all the fine bones. Cook them quickly in the pan before you add the Marsala, then flake them when the sauce has bubbled a bit. But this is only a suggestion; I stick happily to the smoked mackerel option.

I grant you that salted capers, soaked in several goes of cold water then drained, are peppier than the kind of capers that come in jars in a vinegary brine, but I more often than not just reach lazily for the jar. The banana shallot is so easy to peel and quick to cook that I am happy to use it even on busy nights or when under stress, but I'd willingly suggest 4 fat or 6 thin sliced spring onions if the banana shallot eludes you and a regular onion defeats you. I know those kinds of days, too.

PASTA WITH MACKEREL, MARSALA & PINE NUTS

SERVES 2

50G GOLDEN (OR REGULAR)
  SULTANAS
200G LINGUINE
SALT FOR PASTA WATER, TO
  TASTE
2 X 15ML TABLESPOONS
  OLIVE OIL
1 ECHALION OR
  BANANA SHALLOT, PEELED AND
  FINELY CHOPPED

▶

Put water on to boil for the pasta, then put the sultanas into a cup and pour hot water from a recently boiled kettle over them, enough to cover.

Salt the pasta water when it boils and cook the linguine according to packet instructions (though check a good 2 minutes before they're meant to be ready) and start on the sauce once the pasta's in and the water has come back to the boil.

Warm the oil in a frying pan, then cook the chopped shallot for about 2 minutes or until soft.

Add the Marsala and let it bubble, then straightaway add the mackerel flakes, the sultanas (after squeezing out the water), the drained capers and a few scant drops of red wine vinegar. As soon as the mackerel is warm, remove it from the heat. There will be almost no liquid left in the pan: this is a dry sauce, so be prepared.

Just before draining the pasta, remove a cupful of the starchy cooking liquid, which will be used to help the sauce amalgamate with the linguine later.

Put the drained pasta back into its own pan, then tip in the contents of the mackerel pan along with half the dill and half the pine nuts and a tablespoon or so of pasta-cooking liquid, and toss gently but thoroughly to combine. Taste to see if you want any more vinegar.

Divide between 2 warmed bowls and scatter the remaining dill and pine nuts on top. ◼

60ML MARSALA

2 FILLETS (170G TOTAL) SMOKED MACKEREL, SKINNED AND FLAKED

2 X 15ML TABLESPOONS DRAINED CAPERS

FEW DROPS RED WINE VINEGAR

HANDFUL FRESH DILL, TORN INTO FRONDS

25G TOASTED PINE NUTS

I HAVE NOTHING AGAINST THE SORT of unsauced prawn pasta that relies on the prawns themselves, along with some chilli and maybe a splosh of wine and some halved cherry tomatoes; indeed, I once wrote a recipe for just this. But, as with the Fettuccine with Mushrooms, Marsala & Mascarpone on **p.12**, at times I long for something less robust, more soothingly creamy. Actually, this recipe combines both virtues as, beneath the mascarpone-creamy sauce, lie the electric edginess of dried chilli flakes and the acid tongue of tomato purée. Of course, it does amuse me that the sauce, whisked up pretty well instantly in a bowl, looks just like the Marie Rose you'd use to dress a classic prawn cocktail, but its conception is no flight of whimsical fancy or culinary joke. And I'm also serious about the pink drink: I really do think it is worth investing in Martini or Cinzano Rosato, the Italian rosé vermouth. It gives the sauce a sweet blossominess that white vermouth or even rosé wine wouldn't quite convey. Still, brandy works in a retro way, too.

I generally use organic raw prawns that I find at the supermarket, or else little cooked prawns that come frozen. If you use frozen prawns, they might come in slightly bigger packets, but just bung 'em all in. They will give off some water, but the thing about this pasta is that it sucks up almost as much sauce as you can throw at it, as you can see in the photograph.

Talking of which: yes, this is a rich sauce, and I've cooked more pasta (the egg pasta is particularly filling) than I would normally allocate per head, but that is mainly because these egg taglierini – think ultra-fine tagliatelle – tend to come in packets of 250g, and it seems bonkers to hold back 50g.

PRAWN PASTA ROSA

SERVES 2

1 X 15ML TABLESPOON TOMATO
   PURÉE
4 X 15ML TABLESPOONS MILK
4 X 15ML TABLESPOONS
   MASCARPONE
1 X 15ML TABLESPOON
   GARLIC OIL
¼ TEASPOON DRIED CHILLI
   FLAKES
150G RAW PEELED PRAWNS (OR
   SMALL COOKED PRAWNS)
75ML MARTINI OR CINZANO
   ROSATO (SEE INTRO)
250G EGG TAGLIERINI
SALT FOR PASTA WATER

Put copious water on for the pasta, adding salt later, when it comes to the boil.

In a bowl, whisk together the tomato purée and milk, then dollop on the mascarpone, whisk it in, and set to one side.

In a wok or large pan, warm the garlic oil and add the chilli flakes, giving a stir in the heat, before tipping in the prawns and stir-frying for a minute (or longer, if frozen), by which time they should be pretty well cooked through and hot.

Pour in the pink vermouth and let it bubble up excitedly. When it's reduced a little, add in the pink sauce from its bowl and cook, stirring, till it's hot throughout (and check that the frozen prawns, if used, are cooked through and piping hot, too).

Meanwhile, add the taglierini to the salted boiling pasta water and cook them; this should take about 3 minutes. Be vigilant.

Drain the pasta, though not too well, then tip it into the pink sauce and toss gently but thoroughly to combine. Divide between 2 warmed plates or bowls and serve immediately. ■

I AM ONE OF THE FEW PEOPLE I know who does not like canned tuna, and so I surprise myself by the fact that I love this instant pasta sauce made with the stuff. Maybe it's the sharpness provided by the lemon, the heat of the chilli flakes, the sprightliness of the spring onions and the tender pepperiness of the rocket, but this supper – the easy result of a quick forage in fridge and kitchen cupboard – is a regular fixture in my eating diary. As, I trust, it will be in yours.

SPAGHETTI WITH TUNA, LEMON & ROCKET

SERVES 2

200G SPAGHETTI

SALT FOR PASTA WATER, TO TASTE

1 X 150–200G CAN TUNA IN OLIVE OIL (*VENTRESCA* IF BUDGET AND OPPORTUNITY ALLOW), DRAINED

ZEST AND JUICE 1 UNWAXED LEMON

½ CLOVE GARLIC, PEELED

3 SPRING ONIONS, FINELY SLICED

¼ TEASPOON DRIED CHILLI FLAKES, OR TO TASTE

½ TEASPOON SEA SALT FLAKES OR ¼ TEASPOON POURING SALT, OR TO TASTE

1 X 15ML TABLESPOON EXTRA-VIRGIN OLIVE OIL

25G ROCKET LEAVES

Put a big pan of water on to boil for the pasta and, once boiling, salt the water and add the spaghetti, cooking according to packet instructions, though it's best to start checking 2 minutes before it should be ready.

While that's cooking, fork the drained tuna into a large bowl, and add the lemon zest and juice and grate in (or mince and add) the garlic.

Still using your fork, add and mix in the sliced spring onions, then season to taste with the chilli flakes and salt and, finally, add the extra-virgin olive oil, beating with your fork to combine.

Before draining the spaghetti, scoop out a little pasta-cooking liquid, then toss the drained pasta into the bowl of tuna, onions etc., and mix together really well, adding a spoonful or so of pasta-cooking water to bring some starchy creaminess to the sauce. Add the rocket leaves and gently work them through the pasta before dividing it between 2 bowls. ■

AT THE TIME OF WRITING, I confess you will need to go to an Italian deli or specialist food outlet for fregola, the sun-dried and toasted Sardinian couscous specified for this recipe. This is not an insurmountable obstacle, of course. What I suggest is that you buy a decent stock of the stuff (along with farro, see **p.44**, and any other more recondite pasta shapes you might be hankering after) in one go, so that you always have the wherewithal to hand.

I wouldn't substitute regular couscous for the fregola (or "fregula", as it is sometimes written) which is rather more like dense pasta peas than semolina grains, and thus most comparable to the larger Middle Eastern or Israeli couscous, which *could* be used in its stead. However, if you can't find fregola, I would suggest you try a chunky soup-pasta shape such as ditalini, which is more readily available.

Fregola itself, though, brings a distinct quality: when cooked, it certainly softens but also retains a singular chewiness and nuttiness, which is perfect in this light but clam-rich, spiced and tomato-hued soup.

SARDINIAN COUSCOUS WITH CLAMS

Soak the clams in a large bowl of cold water, and sort through them, discarding any shells that remain open or are cracked or smashed.

Heat the oil in a large, heavy-based pan that comes with a lid, then add the chopped shallot, stirring for a minute, grate in (or mince and add) the garlic, and add the chilli flakes, stirring again over the heat so that it sizzles, though not long enough to let the garlic brown.

Stir in the tomato purée, then add the stock and the vermouth and let it come to the boil.

Add the fregola – it should be covered completely by the liquid – and let it simmer, still uncovered, for 10–12 minutes (or as instructed on the fregola packet).

Check that the fregola is nearly ready and then add the drained clams, and cover the pan with the lid. Leave to cook for 3 minutes at a fast simmer, then uncover the pan to check that the clams have opened. Any clams that, once cooked, stay closed should be discarded.

Sprinkle in the chopped parsley and stir to let everything combine before ladling into 4 warmed bowls to serve, sprinkling with a little more chopped parsley as you go. ■

SERVES 4

1KG SMALL CLAMS, SUCH AS
   PALOURDES
2 X 15ML TABLESPOONS OLIVE
   OIL
1 ECHALION OR BANANA
   SHALLOT, PEELED AND FINELY
   CHOPPED
2 CLOVES GARLIC, PEELED
½ TEASPOON DRIED CHILLI
   FLAKES
1 X 15ML TABLESPOON TOMATO
   PURÉE
750ML LIGHT CHICKEN STOCK
   (MADE UP WITH LESS POWDER
   OR CONCENTRATE TO WATER
   THAN USUAL)
60ML DRY RED VERMOUTH
200G FREGOLA
3 X 15ML TABLESPOONS
   CHOPPED PARSLEY, PLUS MORE
   FOR SPRINKLING

CRAB, LEMON AND CHILLI: THESE, FOR ME, are the tastes of the Tuscan seaside. This fresh, sweet, spiky combo works as a pasta sauce (and indeed I've written one in an earlier book), as a salad and as a topping for crostini (see **p.198**), such as I remember vividly from a summer holiday, years ago in Porto Santo Stefano. I can't remember how it morphed, in my kitchen, into a risotto, but it did, and convincingly so.

Had I time, I would certainly love to have the crab fresh from the sea in its shell, and the coral carapace in my kitchen to make a shellfish-scented stock. Or maybe I just kid myself. Still, it hardly matters, since I don't have the time and nor, I presume, do you, so I buy the crabmeat ready out of the shell, and tint and flavour a weak chicken stock (a concentrate made up to half strength) with saffron instead. It may seem to make more sense to buy readymade fish stock, but I find it rudely invasive here.

At my local supermarket, I can buy both brown and white crabmeat separately; if you can't find, or stubbornly resist, the pâté-like brown meat, then increase the weight of the white to 200g; and do give the white crabmeat a quick check for stray bits of shell before you start.

CHILLI CRAB RISOTTO

SERVES 2 Ⓝ

1 LITRE LIGHT CHICKEN STOCK
   (MADE UP TO HALF STRENGTH)
¼ TEASPOON SAFFRON STRANDS
2 X 15ML TABLESPOONS
   GARLIC OIL
4 SPRING ONIONS, FINELY SLICED
1 FRESH RED CHILLI, DE-SEEDED
   AND FINELY CHOPPED
200G RISOTTO RICE
75ML DRY WHITE WINE OR
   VERMOUTH
100G BROWN CRABMEAT
100G WHITE CRABMEAT
ZEST AND JUICE ½ UNWAXED
   LEMON, PLUS ½ LEMON TO
   SERVE
SALT AND PEPPER, TO TASTE
50G ROCKET LEAVES

Make up the stock, adding the strands of saffron, and put it in a saucepan over a low heat, to keep it hot.

Heat the garlic oil in a heavy-based pan, which has a lid, and when warm add the sliced spring onions and most of the chopped chilli and cook over a medium to low heat, stirring, for a minute or so.

Turn the heat up and add the rice, stirring it into the chilli and spring onions.

Add the white wine or vermouth and let this bubble up and be absorbed into the rice. Now add a ladleful of the hot, tinted stock and cook, stirring all the while, until it too is absorbed.

Turn the heat down and add another ladleful of hot stock and cook, stirring constantly, until it is absorbed into the rice, then continue in this surprisingly peaceable manner until all the stock is absorbed and the rice is cooked. I reckon on this taking around 18 minutes.

Take the pan off the heat, add the crabmeat and the lemon zest and juice and stir, then taste for seasoning. Now stir in the rocket leaves, put the lid on, with the pan still off the heat, and let it stand for a minute. While you wait you can cut the untouched half lemon into quarters, so you can each spritz more juice into your bowl as you eat – though this is as much to avoid waste as anything else.

Divide the risotto gooily between 2 warmed shallow bowls or plates, sprinkle with the remaining chilli, and set to lustily. ■

MANY YEARS AGO, I WROTE A RECIPE (never published in book form) for what I then styled "trompe l'œil risotto", using rice-shaped pasta, called variously orzo, risoni, semi de melone or puntarelle. The version here is markedly altered, not least because rather than cooking the pasta and then dressing it in a creamy sauce so that it *looks* like risotto, here I actually cook the pasta much as I would if I were making a traditional risotto. But there are differences and they are all helpful ones. That you use less water to pasta than you would with rice probably doesn't interest you enormously. That you don't have to stir constantly and that the pasta takes only 10 minutes to cook are obvious benefits to the harried midweek cook.

You should also know that much as Italy respects its traditions, this way of cooking pasta – pasta *risottata* – is actually quite the new, cool thing, "*sciccoso*", as the recently coined Italian word (pronounced "chic-oso"), has it. When I've come across this way of cooking pasta in Italy, it's not in fact involved orzo or other rice-shaped pasta; the "risottata" part refers to the method, not the pasta or the end result. Pennette (see Mini Macaroni Cheese all'Italiana, **p.14**) or macaroni or other similarly small pasta would also work, though cooking times may vary a little. But I love the rice-shaped pasta here most of all: the orzo oozes its starchiness out into the sauce rather than being flushed down the sink via the colander and – what's more – you need only the one pan. I advise that the pan be heavy-based: a small enamelled cast-iron casserole would be perfect although often as not I use a thick-bottomed saucepan.

Many Italian recipes don't specify amounts of water, merely instructing you to cover the pasta, just. I feel it's easier to begin only with an idea of how much water you'll need, but please regard this as a starting point only: you may need to add more if the pasta's absorbed all the water before it's cooked.

PASTA RISOTTO WITH PEAS & PANCETTA

Warm the oil in a heavy-based pan that will take everything later; a casserole or saucepan of 22cm diameter should be plenty big enough.

Cook the pancetta, stirring, until it becomes crisp and bronzed, then add the peas and stir for a minute or so until the frozen look leaves them.

Add the pasta and turn it about in the pancetta and peas then pour in the boiling water; I use cup measures – 2½ cups – for ease. Add salt (cautiously, especially if this is for children – the pancetta is salty, as is the Parmesan later); then turn down the heat and leave to simmer for 10 minutes, though check on it a couple of times and give a stir or two, to stop it from sticking and to see if you need to add a little more water from the kettle.

When it's ready, the pasta should be soft and starchy and the water absorbed. Beat the butter and Parmesan into the pan, check the seasoning and serve immediately into warm waiting bowls. ■

SERVES 2 HUNGRY GROWN-UPS, OR 4 SMALL CHILDREN

2 X 15ML TABLESPOONS GARLIC OIL
150G PANCETTA CUBES
150G FROZEN PETITS POIS
250G ORZO PASTA
625ML BOILING WATER
SALT, TO TASTE
1 X 15ML TABLESPOON (15G) SOFT
    UNSALTED BUTTER
2 X 15ML TABLESPOONS GRATED
    PARMESAN
PEPPER, TO TASTE

FARRO RISOTTO WITH MUSHROOMS

I MAKE NO APOLOGY FOR THROWING such a little-known ingredient at you. You may not be aware of farro now, but believe me, once you've found it, cooked with it, eaten it, you will understand why I urge it upon you. Those who are already familiar with it need no convincing. (But do note that I'm talking here of farro *perlato* – pearled – and not "whole farro" with the husk still on.)

I stick to the Italian appellation, since the customary translation into English as "spelt" is not quite correct. It's not entirely unhelpful, as that's probably the nearest thing we've got, but actually farro is emmer wheat, an ancient grain and staple of the Roman Empire. In fact, I had a good mind to call this "Ancient Roman Risotto"; it would have a certain allure, at least for me who is obsessed by All Things Rome.

I don't suggest spelt as a substitute if you can't find farro, as spelt doesn't seem much easier to come by; instead, consider replacing the farro here with pearl barley. Mind you, I'm ready to start a campaign to make farro more widely known and available. What I love particularly is its nutty wholegraininess but without the hessian-weave connotations.

It's true, it doesn't make a risotto (I don't call it a "farrotto", though I gladly call a pearl barley risotto an "orzotto") in the conventional succulently soupy sense; it is really more of a pilaff. But whatever it is, it works. The lack of gluten in the grain means it won't get sticky and starchy, and the upside here is that you don't need to stir while it cooks, as you do with risotto rice. You bung it into a pan, stock in, lid on – and you're done, pretty much. Regard this as a blueprint for further farro risotti but also consider the farro itself as a pastina-substitute in soups.

Were I in Italy, in the right season of course, I'd plump for the gorgeous treat of fresh porcini, but my compromise (though none in flavour) is to use dried porcini boosted with chestnut mushrooms which, when sliced, reveal beautiful bronze-edged white flesh, firm and compact. And the garlicky, thyme-scented, bosky smell of the mushrooms as they cook is heady heaven. If you find yourself in an Italian deli, do pick up some porcini stock cubes, but otherwise use vegetable or chicken stock here, depending on whether you need this to be vegetarian or not.

I cook this as a meal in itself, but it could as easily be brought out as a side dish. And it reheats wonderfully, so not only are leftovers (unlike with a conventional risotto) a positive blessing but you can cook it in advance, which makes it a real boon when you have people over for supper.

Cover the dried porcini with 125ml of recently boiled water, then fill the kettle and switch it on again if you are making up the stock with concentrate, cube or powder.

In a wide, heavy-based pan (that comes with a lid) add 2 tablespoons of the oil and the fine jade tangle of leek, and cook, stirring frequently, for about 5 minutes or until the leeks are softened.

Drain the porcini, reserving the soaking liquid, then chop them and add them to the pan.

Stir well, then add the farro and turn it gently but thoroughly in the pan. Tip in the Marsala and porcini-soaking water and let it bubble up.

Make up the stock as wished and add this to the farro pan, stir, bring to the boil and then clamp on a lid, turn down the heat and let it cook at a simmer for 30 minutes until the farro is cooked and all the liquid absorbed.

While the farro is cooking, warm the remaining 2 tablespoons oil in a medium-sized frying pan and cook the sliced chestnut mushrooms for about 5 minutes or until they begin to soften – they will first seem alarmingly dry – at which point add the thyme, grate in (or mince and add) the garlic, and cook for a further 5 minutes or until the mushrooms are juicy and soft. Remove from the heat if there is still time on the clock for the farro.

Once the farro is cooked, take it off the heat, too, and add the cooked mushrooms.

Stir in the ricotta and Parmesan – they will melt in the heat of the farro – until the farro is creamy, then sprinkle with parsley and serve. ■

SERVES 4–6 Ⓝ

10G DRIED PORCINI

125ML RECENTLY BOILED WATER

4 X 15ML TABLESPOONS
   OLIVE OIL

1 LEEK (WASHED AND TRIMMED),
   HALVED LENGTHWAYS AND
   FINELY SLICED

500G PEARLED FARRO (*PERLATO*)

60ML MARSALA

1.25 LITRES STOCK, VEGETABLE,
   CHICKEN OR PORCINI

250G CHESTNUT MUSHROOMS,
   SLICED

LEAVES FROM A FEW SPRIGS
   FRESH THYME OR ½ TEASPOON
   DRIED THYME

1 CLOVE GARLIC, PEELED

4 X 15ML TABLESPOONS RICOTTA

4 X 15ML TABLESPOONS GRATED
   PARMESAN

APPROX. 3 X 15ML TABLESPOONS
   CHOPPED FRESH PARSLEY, TO
   SERVE

AND SEE ALSO...

As mentioned in the Introduction, I have other pasta recipes not in this pasta chapter, but dotted about elsewhere, and these are:

Gnocchi Gratin on **p.131**; Pappardelle with Chestnuts & Pancetta on **p.212**; Hearty Wholewheat Pasta with Brussels Sprouts, Cheese & Potato on **p.214**; Mountain Macaroni on **p.216**; Pasta & Lentils on **p.263**.

And – although it comes earlier in the book than some of the above, I do feel it needs solo star billing – Chocolate Pasta with Pecans & Caramel on **p.192**.

But there are suggestions I've made, too, for turning other recipes into pasta sauces and dishes, which you'll see when you come across Squid & Prawns with Chilli & Marjoram on **p.80**; Cod with Broccoli & Chilli on **p.82**; Chicken with Tarragon Salsa Verde on **p.94**; Cherry Tomatoes with Olives on **p.104**; Peas with Pancetta on **p.106**; Garlic Mushrooms with Chilli & Lemon on **p.119**; Chilli Tomato Sauce on **p.209**; and Spaghetti Spice on **p.235**.

FLESH, FISH & FOWL

LAMB CUTLETS WITH MINT, CHILLI & GOLDEN POTATOES

THERE ARE FEW THINGS MORE CHEERING than a platter piled with food. This sentiment is not entirely fuelled by greed: I always feel uplifted by a welcoming sense of plenty; I get pleasure from being able to bring good things to the table. The joy of this supper is that it is not just the eater who is cheered, but the cook, too; an essential deal, when you come to think of it.

If you put your halved baby potatoes on to steam before you get started on the lamb chops, you can fairly effortlessly rely on a proper meat-and-potato supper in around 20 minutes (plus a little marinating time). Steaming the potatoes is, for me, an important stipulation: a steamed spud is a sweet spud; more than that, cooked this way, rather than by boiling, the potatoes are dry when done, which makes them easy to fry to crisp bronzedness, without spitting, later. It's important, though, that you don't fill your pot with too much water first. If new potatoes aren't around, then use a couple of baking potatoes, cut into 1cm dice. Steaming here would be obligatory rather than merely desirable, as the potato chunks would dissolve into mush in boiling water.

As for what else to serve with this: as ever, I'd suggest strewing some rocket over the platter first (about 100g should provide enough leafage to make this a salad rather than a garnish), but any leaves that are good and in season will do. I am always on for radicchio of some variety (and see **p.229**).

I concede that celery salt, essential component of Bloody Mary and condiment for gulls' eggs, is not an intrinsic part of the Italian larder, but celery itself is a pervasive back-note of the savoury cooking of Italy, indeed it's one of the famous *odori*, the bunch of essential herbs and flavourings you can get from greengrocers there. If celery salt is not to hand, though, do not give it another thought: just sprinkle a little sea salt in its place.

Put the halved baby potatoes on to steam.

Get out a large dish – in which the lamb cutlets will fit in a single layer – and first pour into it the olive oil and sprinkle in the chilli flakes, dried mint and celery salt.

Using 1 lamb cutlet as if it were a wooden spoon, smoosh the oil with its sprinklings around a bit, so that it is rather better mixed, then place the lamb cutlets in a single layer, turn them instantly, and leave to marinate for 10 minutes.

Heat a large, heavy-based, non-stick frying pan – big enough (about 28cm diameter) for all the cutlets to fit in – then duly place them all in it (the oil that clings to them from the marinade is plenty enough for them to fry in) and fry over a medium heat for 5 minutes. While the cutlets cook, check that the potatoes are tender, which they should be by now; in which case, turn the heat off under your steamer, pour off the water and let the potatoes stand, drying, while they wait.

Using tongs (for ease), turn the cutlets over and cook for a further 3 minutes. If you are going to make this an entire one-plate meal, strew the bottom of a large serving platter with rocket, or any other leafage you desire, and when the lamb cutlets are cooked, but still juicily pink, remove them to the salad-lined (or, indeed, naked) plate. Obviously, cook for longer if you like your lamb well done.

Tip the steamed potatoes into the pan and fry for 3 minutes, then turn them over and fry for another 3 minutes, shaking the pan every now and again to make them tumble and turn in the hot, spiced fat.

Using a slotted spatula or similar, transfer the potatoes to the plate of cutlets and sprinkle with 1 teaspoon of sea salt flakes (I like these plenty salty, but if you have more austere tastes or are feeding small children, then decrease the salt or ignore the command altogether) along with the chopped parsley and mint. ■

SERVES 4

500G BABY NEW POTATOES, HALVED BUT NOT PEELED

3 X 15ML TABLESPOONS OLIVE OIL

½ TEASPOON DRIED CHILLI FLAKES

1 TEASPOON DRIED MINT

½ TEASPOON CELERY SALT

8 LAMB CUTLETS, FRENCH TRIMMED

100G ROCKET, TO SERVE (OPTIONAL)

1 TEASPOON SEA SALT FLAKES OR ½ TEASPOON POURING SALT, OR TO TASTE

1 X 15ML TABLESPOON CHOPPED FRESH PARSLEY

1 X 15ML TABLESPOON CHOPPED FRESH MINT

THIS MAY BE A RECIPE THAT CONTAINS only a handful of ingredients and one, moreover, that takes scarcely 10 minutes from the time you kick off at the stove till supper's on the table, and yet it conveys real richness of flavour and punchy elegance. There is something about the saltiness of anchovies with the sweetness of lamb that works with barely any effort on your part. I love the floral fragrance of the rosé vermouth at the end, but if you can't get hold of that, a sweet – but not cream – sherry along with a sprinkling of lemon or orange zest should do the trick. Anchovy-phobes, poor creatures, can dispense with them but add salt, to taste, along with the vermouth.

I like this – yet again – with nothing more than some peppery rocket, but the fierce flavour of the de-glazing juices really makes tomatoes zing, too. And I would never rule out some wilted spinach or good bread, either.

LAMB STEAKS WITH ANCHOVIES & THYME

Warm the garlic oil in a heavy-based, non-stick frying pan and fry the lamb steaks for about 2 minutes a side, or until they are as pink (or not) as you like.

Remove the steaks to a board lined with foil and turn up the ends so any meat juices that run out are contained.

Off the heat, add the anchovy fillets to the pan and stir until they start to break up and begin melting into the pan. Put it back on the heat and, still stirring, add the thyme leaves.

Now add the pink vermouth and let it bubble up in the pan, then pour in the juices that have collected from the lamb steaks, placing the steaks on a couple of warmed plates as you do so. Let the sauce continue boiling until it's thickened – 30 seconds should do it – and pour it over the waiting steaks. Eat immediately and with gusto. ■

SERVES 2
1 X 15ML TABLESPOON
    GARLIC OIL
2 BONELESS LAMB LEG STEAKS
    (APPROX. 100G EACH)
4 ANCHOVY FILLETS
LEAVES FROM A FEW SPRIGS
    FRESH THYME (APPROX.
    1 TEASPOONFUL)
60ML MARTINI OR CINZANO
    ROSATO

A ROAST, BONED, BUTTERFLIED LEG OF LAMB is just about the easiest, speediest way to cook a joint of meat. Plus, you dispense with all the difficult carving (I am an embarrassingly inept carver myself) as all you need to do is slice the boned meat once it's cooked, which even I can manage without stress.

I've cooked this a number of ways over the years, probably most often with rosemary and lemon and I am tempted to borrow the anchovy, thyme and pink vermouth approach from the lamb steaks on the previous page, too, but this less in-your-face marinade highlights the sweetness of the lamb and imbues it with a definite but not intrusive flavour that makes it more universally appealing, which is a crucial factor when cooking for greater numbers.

I say marinade, but really, I just leave the lamb – which I get from my butcher, boned and butterflied – to steep in the tin while it comes to room temperature. From then on in, it's only a half-hour blitz in the hot oven, followed by quarter of an hour's rest. It could hardly be simpler.

The heat of the oven, with the sugar in the vinegar, does mean that you will get scorched, even blackened, spots on the tin. This doesn't bother me unduly, but you might want to line the tin with foil first.

BUTTERFLIED LEG OF LAMB WITH BAY LEAVES & BALSAMIC VINEGAR

SERVES 8 Ⓝ

1.5KG (APPROX.) BONED AND BUTTERFLIED LEG OF LAMB

6 FRESH BAY LEAVES, SNIPPED, PLUS WHOLE LEAVES (OPTIONAL), TO SERVE

2 TEASPOONS SEA SALT FLAKES, OR TO TASTE

4 X 15ML TABLESPOONS OLIVE OIL

2 X 15ML TABLESPOONS BALSAMIC VINEGAR

3 GARLIC CLOVES, PEELED AND SLICED FINELY

Preheat the oven to 220°C/gas mark 7. Get out a shallow but sturdy roasting tin and put the butterflied leg of lamb in it, skin-side down.

Scatter with the snipped bay leaves and half the salt and pour the oil and vinegar over the lamb, then push the garlic slices into crevices where you can and lay the rest on top. Leave to marinate just until the lamb gets to room temperature.

Turn the lamb over, so it is now skin-side up, sprinkle with the remaining salt flakes and roast in the hot oven for 30 minutes.

Remove from the oven, tent with foil, and let it stand for 15 minutes: this will give you lusciously pink lamb; if you want the meat slightly less pink, then let it stand, under its foil, for 30 minutes.

I like to slice the meat and serve it in its piquant juices in the tin, but if you prefer – and for more formal occasions it does make sense – you can arrange the meat on a warmed serving platter and add a little boiling water – maybe an espresso cupful or so – to the juices in the tin before pouring them over the meat on the platter. A few more fresh bay leaves strewn over the meat will add to the aesthetic pleasure of the arrangement, too. ■

PORK CHOPS WITH FENNEL SEEDS & ALLSPICE

IN AN EARLIER BOOK, *FOREVER SUMMER*, I presented my domestic take on that aromatic Italian marketplace staple, *porchetta*, in the form of a boned and butterflied shoulder of pork, smeared with a paste made of onions cooked with garlic, fennel seeds, rosemary, bay, cloves and peppercorns, to be rolled up, roasted and, after its low and slow cooking, cut into melting slabs and eaten in a split ciabatta roll. What I give you here is the quick-time, pared-down version. Or, if I'm honest, not so much a version as an everyday recipe inspired by it. I'm happy with that: the *porchetta* needs around 30 hours for optimal results; the recipe below gives you a fennel-flavoured, glossy-gravied supper in about 15 minutes.

I'd be all in favour of adding some rosemary (or sage) to the dredging mixture, but without the long time in the oven that a great big rolled joint of meat gets, you do need to oomph up the deeper, more aromatic spices, which means adding allspice to the pinch of cloves. The celery salt is authentic neither to Italy in general, as I've mentioned earlier, nor *porchetta* in particular, but it provides punch and flavoursome feistiness. Spicing may be a matter of taste, and one that withstands infinite variation, but I cannot be quite so relaxed about everything. So listen up: it is vital that the pork chops have some fat to them; I don't mean the strip that runs alongside the chops – you can trim that – but the marbling in the meat itself. Without this fat, the meat will be tasteless and as densely woven as a jumper that's gone through the hot wash by mistake (and about as good to eat). Pork in the UK, especially in supermarkets, is reared to be indigestibly lean. Luckily, there is the beginning of a backlash. Be part of it.

It's also important that the pan you use is a neat fit for the chops; any bit of pan that is over the heat but uncovered with meat will just start to make your kitchen smoky. I find a 23cm frying pan perfect here; it helps that it is heavy-based and non-stick.

And a last bit of fine-tuning: I do know that the amounts of flour, modest as they are, will give you some left over but, if there is any less, it is too difficult to dredge the pork chops properly. I am not an advocate of waste, indeed I disapprove very fiercely of even a hint of it, but I can live with throwing away a spoonful of flour.

I'd suggest with this, if you have time, mashed potatoes (along with some steamed spinach or green beans); as it is, I gladly refer you to the Mock Mash on **p.136**.

Cut the rind and most of the outer fat off the pork chops. A terrible shame, I know, but the fat is unlikely to cook in time. (As said above, it is the filigree network of fat in the meat that you need here.)

Mix the flour, spices and seasonings, including a good grinding of pepper, in a small, flat dish and dredge the pork chops thoroughly all over.

Leave the chops sitting in their floury dish while you warm the garlic oil in a heavy-based frying pan, preferably non-stick, in which the 2 chops fit snugly. Duly add and cook the pork chops for 5 minutes on one side, making sure the heat is not so hot that the chops burn.

Turn the chops over and cook for another 5 minutes, then pour in the Marsala and give the chops a further 5 minutes on a low-medium heat, testing to see they are cooked through before removing them to a couple of warmed plates.

Give the sauce a swirl in the pan over the heat, checking to see that it has thickened and become a rich, glossy chestnut, then pour it over the chops. Serve immediately. ■

SERVES 2

2 PORK CHOPS, NOT TOO LEAN
  (SEE ABOVE)
3 X 15ML TABLESPOONS FLOUR
2 TEASPOONS FENNEL SEEDS
½ TEASPOON GROUND ALLSPICE
½ TEASPOON CELERY SALT
PINCH GROUND CLOVES
FRESHLY GROUND PEPPER
2 X 15ML TABLESPOONS
  GARLIC OIL
75ML MARSALA

PORK LOIN WITH PARMA HAM & OREGANO

ONE DAY I WOULD LOVE TO learn a bit of butchery, but in the meantime I am more than happy, grateful even, to defer to the experts. That's to say, I ask my butcher for a loin of pork, requesting that, once boned and with the rind off, it weigh around 1.5kg, and then I throw in that I want it opened out "like a book", as I want to stuff it and roll it up.

Sometimes, I have to take a knife to it myself just to open up one end part, if I feel there is an uneven chunkiness. I am not going for professional uniformity, but I need a slab of meat with room to have some thin slices of ham lining the inside and that can then be rolled into a log and tied. Probably it's better I don't try to explain any more here. You'll see the end result in the picture opposite.

It's certainly a simple recipe to do. And that's why it's here, despite the fact that it needs about 1¼ hours to cook. The thing about this is that it is quick to stuff and roll and then you've got nothing to do, which means it is perfect for keeping you calm and your guests contented when you have people over for supper.

Furthermore, the end result provides a gravy that more or less makes itself. The onions, which are sliced to provide a podium for the pork – a flavour-platform – drip their juices into the pan as the meat roasts, and from the meat, too, come the intense drips of Parma ham, oregano and garlic. As the meat rests, I throw vermouth and hot water into the pan, and because vermouth (unlike wine) doesn't need mellowing out, you can at this stage just walk away and let the liquid do its work without you.

I love to set these flavoursome rounds on a bed of peppery rocket – and I know this suggestion is one you hear often from me. To make life even rosier, may I suggest some plain green beans and Mock Mash (see **p.136**) alongside?

And there's one more thing. You may have noticed that I said the pork loin should be de-rinded. However, you do still want the rind, or I certainly do. Although crackling may not be renowned as an Italian delicacy, the *ciccioli* (pronounced, rather enchantingly, "cheecholli") – as Italian pork scratchings (give or take) are known – make for a very fine aperitivo-accompanying morsel (my vote here goes to Prosecco, tinted orange with Aperol). What I like to do, before the pork gets its roasting, is to cook the rind in the oven, preheated as overleaf, for 30 minutes on a rack above a tin, then I break up the pieces and put them out on a few saucers, sprinkled with sea salt flakes, for people to crunch on and keep their dentists in business. Speaking of which, if you've got your pork from the butcher, you should take the bones that have been removed, too, and cook them in the tin with the rolled joint. I like to gnaw on these privately: cook's treat.

Preheat the oven to 200°C/gas mark 6. Open up the loin of pork, ready for stuffing, by laying it out in front of you vertically so that the thick part is on the left (I'm right-handed). Now, starting at the top, cut through this thick part of the loin, all the way down, so that you can open it out to the left like a book. This will give you a larger surface area to lay the filling on.

Grate or mince the garlic cloves, and spread the pungent purée all over the meat. Then take the leaves from a few sprigs of oregano and dot them about too; keep the stalks.

Lay the pieces of ham horizontally over the pork loin; this way it will roll up more easily as the roll will follow the long length of the ham slices.

Sprinkle the chilli flakes over the ham and then roll up the loin, starting from the opened end side, keeping as tight a roll as you can. Secure the meat with string at 3 or 4cm intervals, knotting the lengths of string firmly. If you're using stationer's string rather than cook's twine, dampen it first. I wish I could instruct you as to how to tie proper knots, but I do very bad knots myself. Were you to have the offer of a friendly hand – or rather finger – to hold the knot down as you tie it, take it gratefully.

Cut the onion into thick slices without peeling it, and sit them in the bottom of a roasting tin to make the flavour-platform for the pork. Add the reserved stalks from the oregano, sit the loin on top and drizzle with the oil.

Cook for 1¼ hours; when it's cooked, the juices must run clear when you put a skewer into the centre and a meat thermometer should read 71°C.

Transfer the tin to a heatproof kitchen surface, immediately pour the vermouth and boiling water into the tin and scrape all around the bottom of the tin so any oniony, meaty stuck-on bits dissolve into this instant gravy. You can let the meat rest in this sauce for 15 minutes or so.

When you are ready to slice the pork, remove it to a board and warm the gravy (removing the onion bits) if it's cooled. Cut the meat into approximately 2cm slices, in other words, thick enough for the slices to keep their shape and hold the filling. Discard the string as you go. This size joint should give you 10 good slices plus the misshapen end pieces.

Arrange these sturdy slices on a bed of rocket with the gravy served separately in a little jug, or just sit them on a warm platter and pour over them a little gravy or any extra juices the meat has made. Take some more oregano leaves and strew them over the pork slices before serving. ■

SERVES 6

1.5KG BONELESS AND RINDLESS LOIN OF PORK

2 FAT CLOVES GARLIC, PEELED

FEW SPRIGS FRESH OREGANO, PLUS MORE TO SERVE

100G PARMA HAM, FINELY SLICED

¼ TEASPOON DRIED CHILLI FLAKES

1 ONION, UNPEELED

2 X 15ML TABLESPOONS OLIVE OIL

60ML DRY WHITE VERMOUTH

60ML BOILING WATER

VENETIAN STEW

THERE IS AN OLD VENETIAN DISH called, in dialect, *Manai*, that is the inspiration for this. And I emphasize the word "inspiration": *Manai*, which broadly speaking involves polenta with beans, bacon and local raisins, is the fruitful starting point for my pink-hued stew, with its beans and bacon and radicchio (my innovation, but it does come from Venice), echoing the cinnamon-rose colours of the *palazzi* that line the Grand Canal.

I suspect that the original stew would have used speck (think along the lines of smoked bacon) rather than the unsmoked pancetta, but either will do. If you can, though, do buy a good Italian can of borlotti beans as the juice they come in is usable; the gloop in cheaper supermarket own-label brands can be disconcertingly smelly and frankly unfit for consumption. Still, if the only beans you can find need to be rinsed vigorously, you will have to add more water to make sure the beans are covered as they cook. That in turn will make for a runnier stew, so maybe mash some of the beans at the end just to help thicken it.

I adore this salty stew ladled in bowls over a mounded pile of sweet yellow polenta. Or you could consider the Mock Mash on **p.136**, though some unsalty Italian bread with it is enough for me; either way, this is a pretty well instant, soothing and substantial supper.

SERVES 2

25G RAISINS

125ML BOILING WATER

2 TEASPOONS GARLIC OIL

150G PANCETTA CUBES OR DICED
 SPECK OR JAMON SERRANO

1 ECHALION OR BANANA
 SHALLOT, FINELY CHOPPED

½ TEASPOON GROUND CUMIN

1 X 400G CAN BORLOTTI BEANS

½ HEAD RADICCHIO (APPROX.
 125G), FINELY SHREDDED

FOR THE POLENTA:

675ML WATER

1 TEASPOON SEA SALT FLAKES OR
 ½ TEASPOON POURING SALT,
 OR TO TASTE

100G INSTANT POLENTA

2 X 15ML TABLESPOONS GRATED
 PARMESAN

1 X 15ML TABLESPOON (15G)
 UNSALTED BUTTER

Put the raisins into a cup or bowl and pour the 125ml boiling water over them.

Put 675ml water in a pan for the polenta and set it on to boil.

Heat the garlic oil in a heavy-based frying pan of about 28cm diameter (that has a lid) and cook the pancetta (or other) cubes for 3–5 minutes, stirring every now and again, then add the chopped shallot and cook for another 3–5 minutes, until the pancetta is bronzed and the shallot soft.

Stir in the cumin (not Italian, but Venice was the hub of the spice trade so I allow its inauthentic addition) then add the raisins with their soaking water and let it bubble up before tipping in the borlotti beans and their liquid (but see introduction above if your bean gloop is unusable).

Bring to the boil, then add the shredded radicchio and, once the stew starts bubbling again, turn off the heat, put on the lid, and get on with the polenta.

Add salt (to taste) to the now bubbling polenta water, then stir in the polenta, pouring it into the pan in a steady but gentle stream, and cook till smooth and thickened. I use more than the usual ratio of water to polenta here, as I want the finished polenta creamy not set. Once it is cooked, take the pan off the heat and beat in the Parmesan and butter, seasoning to taste. Decant into a warmed serving bowl.

Check the bean stew seasoning, then bring it to the table with the golden polenta. ∎

ITALIANS ARE VERY GOOD AT FINDING WAYS of elevating the less costly cuts of meat in their cooking. Although beef pizzaiola emanates from Naples, you'll find it (and, more commonly, veal as well as fish steaks cooked this way) throughout Italy. It's a cheerful, punchy little number, taking its name, as is self-explanatory, from the fact that it tastes rather like a pizza topping. Tomatoes, oregano and garlic are pretty much always in evidence, with frequent sightings of olives and capers; I like to add anchovies and a sprinkle of hot chilli flakes too.

Originally, cheap slices of meat or fish would have been cooked in the sauce whose acidity would have tenderized tough meat. But although I keep faith with the thrifty origins of the recipe by making 350g of steak feed up to 4 people, I don't buy my meat cheap, and I fry the thin slices of steak first, wrap them in foil to keep them warm and then rustle up the sauce in the hot pan. Actually, I have used British rose veal escalopes here, and pointedly so. There is such widespread revulsion at the idea of eating veal, but it is crucial to know that both the RSPCA and Compassion in World Farming are urging us to eat veal, so long as it is labelled "rose veal" (which is humanely reared), otherwise countless animals are needlessly destroyed. It is time to rethink our prejudices. Lecture over. And whether beef or veal, all in all, this takes about 5 minutes to cook, so even if you're not saving money, you're certainly saving time.

BEEF PIZZAIOLA

Warm the garlic oil in a non-stick frying pan that will contain all 4 steaks or escalopes snugly; I use one with a diameter of 28cm.

When the oil is hot, fry the steaks or escalopes over a high heat for 30 seconds a side (for medium-rare, longer if you must), then take the pan off the heat, transfer the steaks to a large piece of foil and make a loose but tightly sealed parcel. I don't salt the meat at this stage, as I would do normally, since the dry-packed olives are intensely salty. If using regular pitted olives, add a pinch of salt to each steak.

Put the pan back on the heat and add the anchovy fillets, stirring and squishing them down with a wooden spoon or similar until they start to dissolve into the oil. Stir in the dried oregano and chilli flakes.

Now tumble in the halved tomatoes along with the olives and capers and the red vermouth, and cook for 2 minutes. Add the water and cook for 1 further minute.

Acting fast, while the sauce is cooking, unwrap the steak slices and arrange them on a platter, pouring the juices that have collected in the foil into the pan. Now pour the contents of the pan over the steaks, and sprinkle with the parsley.

Serve immediately, and if you want to feed 4 rather than 2, I'd simply add more than one side dish, remembering that the piquancy of the sauce already helps it to go further. ∎

SERVES 2–4

1 X 15ML TABLESPOON GARLIC OIL

4 THIN-CUT SIRLOIN STEAKS OR ROSE VEAL ESCALOPES (APPROX. 350G TOTAL)

4 ANCHOVY FILLETS

1 TEASPOON DRIED OREGANO

¼ TEASPOON DRIED CHILLI FLAKES

250G CHERRY TOMATOES, HALVED

60G PITTED BLACK OLIVES, PREFERABLY DRY-PACKED

2 X 15ML TABLESPOONS DRAINED CAPERS

2 X 15ML TABLESPOONS DRY RED VERMOUTH

2 X 15ML TABLESPOONS WATER

1 X 15ML TABLESPOON CHOPPED FRESH PARSLEY, TO SERVE

THE FRENCH AND THE AMERICANS may be proud of their steaks but, for me, the Italians win hands down. Nothing can compare to a *tagliata* (pronounced "tallyata") in its full glory: a vast, juicy, rare steak, big enough for a tableful of people, cut into thin slices (*tagliare* simply means to cut) and served most often over rocket and with some Parmesan shaved on top. I've given recipes for just such a dish before, but it seemed to me that it might be possible to downsize a little, making this a more easily accomplished dish for a midweek meat-feast.

That's to say, instead of going to the butcher and asking for a huge hunk of steak cut specially, you can make 1 supermarket sirloin steak (it still should be good meat, or don't bother) stretch to feed 2 of you with no suggestion of scrimping; and the "marinade" is really a post-cooking dressing, so can happily be used as such. This is fabulously fiery, and the cherry tomatoes somehow serve as both condiment and accompaniment. Of course, you could add potatoes – steamed would be good to stab with a fork and use to soak up the piquant juices, though the Tuscan Fries on **p.138** are the greedy person's obvious choice – but I am happy with nothing more than some bread alongside. My son (whose absolute favourite this is) thinks likewise.

TAGLIATA FOR TWO

SERVES 2

2 X 15ML TABLESPOONS EXTRA-VIRGIN OLIVE OIL, PLUS SOME FOR OILING

½ TEASPOON DRIED CHILLI FLAKES

1 TEASPOON DRIED OREGANO

JUST UNDER A TEASPOON SEA SALT FLAKES OR ½ TEASPOON POURING SALT, OR TO TASTE

2 TEASPOONS RED WINE VINEGAR

1 SIRLOIN STEAK (APPROX. 300G)

250G CHERRY TOMATOES, HALVED

FEW SPRIGS FRESH OREGANO, TO SERVE (OPTIONAL)

Heat a griddle, or cast-iron or heavy-based non-stick frying pan.

In a small dish that can take the steak snugly later, combine the extra-virgin olive oil, chilli flakes, dried oregano, salt and red wine vinegar.

Oil the steak lightly and put it on the hot griddle (or in the hot pan) and cook for 2 minutes on each side, then remove it to the dish of chilli marinade and sit the cooked steak for 2 minutes a side in the dish. Your steak will be rare, but that's the way it's meant to be – although if you want to cook it for longer, I won't stop you.

Remove the steeped steak to a board, ready for slicing, and while it sits there, arrange the cherry tomatoes, cut-side down, in the marinade dish. Cut the steak into thin slices on the diagonal and arrange on a serving dish or 2 dinner plates.

Smoosh the tomatoes around in the marinade, then pour them, and the marinade, over the ribbons of meat. Add a few leaves of fresh oregano, if you can get them, and serve immediately. ■

MEATZZA

OF ALL THE RECIPES IN THIS BOOK (and, of course, this statement is made prior to publication) this is the *numero uno* so far, in terms of repeat requests and general all-round joyous reception it gets at home. (I concede that since my on-hand sample demographic is the teenage market, factors are skewed in its favour.) It amuses. But then, a culinary pun, it is intended to amuse: it looks like a pizza, but its base is made out of meatball mixture, moreover a meatball mixture you don't have to roll into balls but can simply press into a tin, rather like a juicy disc of meatloaf, or *polpettone*.

I first came across this idea in the form of Giuliano Hazan's Meat Pie Pizza Style (though mine is a characteristically lazy, simplified version) in his book *Every Night Italian*, but it was the great Ed Victor, consumer of bonnes bouches and producer of bons mots (if you'll forgive my French) who named it Meatzza.

I have been struggling with the problem of conveying this particular pun in Italian, and the best I can come up with (so far) is *polpettizza* but maybe this isn't a particularly Italian joke, anyway. Quite rightly, Italians take their traditions seriously, but I am untroubled and hope they will be, as this is seriously delicious. What's more, I find it more and more helpful in the repertoire as so many children – small children at any rate – seem to be kept on strict wheat-free diets by their parents these days; this is why I've given the option of replacing the breadcrumbs with porridge oats, and very well it works, too. All in all, it is just about the perfect children's tea. My own children favour a Meatzza Margherita so I've kept it simple, but of course you could add any other toppings you like.

SERVES 4–6

500G MINCED BEEF
3 X 15ML TABLESPOONS GRATED PARMESAN
3 X 15ML TABLESPOONS BREADCRUMBS OR PORRIDGE OATS (NOT INSTANT)
3 X 15ML TABLESPOONS CHOPPED FRESH PARSLEY
2 EGGS, LIGHTLY BEATEN
1 CLOVE GARLIC, PEELED
SALT AND PEPPER, TO TASTE
BUTTER, FOR GREASING
1 X 400G CAN CHOPPED TOMATOES, DRAINED
1 TEASPOON GARLIC OIL
1 TEASPOON DRIED OREGANO
1 X 125G BALL (DRAINED WEIGHT) MOZZARELLA (NOT BUFFALO), HALVED THEN SLICED
FEW LEAVES FRESH BASIL

Preheat the oven to 220°C/gas mark 7.

In a large bowl, using your hands, combine the mince, Parmesan, breadcrumbs or oats, parsley and eggs. Grate in (or mince and add) the garlic and add some salt and pepper. Do not overwork it, just lightly mix together, or the meat will become compacted and dense.

Butter a shallow, round baking tin of about 28cm diameter and turn the meat into it, pressing the mixture lightly with your fingers to cover the bottom as if the seasoned minced meat were your pizza crust.

Make sure you've drained as much runny liquid as possible out of your can of chopped tomatoes, then mix the tomato with the garlic oil, oregano and some salt and pepper and spread, using a rubber spatula, lightly on top of the meat base. Arrange the mozzarella slices on top, and then put in the oven for 20–25 minutes, by which time the meat should be cooked through and lightly set and the mozzarella melted.

Remove from the oven and let it sit for 5 minutes, then adorn with some basil leaves and bring it to the table before cutting into wedges, like a pizza. ∎

THERE IS ALWAYS GREAT JUBILATION IN MY HOUSE when meatballs are on the menu, and with this recipe it is easy to rustle them up in minutes. Instead of making up a meatball mixture with minced meat or meats, Parmesan, garlic, parsley and egg, I simply squeeze the stuffing out of about half a kilo of Italian sausages and roll it into cherry-tomato-sized balls. It's not so much that the making process is simplified, it's that this recipe is easier on the shopping and fridge-stocking front. I'm not sure that, now, my children don't prefer this version.

But don't worry if you can't get Italian sausages easily; I gave this recipe to an Italian friend of mine (who lives in London) and she – ironically – chooses to fashion hers out of everyday English Porkinsons. And if that's good enough for her…

SHORTCUT SAUSAGE MEATBALLS

Squeeze the sausage meat from the sausages and roll small cherry-tomato-sized meatballs out of it, putting them onto a clingfilm-lined baking tray as you go. Your final tally should be around 40.

Heat the oil in a large, heavy-based pan or flameproof casserole and add the meatballs, frying them until golden; as they become firmer, nudge them up in the pan to make room for the rest, if you can't fit them all in at first.

When all the meatballs are in the pan and browned, add the spring onion and oregano and stir about gently.

Add the wine or vermouth and chopped tomatoes, then fill half of one of the empty cans with cold water and tip it into the other empty can, then into the pan. The can-to-can technique is just my way of making sure you swill out as much of the tomato residue as possible.

Pop in the bay leaves and let the pan come to a fast simmer. Leave to cook like this, uncovered, for 20 minutes until the sauce has thickened slightly and the meatballs are cooked through. Check the sauce for seasoning, adding some salt and pepper, if you like.

During this time you can cook whatever you fancy to go with the meatballs, whether it be pasta, rice, whatever.

Once the meatballs are ready, you can eat them immediately or let them stand, off the heat but still on the stove, for 15 minutes. The sauce will thicken up a bit on standing. Should your diners be other than children who baulk at green bits, sprinkle with parsley on serving. ■

SERVES 4, *MAKES APPROX. 40 MEATBALLS*
450–500G ITALIAN SAUSAGES
2 X 15ML TABLESPOONS GARLIC OIL
4 FAT OR 6 SPINDLY SPRING ONIONS, FINELY SLICED
1 TEASPOON DRIED OREGANO
60ML WHITE WINE OR VERMOUTH
2 X 400G CANS CHOPPED TOMATOES, PLUS WATER TO RINSE ½ CAN
2 BAY LEAVES
SALT AND PEPPER, TO TASTE
CHOPPED FRESH PARSLEY, TO SERVE (OPTIONAL)

THIS IS ANOTHER RECIPE THAT USES ITALIAN SAUSAGES, and I specify them advisedly; being 100% meat and loosely packed, they cook much faster than the densely-woven, finer-textured English sausage. I've used regular Italian *salsicce* below but, given that this recipe already has a bit of the gangster food air about it (I feel I should be called Knuckles Lawsoni and be packing a piece when I eat it), here might be the place to choose the spicier fennel sausages, instead.

Feel free to use whatever canned beans you have in the cupboard; borlotti or cannellini would be just fine, too. Similarly, standard canned tomatoes can replace the cherry tomatoes. Don't be tempted, however, to omit the flame-roasted peppers. Their flavour – the sweetness and smokiness – is essential.

SAUSAGES WITH BEANS & PEPPERS

SERVES 4

1 X 15ML TABLESPOON
   GARLIC OIL

450G ITALIAN SAUSAGES (5–6 IN
   NUMBER)

60ML DRY RED VERMOUTH

2 X 400G CANS BUTTERBEANS,
   DRAINED

1 X 290G JAR (190G DRAINED
   WEIGHT) FLAME-ROASTED
   PEPPERS, DRAINED AND
   SCISSORED INTO BITE-SIZED
   PIECES

1 X 400G CAN CHERRY
   TOMATOES IN JUICE

3 BAY LEAVES

SALT AND PEPPER, TO TASTE

Heat the garlic oil in a shallow, flameproof casserole or heavy-based saucepan that comes with a lid, and brown the sausages, bearing in mind that Italian sausages do not colour hugely.

Take the pan off the heat for a moment, and pour in the red vermouth, then put it back on the heat and let the vermouth bubble up a bit, before adding the drained beans, the drained, snipped peppers and the can of tomatoes.

Now, take the emptied can of tomatoes and half-fill with water, then throw this in, too, before adding the bay leaves, and salt and pepper to taste.

Bring to a bubble, then turn the heat down to low, clamp on a lid and let it simmer for 15 minutes until the sausages are cooked through.

Remove the lid, turn up the heat a bit and simmer robustly for 5 further minutes until the sauce has thickened slightly.

Now, take off the heat altogether, then – using tongs, for ease – remove the sausages to a chopping board and cut them into thick slices, on a gentle diagonal if you can. You can leave them whole, but they go further sliced. Return the sausage slices to the pan and dish out from there, *or* ladle the beans into shallow bowls, adding the sliced sausages on top. Either way, serve with hunks of bread for people to *fare la scarpetta* – dunk – as they eat.

I AM FULLY EXPECTING A PHONE CALL from the 1980s asking for its menu back, but in my defence this is simple, superfast (to prepare) and sensational (to eat, which is what counts) and I am not suggesting you serve it with kiwi fruit discs or a raspberry vinaigrette.

What I do is to slice the cooked monkfish thickly, so it holds its shape, and arrange these chunky medallions (I am keeping period here) on a platter, or couple of plates, lined with rubied radicchio leaves: they make for exquisite bite-sized wraps.

All in all, were you in the market for a romantico little dinner, this would be the recipe I'd steer you towards.

MONKFISH WRAPPED IN ROSEMARY, LEMON & PARMA HAM

Preheat the oven to 220°C/gas mark 7.

Scatter the chopped rosemary and the lemon zest onto a chopping board, and then roll the monkfish fillets in the delicate mixture. The dampness of the fish should make everything stick.

Wrap the monkfish fillets with the cat's-tongue-pink prosciutto, rather as if you were putting on a ham bandage, letting the thin pieces overlap a little so that the fish stays covered.

Drizzle the oil in a shallow roasting tin and place the Parma-ham-covered fish in the tin. Roast for 15 minutes or until the fish is just cooked.

Take the tin out of the oven, transfer the fish to a board and let it rest for 2 or 3 minutes, while you arrange a bed of red leaves on a serving platter (dribbling a little extra-virgin olive oil and squeezing some lemon juice over the salad, if wished). Then carve the fish into chunky diagonal slices, taking care to keep the ham in place around it (this is not as difficult as it sounds), place these on the leaves and serve immediately. ■

SERVES 2

2 SPRIGS ROSEMARY, LEAVES
  STRIPPED AND CHOPPED
ZEST ½ UNWAXED LEMON
2 MONKFISH TAIL FILLETS
  (APPROX. 150G EACH)
75G PARMA HAM OR
  PROSCIUTTO DI SAN DANIELE,
  FINELY SLICED
1 X 15ML TABLESPOON OLIVE OIL
RADICCHIO OR OTHER RED
  LEAVES, TO SERVE (OPTIONAL)
EXTRA-VIRGIN OLIVE OIL AND
  LEMON JUICE, TO SERVE
  (OPTIONAL)

SQUID & PRAWNS WITH CHILLI & MARJORAM

IF I DIDN'T HAVE A SPEEDY SEAFOOD SUPPER in an earlier book (*Kitchen*), that surely would have been the title of this recipe. This is nothing if not a fast feast: I reckon that if you get all the bits and pieces out in front of you, ready to go, you can get this cooked in around 5 minutes. Not that there is a great deal to get ready: 1 chilli and a handful of herbs to chop, plus a little light grating of garlic and lemon zest. I buy the prawns ready-peeled and the squid cleaned and cut into rings.

Indeed, if you keep a packet of prawns and some squid in your freezer (always advisable) and then stick them in the fridge to defrost before you go off to work in the morning, you can be moments away from a really elegant and luscious supper once you get back, which makes this an instant de-stressor in the face of midweek entertaining.

If you want to make this a smaller supper for ordinary, everyday eating (though, tasting like this, it is never quite going to be *ordinary*), you can simply halve the quantities of seafood, or use only the squid or only the prawns.

If time allows, then I love to serve this along with plain, boiled Italian black rice (see **p.xii**), which I advise for its drama as well as its sauce-soaking capacity. But if you want to stretch the amounts below to feed more people, then cook a packet of spaghetti and toss the lemony, chilli-flecked and marjoram-scented seafood through it, making sure you use a little pasta-cooking water to help the sauce emulsify.

In summer, or when ease and speed are major considerations, simply line a platter (with a lip to stop any lemony juices escaping) with rocket.

Marjoram – *maggiorana* in Italian – has a more tender leaf and slightly sweeter scent than the oregano it is related to, but nothing dreadful would happen were you to use oregano instead.

SERVES 4

3 X 15ML TABLESPOONS OLIVE OIL

1 RED CHILLI, DE-SEEDED (IF WISHED) AND FINELY CHOPPED

ZEST AND JUICE 1 UNWAXED LEMON

1 CLOVE GARLIC, PEELED

FINELY CHOPPED LEAVES (APPROX. 3 X 15ML TABLESPOONS) FROM SMALL BUNCH PARSLEY

FINELY CHOPPED LEAVES (APPROX. 2 X 15ML TABLESPOONS) FROM SMALL BUNCH MARJORAM

350G PREPARED SQUID (DEFROSTED IF FROZEN), SLICED INTO RINGS

20 (APPROX. 300G TOTAL) RAW PEELED KING PRAWNS (DEFROSTED IF FROZEN)

1 TEASPOON SEA SALT FLAKES OR ½ TEASPOON POURING SALT, OR TO TASTE

Warm the oil in a wok or similarly wide, capacious pan, then add the chopped chilli (with seeds if you like it fiery) and lemon zest, turning them as they sizzle in the hot oil. This is a moment of fragrant joy.

Now grate in the garlic, or mince and add it, along with about a third of the chopped parsley and marjoram and give a quick stir, before tumbling in the prepared squid and prawns. Stir-fry in the pan for 2–3 minutes until the seafood is just cooked through.

Add the juice of half the lemon and most of the remaining herbs and cook, stirring, for another 30 seconds or so. Taste to see if you need any salt or more lemon juice, before turning the seafood out onto a warm platter and scattering it with the last remaining bits of chopped parsley and marjoram. ∎

I WAS READING THE COMMUNITY RECIPES on my website one evening, when I came across one for Tuscan Steak Tartare. I liked the sound of it, but I knew that it would not be something I'd make at home. It's entirely illogical, to the point of nonsensical, but, for some counterintuitive reason, I feel more comfortable doing raw meat in a restaurant. Equally illogically, I don't feel the same way about fish, and that is how my Tuscan Tuna Tartare came into being.

I have a proviso: I have to get the fish from a fishmonger, not the supermarket. Moreover, I do inform him first that I will be eating it raw, and thus require sashimi-grade tuna. I find it easier if the tuna comes in slices about 1cm thick, but this is not imperative. What *is* crucial is that when you chop it, you *really* chop it, whether it be with a knife or a mezzaluna: *never, ever* mince it or put it in a processor.

For me, this is the perfect summer supper with a girlfriend. I'm thinking crisp, cold white wine or rosé first (and during), then toasted bread, be it hearty farmhouse slices or small white-toast triangles, with. I really, really love this, though, with some searingly hot Tuscan Fries (see **p.138**) but then of course it's no longer a no-cook supper. To end, some perfect white peaches. Or, if you insist, the Liquorice Pudding on **p.152**. What happiness just the idea of all this brings.

TUSCAN TUNA TARTARE

Arrange the rocket on 2 dinner plates or a serving platter, like a messy wreath, with some of the leaves falling into the centre too.

Using a sharp knife, cut the tuna into small chunks and then (with a mezzaluna, if you have one), chop it finely.

While the tuna is still on the chopping board, zest the lemon over it and add the sliced spring onions, capers, salt and a good coarse grinding of pepper. Mix gently and briefly with your hands, and then carry it over to the centre of the waiting plate(s) in a messy heap.

Drizzle the olive oil over the rocket and the tuna, and squeeze half the lemon over the circling frame of rocket. Don't spritz the tuna yet or it will whiten. Cut the remaining piece of lemon in half so that each person can have a wedge to squeeze over their tuna as they eat. ■

SERVES 2

50G WILD ROCKET

300G RAW SASHIMI-QUALITY TUNA

1 UNWAXED LEMON

1 THIN OR 2 FAT SPRING ONIONS, FINELY SLICED (CUT FAT SPRING ONION LENGTHWAYS FIRST)

2 X 15ML TABLESPOONS DRAINED CAPERS

1 TEASPOON SEA SALT FLAKES OR ½ TEASPOON POURING SALT, OR TO TASTE

GROUND PEPPER

2 X 15ML TABLESPOONS EXTRA-VIRGIN OLIVE OIL

EVERYBODY LOVES A TRAYBAKE. It's not just the ease – though I admit that's a great part of it – but how cooking everything together makes the flavours juicily commingle. There are no official writings on traybakes in Italy, or none that I am aware of, but one-pot cooking is as old as the Tuscan hills, so this recipe makes perfect sense to me and to everyone (Italians included) who has eaten it.

It is "Italian" in its flavourings – the rosemary and lemon that waft gorgeously through the house as you cook – and in deference to the Italian sausages I use in it. You can go for the milder sausages, often sold as "sweet", or the hotter chillified fennel sausages, as you please. Indeed, should you be unable to find the appropriate Italian *salsicce*, it will not be the end of the world if you use regular bangers. If you would prefer to use a whole chicken, butchered into portions, rather than just the thighs, I'd go along with that, too. What I wouldn't recommend here is boneless chicken, especially not breast fillets.

So that's the chicken and the sausages. What I need to tell you most urgently though is that the potato chunks soak up the meaty, lemony juices as they cook. So set your mind not to expect crunchy roast potatoes, but rather soft-soused chunks, scorched crisp at the corners.

I use a large, shallow baking tray, in which everything below fits. It's a tight fit, but nothing suffers. Otherwise, use 2 regular baking trays; it's important that they be low-sided, as a deep tin will stop the meat and potatoes from browning desirably. This is not just an aesthetic consideration; it will have an impact on texture, too.

For all that there are potatoes included, I do like this with bread. I also like lentils alongside (but only if there's no bread on the table) and if that appeals to you, too, check out the recipe on **p.128**. And for an instant accompaniment, consider a couple of jars of flame-roasted peppers, drained and dressed with good olive oil, red wine vinegar and parsley. *Buon appetito!*

ITALIAN TRAYBAKE

SERVES 4–6 ⊘

3 BAKING POTATOES (APPROX. 750G TOTAL), UNPEELED AND CUT INTO 2CM CHUNKS

8 CHICKEN THIGHS, BONE IN AND SKIN ON

8 ITALIAN SAUSAGES (APPROX. 750G TOTAL)

▶

Preheat the oven to 220°C/gas mark 7.

Put the potatoes into a large, shallow baking tray and add the chicken thighs and sausages. If using 2 trays, divide everything between them (and also swap the trays over and turn them round halfway through cooking time).

Arrange about 4 sprigs of the rosemary among the chicken and sausages, then finely chop the needles of another 2 sprigs, to give you about 2 teaspoons of finely chopped needles, and sprinkle these onto the chicken pieces.

Zest the lemon over everything, and season with the salt and a good grinding of pepper. Drizzle with the oil and bake for 50–60 minutes, or until the chicken skin and sausages are golden and the potato pieces are cooked through. It's fine to let all of this stand for up to 30 minutes once cooked, prior to serving. ∎

SMALL BUNCH (6 OR 7 SPRIGS)
  FRESH ROSEMARY
ZEST 1 UNWAXED LEMON
1 TEASPOON SEA SALT FLAKES OR
  ½ TEASPOON POURING SALT
GROUND PEPPER
4 X 15ML TABLESPOONS
  OLIVE OIL

I LOVE THE ITALIAN "POLLO AL MATTONE" (which means "chicken cooked with a brick"), and although I am given to believe it is Italo-American rather than old-country authentic, I have been recently admonished and told it is in fact a dish that originates with the Etruscans. Hmm. Does it matter? It is a glorious creation: salty, lemony and either fiercely peppery or afire with crushed chilli.

The particular pollo al mattone I love dearly is the incredibly tender, melting-fleshed, super-lemony and thyme-scented version served at Sfoglia, in New York. Inspired by a recent visit, I knew I had to make it my own, and this is what I'm now giving you. In a domestic oven, I feel this works best, with 2 poussins rather than 1 chicken, which makes it not quite chicken under a brick, but you get the gist. This is not an instant recipe by any means, but it is a very simple one. It is certainly streamlined from the original, if that counts. And even if it doesn't, I wouldn't feel happy keeping it from you.

CHICKEN UNDER A BRICK

SERVES 2

2 POUSSINS
ZEST AND JUICE 2 UNWAXED
   LEMONS
8 SPRIGS THYME
1 TEASPOON SEA SALT FLAKES OR
   ½ TEASPOON POURING SALT,
   OR TO TASTE
½ TEASPOON COARSELY
   GROUND PEPPER OR DRIED
   CHILLI FLAKES.
60ML OLIVE OIL
2 CLOVES GARLIC, PEELED

2 X FOIL-COVERED BUILDERS'
   BRICKS

Cut along the backbone of each poussin to open them out flat: you can do this with a pair of strong kitchen scissors.

Zest and juice the lemons into a large freezer bag, then pull off the thyme leaves, dropping them in too.

Sprinkle in the salt and either grind in the pepper or shake in the chilli flakes, then pour the oil into the bag and, finally, grate in (or mince and add) the garlic.

Add the spatchcocked poussins, then seal the bag before squidging the marinade all over the flattened birds as efficiently (and agreeably) as you can. Put the bag of birds on a dish and pop it into the fridge and leave for a day or overnight.

When you are ready to cook the poussins, preheat the oven to 200°C/gas mark 6, and let them come to room temperature.

Heat a griddle or roasting tin that can go into the oven and on the hob. Then take the poussins out of the marinade (reserving it for later) and place them skin-side down on the griddle or in the tin.

Place the bricks on top of the birds and let them cook over a moderate heat for 5 minutes.

Immediately place the poussins in the oven, bricks still on top, and cook for 15 minutes.

Take the tin or griddle out of the oven and, wearing oven-gloves, carefully remove the bricks before turning the poussins over. Pour the reserved marinade over the flattened birds, then put the bricks back on top and roast in the oven for another 15 minutes until the juices run clear.

Take the poussins out of the oven, carefully remove the hot bricks, then carve each bird into 4 pieces, drizzling with any intense pan juices. Bread and a green salad is all I need on the side. ∎

ON THE WHOLE, I'D DESCRIBE MY ITALIAN TASTES as having more of a northern than southern affiliation; it's the non-Mediterranean Italy that has always lured me, not least at the table.

Having said that – and maybe it's the mellowness of age – I seem to be warming to the sunnier approach, cheerfully cooking with tomatoes and peppers and finding myself unfamiliarly delighted with the result. This stew says it all, really: it has spirit-lifting southern gusto, and the rich sweetness of the flame-roasted peppers (a kitchen cupboard must-have for me) keeps the acidity of the tomatoes in check.

If I make this for my children for tea, I most often serve it with a bowlful of orzo pasta (see right); when it's for me, though, some wilted spinach and gorgeous bread are the only accompaniments I require.

CHICKEN WITH TOMATOES & PEPPERS

Pour the oil into a small, flameproof casserole or heavy-based pan – I use my old enamelled cast-iron one with a 20cm diameter – and cook the chopped shallot, stirring frequently, until soft: this should take about 3 minutes; an onion may take longer.

Add the chicken pieces along with the dried oregano and turn them in the hot pan. Add the Marsala and watch it bubble up, then promptly add the canned tomatoes and the salt.

Half-fill the empty tomato can with water and pour it into the pan, swilling out as much of the tomato residue as you can.

Drain the peppers and snip with scissors – for ease – into bite-sized pieces and add to the pan, then bring to a boil before turning down the heat and leaving to cook at a steady simmer, uncovered, for 20 minutes until the sauce has thickened slightly and the chicken is cooked through. Decant into a bowl, or bowls, or just leave in the pan, if you prefer, and serve. ◼

SERVES 3–4

1 X 15ML TABLESPOON
GARLIC OIL

1 ECHALION OR BANANA
SHALLOT, OR 1 SMALL ONION,
PEELED AND FINELY CHOPPED

500G CHICKEN THIGH FILLETS,
CUT INTO BITE-SIZED PIECES

1 TEASPOON DRIED OREGANO

2 X 15ML TABLESPOONS MARSALA

1 X 400G CAN CHOPPED
TOMATOES, PLUS WATER TO
RINSE OUT CAN

1 TEASPOON SEA SALT FLAKES OR
½ TEASPOON POURING SALT,
OR TO TASTE

1 X 290G JAR (190G DRAINED
WEIGHT) FLAME-ROASTED RED
PEPPERS

CHICKEN WITH TARRAGON SALSA VERDE

TARRAGON, THE GORGEOUSLY NAMED "DRAGONCELLO", is actually little used in Italy, despite the country's immoderate passion for all things anise. You find tarragon used only here and there, mainly in Tuscany; indeed, it is sometimes referred to as *erba di Siena*, the herb of Siena.

Its chief appearance in those parts is in the *salsa al dragoncello*, where the herb is pounded with breadcrumbs and garlic and then emulsified with olive oil to produce a fragrant sauce customarily served with plain boiled meats. To be honest, I'm not sure I had that in mind when I first made this: all I wanted was to create a version of that fabulously spiky Italian green sauce, tweaked to suit chicken, which for me (and I hope this display of frankly French influence is forgiven in Italy) means tarragon.

Even though I've always been open about my preference for thigh meat (tastes more and costs less), I specifically need the tender delicacy of the breast meat here. I find that organic corn-fed breast fillets, with the skin still on, make for the most succulent slices later.

There are many good ways to eat this. Obviously hot – or after 10 minutes' post-roast rest – is the first port of call (with some green beans or a crisp salad and either jacket potatoes or steamed baby ones), but in summer I am happy to leave the fillets to cool to room temperature, or somewhere hovering around it (covered and out of the sun, for up to 45 minutes), before slicing them and blitzing up the sauce. And any slices that are left over can, with the sauce and some cooked, drained and cooled fusilli, be turned into a strangely compelling (not terribly Italian) pasta salad.

I always feel slightly silly giving weights of herbs, but I do so to give guidance. Generally a supermarket small bunch (or packet) of fresh herbs weighs in at around 20g. It's really all about proportions though: the amount of tarragon in the sauce should be a quarter of the amount of parsley. It may seem odd to pick out the smaller quantity of the herb as the defining feature of this sauce, but a little tarragon goes a long way. Use too much and a slightly musty farmyard scent is evoked; pitched perfectly, as here, and you get a fragrant herbal hit, at once light and refreshing and warmly mellow.

Preheat the oven to 220°C/gas mark 7.

Pour 1 tablespoon of the oil into a shallow ovenproof dish or roasting tin in which the chicken breast fillets will fit snugly and then arrange them in there skin-side up. Tuck 2 sprigs of tarragon in between the chicken pieces, add a good grinding of pepper and dribble another tablespoon of oil over them, then pop them in the oven for 20–30 minutes, or until the skins are golden and the flesh tender.

Take out of the oven, and let the cooked chicken stand for 5–10 minutes in the tin while you prepare the sauce.

Put the parsley and tarragon leaves, along with the spring onion, lemon zest, salt flakes and 3 tablespoons olive oil into a suitable receptacle and, using a stick blender, whizz to a paste, adding the lemon juice and remaining 3 tablespoons olive oil slowly as you blend. Leave for a mo, while you slice the chicken.

Cut the chicken into thickish – 1cm or so – slices (if you need it to go further, then slice more thinly) and arrange on a platter.

Pour any juices that have collected in the tin into the tarragon salsa and whizz again with your stick blender, tasting for seasoning before dribbling the sauce over the tender sliced chicken. ■

SERVES 6–8

FOR THE CHICKEN:
2 X 15ML TABLESPOONS
  OLIVE OIL
4 CHICKEN BREAST FILLETS
  (PREFERABLY ORGANIC AND
  CORN-FED), WITH SKIN ON
SMALL BUNCH FRESH TARRAGON
  (2 SPRIGS FOR CHICKEN PLUS
  MORE LEAVES FOR SAUCE)
PEPPER (PREFERABLY WHITE
  COARSELY GROUND), TO TASTE

FOR THE SAUCE:
LEAVES FROM SMALL BUNCH
  FRESH PARSLEY (APPROX. 20G)
LEAVES FROM SPRIGS FRESH
  TARRAGON (APPROX. 5G)
1 SPRING ONION (INCLUDING
  GREEN PART), ROUGHLY
  CHOPPED
ZEST 1 UNWAXED LEMON AND
  JUICE ½ LEMON
1 TEASPOON SEA SALT FLAKES OR
  ½ TEASPOON POURING SALT,
  OR TO TASTE
6 X 15ML TABLESPOONS
  OLIVE OIL

A ROAST CHICKEN ALWAYS FEELS CELEBRATORY; indeed, a roast chicken always *is* celebratory. The vibrantly coloured and intensely flavoured vegetables that are cooked alongside here seem only to underline this, offering their own brightness and brio, sunny in taste as well as mood.

If you had a really huge roasting tin – and a really huge oven to put it in – you could happily double the amount of vegetables; as it is, think of the soft tangle of leeks and peppers, punctuated by the salty olives, more as an accompanying sauce. The chicken will feed 4, and could stretch to 6 but that will give you only a spoonful of the vegetables each. I add a crisp green salad and a Pugliese loaf, or any other good bread I can use to soak up the scant but flavoursome vegetables and their juices. My children like some simply cooked soup pasta – orzo or miniature bow ties – dressed in a little butter or olive oil and served alongside, as well.

ITALIAN ROAST CHICKEN WITH PEPPERS & OLIVES

SERVES 4–6

1 CHICKEN (APPROX. 1.5KG, OR SLIGHTLY MORE), PREFERABLY ORGANIC AND CORN-FED

1 UNWAXED LEMON, CUT IN HALF

4 SPRIGS ROSEMARY

3 LEEKS, WASHED AND TRIMMED

2 RED PEPPERS

1 ORANGE PEPPER

1 YELLOW PEPPER

100G PITTED DRY-PACKED BLACK OLIVES

60ML OLIVE OIL

SEA SALT FLAKES AND PEPPER, TO TASTE

Preheat the oven to 200°C/gas mark 6. Untruss the chicken, sit it in a roasting tin and put the lemon halves and 2 of the rosemary sprigs into the chicken's cavity.

Cut each leek into 3 logs, then slice lengthways and add to the tin. Now, remove the core and seeds of the peppers and slice them into strips, following their natural curves and ridges, and add these to the tin.

Tumble in the olives, and now pour the olive oil, mostly over the vegetables but a little over the chicken, too. Add the remaining rosemary sprigs to the vegetables, along with some sea salt flakes and freshly ground pepper, to taste, and, using a couple of spoons or spatulas, gently toss the vegetables about to help coat them with the oil and make sure everything's well mixed up.

Sprinkle some sea salt flakes over the chicken and put it in the oven for about 1– 1¼ hours, by which time the chicken should be cooked through, and its juices running clear when you cut into the flesh with a small sharp knife at the thickest part of the thigh joint. The vegetables should be tender by now, too, and some of the leeks will be a scorched light-brown in parts.

Remove the chicken to a carving board and, while it rests (for about 10 minutes), pop the pan of veg back in the oven, switching the oven off as you do so.

Cut the chicken up chunkily, transferring the pieces to a large warmed platter. Now take the pan back out of the oven and, with a slotted spoon or spatula, remove the vegetables to the large platter and when all is arranged to your aesthetic delight, pour over it all the bronze, highly flavoured juices that have collected in the pan. ■

VEGETABLES
& SIDES

I REMEMBER, WHEN I WAS IN the south of Italy, eating aubergines that had been roughly chopped, sprinkled with dried wild oregano, doused with olive oil and then roasted with a little garlic and a lot of red onions. Indeed, a friend of mine from Campania says this is the way her mother always cooks aubergines, sometimes throwing chopped potatoes into the oven pan at the same time.

This below, is my version: quicker, yes, but I also like the way it can be eaten as a starter or part of an antipasti table, and even as a main course, sprinkled with some ricotta salata (the deliciously salted, semi-dried kind) or crumbled feta, or as an accompaniment to meat and fish. If you are adding cheese, then sprinkle it over before topping with the onions, which are turned a glorious, luminescent puce by their red wine vinegar marinade (an old and favourite trick of mine).

BABY AUBERGINES WITH OREGANO & RED ONION

SERVES 6, *AS A SIDE DISH*
500G BABY AUBERGINES
3 X 15ML TABLESPOONS
  REGULAR OLIVE OIL
2 TEASPOONS DRIED OREGANO
1 SMALL RED ONION, CUT INTO
  THIN HALF-MOONS
3 X 15ML TABLESPOONS RED
  WINE VINEGAR
1 TEASPOON SEA SALT FLAKES OR
  ½ TEASPOON POURING SALT,
  OR TO TASTE
4 X 15ML TABLESPOONS EXTRA-
  VIRGIN OLIVE OIL
1 CLOVE GARLIC, PEELED
1½ X 15ML TABLESPOONS COLD
  WATER
FEW SPRIGS FRESH OREGANO
  (OPTIONAL)

Preheat the oven to 250°C/gas mark 9.

Slice the baby aubergines in half lengthways, keeping the stalks on; this is an aesthetic consideration, nothing to do with flavour, but humour me.

Pour the 3 tablespoons regular olive oil into a very shallow roasting tin, sprinkle in the dried oregano, add the aubergines, cut-side down, and swirl them gently around. Then turn them so they are cut-side up and put the tray in the hot oven for 15 minutes, by which time they should be tender and turning gold in parts.

As soon as the aubergines are in the oven, put the fine half-moons of red onion in a bowl and cover with the red wine vinegar and salt.

Remove the cooked aubergines to a platter, and now whisk into the vinegary onions the extra-virgin olive oil, then grate in (or mince and add) the garlic and, finally, whisk in the cold water.

Pour this over the warm aubergines, using your hands to arrange the glowingly pink onion over them evenly, then leave it all for about half an hour to cool to room temperature before you eat, scattering with fresh oregano, if you have any, when serving. ■

I CAN FEEL SLIGHTLY SELF-CONSCIOUS fiddling about with traditional pesto recipes, when in its authentic original it is surely unbeatable. But having had such uplifting results with – admittedly still traditional – Sicilian variants (see, in particular, **p.2**), I decided that the uninhibited approach had something going for it – hence the substitution of pistachios for pine nuts in the pesto here. And, frankly, this was born to go with the green beans: it's a riot of verdigloriousness!

It's up to you whether you go with this, or revert to the standard model. I should tell you that when I make this for my only slightly picky children, I leave the nuts out altogether. And perhaps I shouldn't be telling you, but if you use a couple of spoonfuls of shop-bought pesto, instead – so long as it's made fresh in an Italian deli – it's not the end of the world. There is no good argument, really, for not making this, however. It is just so easy – providing you have a simple, inexpensive stick blender – and gives your everyday vegetables a bit of dinner-party dash.

GREEN BEANS WITH PISTACHIO PESTO

Put a pan of water on for the beans, adding salt when it starts to boil.

To make the pesto, put the pistachios, Parmesan, basil and olive oil in a small bowl. Grate in (or mince and add) a little bit of the garlic – about a quarter of a clove – throwing the remaining piece of garlic into the bean water. Using a stick blender, blitz the pesto ingredients to a thick green paste.

Cook the beans to taste (check after 4 minutes), and, before draining, spoon a little of the cooking water (1 or 2 tablespoons is all you need) into the pesto bowl and blitz quickly to mix again with your stick blender.

Drain the beans (discarding the rogue garlic clove), and toss them in the bowl with the pesto, then transfer to a serving bowl, and take them fragrantly to the table. ∎

SERVES 6–8, *AS A SIDE DISH*

600G TRIMMED GREEN BEANS, CUT IN HALF OR INTO SHORT LENGTHS

1 TEASPOON SEA SALT FLAKES OR ½ TEASPOON POURING SALT, OR TO TASTE

3 X 15ML TABLESPOONS SHELLED PISTACHIOS

3 X 15ML TABLESPOONS GRATED PARMESAN

LEAVES FROM SMALL BUNCH FRESH BASIL (APPROX. 20G)

3 X 15ML TABLESPOONS EXTRA-VIRGIN OLIVE OIL

1 CLOVE GARLIC, PEELED

WHERE DO I START WITH THIS? You can see at a glance that it is extraordinarily simple, but the full-on flavours have a gratifying complexity that is not reflected in either the length of the ingredients list or the time and technique needed to make it. Moreover, it easily lends itself to being turned into a sauce for pasta (in which case, consider adding some shredded or diced mozzarella) or for meat and also fish.

My own preferences are markedly – as ever – for the less than ubiquitous dry-packed pitted olives, but you could use any pitted (or unpitted, for that matter, if your guests are forewarned) black olives you wanted. I also feel the floral scent of the pink vermouth is the best balance for the acid tang of the tomatoes, but am not troubled unduly by the idea of your using either red or white vermouth in its place.

And have I said, by the way, how great this is, eaten alone, not to accompany anything, but just with a hunk or three of bread to dunk in it, too?

CHERRY TOMATOES WITH OLIVES

SERVES 4–6, *AS A SIDE DISH* Ⓝ
3 X 15ML TABLESPOONS
 GARLIC OIL
2 TEASPOONS FINELY CHOPPED
 FRESH ROSEMARY
500G CHERRY TOMATOES,
 HALVED
60ML MARTINI OR CINZANO
 ROSATO
75G DRY-PACKED PITTED BLACK
 OLIVES
3 X 15ML TABLESPOONS
 CHOPPED FRESH PARSLEY
SALT AND PEPPER, TO TASTE

Put the garlic oil and chopped rosemary into a thick-bottomed, non-stick wok – or wide, heavy-based pan – that comes with a lid, and put it on a low to medium heat to warm up, letting the rosemary sizzle fragrantly in the oil for 30 seconds.

Add the halved cherry tomatoes and cook, stirring gently, for about 1½ minutes, by which time the tomatoes will start softening and oozing their viscous juices.

Add the pink vermouth and bring to a bubble, then clamp on a lid and let it cook away for a further minute.

Remove the lid, stir in the olives and let it bubble uncovered for another minute, letting the juices reduce a little. Stir in most of the parsley and season to taste, then pour into a warmed serving dish, leaving it to stand for 10 minutes if you can, as the juices will thicken and the flavours mellow.

Sprinkle with the remaining parsley and serve. ▪

PEAS WITH PANCETTA

I LOVE THE WAY ITALIANS COOK PEAS; indeed I love the way they cook all their *verdura*. Sometimes I think that the British tendency to champion crunchy vegetables (often on the challenging side of *al dente*), is a form of subconscious overcompensation for our shamefully suppressed past of under-seasoned and over-cooked greens – the Waterlogged Cabbage Era. Now, these peas are not cooked for an unreasonably long time, but just long enough – around 20 minutes – for them to soften and sweeten; and if their vibrant green has left them by the time they're ready to eat, know that the vividness of taste more than makes up for any drabness of tone.

If you're cooking for vegetarians, or don't want to include the pancetta for any number of reasons, that's fine, too; but in that case I would add another chopped shallot and – without the flavourful fat so generously yielded by the pancetta – also another couple of tablespoons of garlic oil at the beginning, as well as adding some vegetable bouillon powder, or similar, to the water later.

And about that: I know it does seem there is very little liquid for a great deal of peas. That's on purpose: the peas are braised in the scant liquid (remember that as they defrost they give up more of their own, too) and not drained at the end, but rather served in their intense savoury syrup. The trick is to use a pan that you think will be too small. I bring out one of my favourite eBay buys – an old 20cm Le Creuset casserole – and squish everything in. If you do use a larger pan, then you may need more water, but do not add any more than just enough to cover the peas.

Leftovers can be simply recycled as they are (transfer to an airtight container, cool as quickly as possible, cover and refrigerate for up to 2 days), and reheated gently in a pan; or, if you have only a little left, as a sauce for pasta – penne, tagliatelle, whatever you feel like – with or without the addition of cream; if you have a fair amount left, then add water, bring to a boil and cook some soup pasta, such as ditalini, in the pea and pancetta broth until soft, then let it stand, off the heat, for 5–10 minutes before serving.

The mint is an English touch, to be sure, but then – as the great 21st-century philosopher, Lady Gaga, has it – "Baby, I was born this way".

Warm the garlic oil over a medium heat in a smallish, heavy-based pan or flameproof casserole (see introduction, left) that comes with a lid, and fry the pancetta – stirring every now and again – until it is nearly, but not quite, crisp (about 5 minutes).

Add the chopped shallot and cook for another 2 minutes or so, stirring, until the pancetta cubes are crisp and the shallot soft. Stir in the dried mint.

Tip in the frozen peas and turn them in the pan a little (if you're using the requisite small pan you won't be able to do much more than nudge them with your wooden spoon) then, after a couple of minutes or so, when the frozen look has left the peas a bit, turn up the heat, slosh in the vermouth or wine and when you hear it begin to bubble, pour in the water to cover the peas.

Bring to the boil, then turn down the heat to low, cover, and simmer for 15 minutes.

Remove the lid, turn up the heat and let it bubble away for 5 minutes, so that the sweet and salty juices reduce and thicken a little.

Remove from the heat, and – if time and patience permit – let the peas stand, with the lid still off, for 15 minutes before serving. At which time, stir in most of the chopped fresh mint and parsley and then sprinkle the little remaining quantity over the top. I often put out a slotted spoon as well as a regular serving spoon so that those who want the sweet, sticky gravy can have it, and those who don't can let it drain back into the casserole as they help themselves. ■

SERVES 6–8, *AS A SIDE DISH* Ⓝ

1 X 15ML TABLESPOON GARLIC OIL

225G PANCETTA CUBES

1 ECHALION OR BANANA SHALLOT, PEELED AND FINELY CHOPPED

1 TEASPOON DRIED MINT

750G FROZEN PEAS, UNTHAWED

75ML DRY WHITE VERMOUTH OR WHITE WINE

500ML WATER (OR JUST ENOUGH TO COVER THE PEAS)

2 X 15ML TABLESPOONS CHOPPED FRESH MINT

2 X 15ML TABLESPOONS CHOPPED FRESH PARSLEY

IN THE NORTH OF ITALY, you will often find sage-scented squash tossed over pasta, and I often do the same myself. Here, I'm happy enough to enjoy the squash solo.

I eat this two ways: the first pretty well as is, as a substantial and goldenly glowing vegetable course; but if I have no room in the oven while the main course is roasting, I cook this first, leave it in the tin and then, on serving, transfer it to a rocket-lined platter and add a dribble or two of extra-virgin olive oil along with the lemon and pine nuts. I've always got time and the taste for an *insalata tiepida*, or warm salad.

To bolster it into a main course you can go any number of ways but, most commonly, I either toss the hot roast butternut with some lentils (see the recipe on **p.128**) and then sprinkle with sage, but leave out the pine nuts; or I add small dabs of Gorgonzola all over the warm salad of rocket and butternut before sprinkling it with the toasted pine nuts.

ROAST BUTTERNUT WITH SAGE & PINE NUTS

Preheat the oven to 220°C/gas mark 7.

Don't peel, but halve and de-seed the butternut and cut into large, fork-sized pieces, about 3–4cm wedges.

Drizzle the oil into a shallow baking tray and arrange the pieces in the tin, skin-side down.

Tear the leaves off 2 of the sprigs of sage and arrange them around the butternut chunks. Bake in the oven for about 40 minutes, or until the butternut is tender and cooked through.

Heat a small frying pan, pop in the pine nuts and shake them about for a couple of minutes until golden and toasted, and don't leave the pan till they're done.

Transfer the baked butternut to a platter or shallow bowl. Squeeze the lemon juice over it, sprinkle with salt and pepper to taste, and scatter with the toasted pine nuts.

Finally, tear off the leaves from the remaining sprig of sage to decorate, and serve. ∎

SERVES 4–6, *AS A SIDE DISH*

1 LARGE BUTTERNUT SQUASH
  (APPROX. 1KG)
2 X 15ML TABLESPOONS
  OLIVE OIL
3 SPRIGS FRESH SAGE
3 X 15ML TABLESPOONS
  TOASTED PINE NUTS
JUICE ½ LEMON
SEA SALT FLAKES AND PEPPER,
  TO TASTE

BRAISED BROAD BEANS, PEAS & ARTICHOKES WITH THYME & MINT

THE INSPIRATION FOR THIS IS STRAIGHTFORWARD: what we have here is simply the lazy person's *vignarola*. *La vignarola* – for some reason often called *vignole* in British restaurant versions – is the soft, sweetly fragrant Roman spring stew of young broad beans, peas and violet-tipped artichokes; truly, it's a beautiful thing. It's also, made traditionally – properly, you could say – enormously labour-intensive. I don't, however, feel ashamed of this streamlined, shortcut, out-of-a-packet version. No, I exult in it. Besides, if you're in Rome in April (and it's worth it to eat this in seasonal *situ*) you'll see small bags of podded peas, shelled broad beans and prepared artichokes for sale in all the markets. I just happen to keep my little bags of the above in the deep freeze.

I do, nonetheless, like to buy the herbs fresh. I have made it with dried mint and thyme (bolstered with some fresh parsley) but, for best results, use fresh mint, fresh thyme: they make the stew really sing for your supper.

Traditionally, *guanciale* or pancetta would be among the ingredients but, although as a general rule I believe – as one of my favourite book titles has it – *Everything Tastes Better with Bacon*, here I prefer not to go the whole hog.

A couple of notes about the holy trinity of vegetables used here: I buy frozen artichoke bottoms (not to be confused with artichoke hearts) from Middle Eastern stores and stash them (along with the baby broad beans and the peas) in the freezer so that I can always make this without notice; but you can equally well use those that come in jars in oil (drained). The weight I give is because of the packet size I use, so don't be constrained by it. And I know I said this is a lazy take, but I do like my broad beans skinned. This is not hard work, and rather satisfying: you thaw the beans, then it's the work of moments to squish them so that the vivid green beans shoot out, free of their tough outer casing. You don't have to follow suit.

I often make this in advance, but only slightly, preferring to eat it a few beats above room temperature. But if you preferred, you could make it a couple of days in advance and reheat it gently later (see Notes **p.264**).

Should you have any left (though I wouldn't count on it), this makes for the basis of a wholly heavenly risotto *primavera*. (Just follow the method of the Chilli Crab Risotto recipe on **p.40**, omitting the chilli and saffron, and using 1 litre vegetable stock in place of the chicken stock. Add whatever leftover vegetables you have, at the point where the crab is added to the crab risotto.)

Warm the garlic oil and butter in a heavy-based, flameproof casserole that comes with a lid, then add the leaves from about 5 sprigs of the thyme and cook for 30 seconds or so, before adding the frozen peas.

Cook, stirring, until the frozen look leaves the peas – no more than a couple of minutes – then tip in the broad beans and the artichoke slices and stir gently to mix, before adding the white wine or vermouth and the water.

Bring to a bubble, then add salt and pepper to taste, clamp on the lid, turn down the heat and let it simmer for 15 minutes, or until all the vegetables are sweetly soused and tender. You can then hold them like this – with the lid on but heat off – for 10–15 minutes, if you like.

Stir in the chopped mint and parsley and the leaves from another 4 sprigs of thyme just before serving. And, if you want, dribble in some extra-virgin olive oil as well. ■

SERVES 6–8 ℕ

2 X 15ML TABLESPOONS GARLIC OIL

1 X 15ML TABLESPOON (15G) BUTTER

SMALL BUNCH FRESH THYME

500G FROZEN PETITS POIS, UNTHAWED

250G FROZEN BROAD BEANS, THAWED AND POPPED OUT OF THEIR SKINS

350G ARTICHOKE BOTTOMS, CUT INTO APPROX. 1CM SLICES WHILE PARTIALLY FROZEN

60ML DRY WHITE WINE OR VERMOUTH

60ML WATER

SEA SALT FLAKES AND PEPPER, TO TASTE

2 X 15ML TABLESPOONS CHOPPED FRESH MINT

3 X 15ML TABLESPOONS CHOPPED FRESH PARSLEY

EXTRA-VIRGIN OLIVE OIL, TO SERVE (OPTIONAL)

THIS IS ONE OF THOSE RECIPES that, while not quick to cook, is the work of easy minutes to make. Also, because it's best warm rather than hot, you can cook this before getting on with anything else, thus freeing up the oven later, should you need it.

I know that having to peel a kilo of onions doesn't seem like light work, but if you quarter them first, the peel almost falls off. And I never worry about a bit of it here and there in the pan, anyway. I prefer to use smallish red onions, but if you can only find large ones, then cut them into eighths rather than quarters.

This recipe can easily lend itself to being part of a buffet-type arrangement for parties, but is a wonderful supper or lunch accompaniment to roast lamb or, for that matter, any lamb. I also love it alongside a platter of (very unItalian) grilled halloumi. If you want it to be a main course in itself, then crumble or dab over it the cheese of your choice – ricotta salata (the lightly salted, semi-dried version), fresh ricotta, Gorgonzola, Taleggio – just as it comes out of the oven, but before you add the uplifting and scented splendour of the basil.

ROAST RED ONIONS WITH BASIL

SERVES 6–8, *AS PART OF A MEAL* Ⓝ

1KG RED ONIONS (PREFERABLY SMALL), QUARTERED THEN PEELED

125ML OLIVE OIL

1 TEASPOON FENNEL SEEDS

1 TEASPOON SEA SALT FLAKES OR ½ TEASPOON POURING SALT, OR TO TASTE

1 TEASPOON BEST-QUALITY BALSAMIC VINEGAR, OR TO TASTE

LARGE BUNCH (APPROX. 90G) FRESH BASIL

Preheat the oven to 200°C/gas mark 6.

Tip the quartered onions into a roasting tin, pour the olive oil over them, then scatter with fennel seeds, tossing the onions in the tin to coat them thoroughly; then put the tin in the oven for 1 hour, by which time the onions should be soft and cooked through.

Remove from the oven, sprinkle with the salt and drizzle the balsamic vinegar over the onions, then toss them gently and leave (for up to 1 hour) to come to room temperature, though you can eat this hot if you prefer.

On serving, add the basil leaves, torn from their stems, and toss again, seasoning to taste. There is a lot of basil, but think of it as a salad leaf, here, not mere decoration. ■

HERE IS MY ITALIAN VERSION, you could say, of creamed spinach. Actually, it tastes rather like the ricotta and spinach mixture that's used to stuff pasta; of course, given the ingredients, this is scarcely surprising.

For me this is the perfect accompaniment to a grilled steak or roast chicken but then I could spoon this soft, eggy spinach down, swooningly, just as it is.

SPINACH BAKED WITH RICOTTA & NUTMEG

Preheat the oven to 200°C/gas mark 6, and butter a small ovenproof dish: I use a vaguely oval one with a capacity of about 700ml.

In a wok or wide, heavy-based pan, warm the olive oil with the garlic clove and cook until the garlic is bronze.

Over a low heat stir in the spinach, bearing in mind that, though it will look at first as if you can't fit it all in, cooked spinach reduces to a fraction of its raw volume.

Turn up the heat, throw in the wine or vermouth and toss gently until the spinach has wilted – which will take around 30 seconds.

Remove from the heat and stir in the Parmesan and ricotta and season to taste, adding a good grating of nutmeg.

Beat in the eggs, then transfer the eggy spinach to your buttered oven dish – I leave the garlic clove in just out of laziness, but you could remove it at this point – and bake in the oven for 10 minutes until just set. Let it stand for at least 5 but no longer than 15 minutes, before serving. ■

SERVES 2, *AS A SIDE DISH*
BUTTER FOR GREASING
1 X 15ML TABLESPOON OLIVE OIL
1 CLOVE GARLIC, PEELED
300G BABY SPINACH LEAVES,
   WASHED AND DRIED
2 X 15ML TABLESPOONS WHITE
   WINE OR VERMOUTH
3 X 15ML TABLESPOONS GRATED
   PARMESAN
2 X 15ML TABLESPOONS RICOTTA
FRESHLY GROUND PEPPER AND
   SALT, TO TASTE
FRESHLY GRATED NUTMEG
2 EGGS, BEATEN

THIS RECIPE IS A HOTCHPOTCH, REALLY. I do equate Savoy cabbage – *verza* – very much with Italy, but then again, whenever I eat it I also think of how my mother used to cook it, halfway between stir-fried and braised, with caraway seeds. The fennel seeds are my way of conjoining the two. On top of that, the potatoes I add give it something of an Italo-Irish spin. You don't need to bother with the potatoes: I used not to; but I did it once, as I had a spare spud around, and couldn't then go back. Nor do you absolutely need the cheese at the end. I add the gooey blobs of Taleggio only when I'm making this as a meal in itself, and if Taleggio eludes you, use any soft but full-bodied cheese that's easier to come by locally: Camembert would be the most obvious option.

Any leftovers, you may like to know, make for a gorgeous frittata the next day. For 100g of cabbage and potato mixture, use 2 eggs, whisk and add to the leftovers, then tip them into a buttery frying pan and once the underside is cooked, give it a flash under a hot grill to cook the top. I happen to adore cold frittata, so a bonus of this recipe could also be a cooked packed lunch for later in the week (but make sure, if that's your plan, that the frittata is cooled, covered and refrigerated quickly).

SAVOY CABBAGE WITH POTATOES, FENNEL SEEDS & TALEGGIO

SERVES 4–6 Ⓝ

2 X 15ML TABLESPOONS OLIVE OIL

250G POTATOES (APPROX. 1
   LARGE POTATO), UNPEELED,
   CUT INTO 1CM DICE

6 SPRING ONIONS, SLICED

2 TEASPOONS FENNEL SEEDS

1 HEAD SAVOY CABBAGE

350ML HOT WATER, FROM A
   RECENTLY BOILED KETTLE

SALT AND PEPPER, TO TASTE

200G TALEGGIO CHEESE, RIND
   REMOVED (OPTIONAL)

Heat the oil in a large pan or heavy-based wok (my preference) that has a lid, then add the diced potato and cook in the hot oil, stirring frequently, for 10 minutes, by which time the potato will be more or less cooked through.

Stir in the spring onions and fennel seeds and cook, stirring, for a further minute.

Meanwhile, shred the Savoy cabbage (by hand, with a knife). Then, when the potatoes have had their 10 minutes, add the cabbage, turning it in the hot pan – I like to use a spatula or spoon in each hand for this, like tossing a salad – and making sure the potato is mixed into it. Pour in the hot water, adding salt and pepper to taste, then give the pan a quick stir, clamp on the lid, turning the heat down, and let it simmer for 10 minutes, or until the potato and cabbage are cooked through.

Remove from the heat, then pinch out blobs of Taleggio (if using) and let them drop into the pan, stirring as you go so that the cheese melts into the cabbage. But if the pan you've cooked everything in can't be brought to the table, then warm a bowl, and tip the cabbage and potato mixture into it first, before adding the cheese, and toss well so that it melts and mixes in the serving dish. ■

THIS IS, IN EFFECT, NOTHING OTHER than the *funghi trifolati* you find all over Italy in the autumn. Perhaps I have been a bit more exuberant with the lemon, but it really brings out the rich, sweet meatiness of the mushrooms. And although *funghi trifolati* means, literally, truffled mushrooms, that isn't to indicate that truffles are included but, rather, that the porcini mushrooms resemble truffles.

I'm not really sure they do, much as I love the image, and anyway, porcini mushrooms are neither easily nor cheaply come by in the UK, and so I use any mixture of mushrooms I can get hold of. (Don't forget that mushrooms should be wiped with a damp cloth or a sheet of kitchen roll, never washed.) The larger mushrooms I slice; others I quarter, halve or leave whole as I see fit; and although I do remove the stems, I then slice and throw them in, too, where I can.

As a main course, this is wonderful alongside a big bowlful of golden polenta (cooked according to packet instructions), the paler Mock Mash or indeed the Gnocchi Gratin (see **pp.136** and **131**) and I wouldn't rule out the Saffron Orzotto (**p.134**) as a supper-party partner, either. Stirred through a tangle of egg tagliatelle, they would be sublime, too.

GARLIC MUSHROOMS WITH CHILLI & LEMON

Pour the oil into a heavy-bottomed pan or flameproof casserole that comes with a lid, and put it on a low to medium heat. Add the parsley, lemon zest and chilli flakes and grate in (or mince and add) the garlic, and let them sizzle fragrantly, but briefly as you don't want them to burn or, really, do anything other than infuse the oil with their heady scent.

Turn up the heat, add the mushrooms, sprinkle with the salt, and give a gentle stir to try to mix in the flavoured oil, then clamp on the lid. Turn the heat down to low and leave everything to simmer for 10 minutes. Although the mushrooms look dangerously dry as you put the lid on, when you remove the lid after these 10 minutes, you will see that they have given off quite a bit of liquid.

Now add the juice of the lemon, give everything a vigorous stir, then put the lid back on for another 10 minutes' simmering until the mushrooms are tender. It's wise to have a look once or twice during that time – just lift the lid and give a bit of a stir.

Scatter a little more parsley over the mushrooms, and serve. ◼

SERVES 4–6

60ML OLIVE OIL

4 X 15ML TABLESPOONS CHOPPED FRESH PARSLEY, PLUS MORE TO SERVE

ZEST AND JUICE 1 UNWAXED LEMON

½ TEASPOON DRIED CHILLI FLAKES

1 FAT CLOVE GARLIC, PEELED

750G MIXED MUSHROOMS (SEE INTRO ABOVE FOR PREP. NOTES)

1 TEASPOON SEA SALT FLAKES OR ½ TEASPOON POURING SALT, OR TO TASTE

WE IN BRITAIN TEND TO CONSIGN Brussels sprouts too readily to the Christmas culinary canon. It's true, of course, that they are a winter vegetable, thriving on frost, as anyone who has painfully picked them on icy mornings can attest.

I am slotting them in here, rather than in the Christmas section, not simply because I am happy to eat them roast, nuttily like this, whenever I can, but because trying to find last-minute oven space as you're about to serve up Christmas lunch could be enough to push one over the edge on a day that already has enough stress and tension. Of course, if you are blessed with a double oven, then augment quantities as needed and go for it.

I have specified smallish sprouts, by which I mean those that are still neatly and tightly furled rather than looser-leaved and blowsy.

ROAST BRUSSELS SPROUTS WITH ROSEMARY, LEMON & PECORINO

SERVES 4–6, *DEPENDING ON OTHER SIDE DISHES*
2 X 15ML TABLESPOONS GARLIC OIL
1 TEASPOON FINELY CHOPPED FRESH ROSEMARY NEEDLES
ZEST 1 UNWAXED LEMON (JUICE OPTIONAL)
500G SMALLISH BRUSSELS SPROUTS, TRIMMED AND HALVED
2 X 15ML TABLESPOONS GRATED PECORINO OR PARMESAN CHEESE
SALT AND PEPPER, TO TASTE

Preheat the oven to 220°C/gas mark 7.

Put the garlic oil in a shallow baking tin, add the chopped rosemary and the finely grated lemon zest, then tumble in the halved sprouts and smoosh everything about in the tin to coat as best you can, before roasting in the oven for 20 minutes.

Taste (being careful not to burn your mouth), to check that the sprouts are cooked through – though a bit of resistance (in this vegetable instance) is not a bad thing – and roast them another 4–5 minutes if they're not quite done; then remove the tin from the oven.

Decant the sprouts into a warmed serving bowl, sprinkle with the pecorino, then toss to combine well before adding salt and pepper to taste. If you want to add some lemon juice, from the lemon you zested earlier, do. ∎

WITHOUT THE LEMON, THIS IS MY children's favourite way of eating broccoli; they have been known to whoop with pleasure when seeing it on the kitchen table. Strange but true. I prefer it with the edge of lemon cutting across the rich saltiness of the Parmesan but, with or without, this does add a bit of Mambo Italiano to the Sunday lunch or weeknight supper veg menu.

For the Cod with Broccoli & Chilli on **p.82** I've specified 250g of tenderstem broccoli for 2 people; here I've reckoned that it will feed 4. This is partly because of the cheese that's added, but mostly because I tend to bring this out as one of a couple of side dishes to accompany a roast or at any rate some main course more robust than a modest cod fillet.

As a main course for 2, divide between 2 bowls and top each with a poached egg.

BROCCOLI WITH LEMON & PARMESAN

Put a pan of water on for the broccoli, adding salt to taste when it comes to the boil, and cook the broccoli until the stalk is tender. Drain and return to the pan, adding the lemon zest and juice, then toss to coat.

Transfer the broccoli to a warmed bowl and add the Parmesan flakes. There's no absolute need to do this – you could add the cheese to the broccoli in the pan – but it helps with the washing-up later. Either use a vegetable peeler to shave off strips or – if laziness dictates – use some ready-flaked, from a tub found in the chill cabinets in supermarkets.

Add the olive oil and toss well so that some of the cheese flakes start melting into the broccoli. Before serving, add pepper – and salt if wished, though it's unlikely any will be needed – to taste. ■

SERVES UP TO 4, *DEPENDING ON WHAT ELSE IS ON THE TABLE*
250G TRIMMED TENDERSTEM BROCCOLI
ZEST AND JUICE ½ UNWAXED LEMON
30G PARMESAN FLAKES (FRESHLY FLAKED OR SUPERMARKET TUB)
1 X 15ML TABLESPOON EXTRA-VIRGIN OLIVE OIL
SALT AND PEPPER, TO TASTE

THIS RECIPE DOESN'T EXACTLY EMANATE FROM Sicily, but the Moorish flavourings, with the saffron and that mixture of sweet sultanas and salty olives, most definitely do. I like the addition of (Sicilian) Marsala, but you can use water in its place, adding the saffron and its water to the sultanas and theirs. As ever, I go for dry-packed pitted black olives, but you can use black or green, pitted or unpitted, spiced or not. I have been known, *in extremis*, to use those retro anchovy-stuffed green ones. I'm not sure this quite counts as a salad, but I've settled on that nomenclature since I like to eat it at a whispering breath above room temperature, or even cold. I often do this salad when I have people over, as it really demands to be prepared ahead, which can make life easier as kick-off approaches.

SICILIAN CAULIFLOWER SALAD

SERVES 4–6, *AS A SIDE DISH* Ⓝ

1 HEAD CAULIFLOWER (APPROX. 1KG)

1 TEASPOON SEA SALT FLAKES OR ½ TEASPOON POURING SALT, PLUS MORE TO TASTE

2 BAY LEAVES

½ TEASPOON SAFFRON THREADS

60ML WATER, FROM A RECENTLY BOILED KETTLE

75G GOLDEN (OR REGULAR) SULTANAS

75ML MARSALA

1 ECHALION OR BANANA SHALLOT, PEELED AND FINELY CHOPPED

1 X 15ML TABLESPOON LEMON JUICE

4 X 15ML TABLESPOONS EXTRA-VIRGIN OLIVE OIL

150G PITTED DRY-PACKED BLACK OLIVES

25G PINE NUTS, TOASTED

SMALL BUNCH FRESH PARSLEY, CHOPPED

Break the cauliflower into florets and put these in a saucepan that comes with a lid. Cover with cold water, add the salt and bay leaves, put the lid on, set the pan on a high heat and bring to a boil; then drain immediately, discarding the bay leaves, and hold the colander bearing the cauliflower under a running cold tap for a moment, before putting it to one side. This will take the edge off the heat, but the cauliflower will still be warm.

Meanwhile, as the cauliflower is heating up in its water, put the saffron threads into a small bowl and pour the 60ml of recently boiled water over them. Leave to steep.

Put the sultanas into a small saucepan with the Marsala and bring to the boil, then immediately remove from the heat.

Put the still-warm cauliflower into a large serving bowl.

Add the chopped shallot to the saffron water, then whisk in the lemon juice and carry on whisking while you add the olive oil – a small hand whisk is all you need for this.

Add the sultanas (with any Marsala that clings to them and any left in the pan) and the olives to the cauliflower, then pour the dressing over them, scraping every drop out, and – first putting on a pair of disposable vinyl gloves, CSI-style – use your hands to toss to combine. Of course you can use external implements, if you prefer. Season to taste.

Leave your salad to come to room temperature (about 30 minutes to 1 hour, or less if you want it warmer) and, while you wait, heat a small frying pan, pop in the pine nuts and shake them about for a couple of minutes until golden and toasted. Don't leave the pan.

Toss most of the toasted pine nuts and chopped parsley through the salad and scatter what's left on top. This turns just about anything into a feast. ■

SHOULD I FEEL BASHFUL ABOUT GIVING a recipe that involves little more than opening a can? Well, if I should, I don't. I can't apologize for speed or ease when the outcome is so enduringly pleasurable.

Even if there are only two of us eating, I still like to make this amount, as it's perfect the next day, cold, and with the addition of some good tuna from another can, makes for a great packed lunch or speedy supper.

CANNELLINI BEANS WITH ROSEMARY

In a non-stick frying pan placed over a medium to low heat, warm the oil, then add the rosemary and lemon zest and let them sizzle aromatically, as you stir, for about 30 seconds.

Now grate in the garlic (or mince and add it) and stir for another 30 seconds, making sure the garlic doesn't colour. Put in the beans with some rinsing water still clinging to them, stirring gently but thoroughly enough to coat the beans in the fragrant oil.

Squeeze in the lemon juice and add salt and pepper to taste, then cook, stirring occasionally, until the beans are hot through – this shouldn't take more than a couple of minutes. Taste for seasoning.

Decant to a warm serving bowl and drizzle with a little extra-virgin olive oil, if wished. ■

SERVES 2–4 Ⓝ

2 X 15ML TABLESPOONS REGULAR OLIVE OIL

1 TEASPOON FINELY CHOPPED FRESH ROSEMARY

ZEST AND JUICE 1 UNWAXED LEMON

1 SMALL CLOVE GARLIC, PEELED

2 X 400G CANS CANNELLINI BEANS (OR OTHER BEANS OF YOUR CHOICE), DRAINED AND RINSED

SALT AND PEPPER, TO TASTE

APPROX. 1 TEASPOON EXTRA-VIRGIN OLIVE OIL (OPTIONAL)

IF YOU HAVEN'T AS YET COME across the small, bronzy-gold Castelluccio lentils from Umbria, you have a treat in store – and I use that last word advisedly here, as I always keep a packet or two of these to hand. Like the French Puy lentils, they are smaller than the generic green or brown lentils, and also – it should be said – more expensive. But, in the same way as their French counterparts, these Umbrian lentils are less earthy and more delicate in flavour than the generic ones and keep their nuttiness and texture better on cooking, too. I adore Puy lentils, and there is something appealing about their slate blue-black colouring, but the antique gold of a bowl of Castelluccio lentils brings a Renaissance opulence to any meal.

I should say that, as often as not, I include *cubetti di pancetta* in any dish of lentils I make, but not always, and it seems sensible to give the recipe without it, and offer you the option. If you do want to add the pancetta – or any bacon, frankly – for 500g lentils, I use 150g pancetta cubes and reduce the garlic oil at the beginning to 1 tablespoon.

This is a go-to recipe in my repertoire, because I find that if I make this – and though it's not instant, it's definitely low-effort – I can dispense with potatoes or any other starch, which lightens the load when entertaining. And these lentils can be made in advance, and then either reheated or served at room temperature, depending on how ahead of yourself you want to get.

Of course, you can use other lentils, but they don't quite capture the celebratory flourish of the Castelluccio gold.

ITALIAN GOLDEN LENTILS

SERVES 6–8, *AS A SIDE DISH* Ⓝ
3 X 15ML TABLESPOONS
    GARLIC OIL
1 LEEK, WASHED, TRIMMED,
    HALVED LENGTHWAYS AND
    FINELY SLICED
2 TEASPOONS DRIED THYME
500G CASTELLUCCIO LENTILS,
    RINSED AND DRAINED
APPROX. 1 LITRE COLD WATER
3 DRIED BAY LEAVES
SALT AND PEPPER, TO TASTE
CHOPPED FRESH PARSLEY OR
    CHIVES, TO SERVE (OPTIONAL)
EXTRA-VIRGIN OR CHILLI OIL, TO
    SERVE (OPTIONAL)

In a medium-sized pan, with a heavy base – or in a flameproof casserole – that has a lid, warm the garlic oil over a medium heat and stir in the pale jade strips of leek. Cook, stirring, for 2–3 minutes, then add the thyme and give a quick stir, before tipping in the lentils. Toss briskly but cautiously, so that the lentils are turned in the leeks and oil.

Pour in the water so that it comes 2–3cm above the lentils, then add the bay leaves, turn the heat up and let everything come to a boil. Clamp on the lid, turn the heat down to low and let it simmer gently for 30 minutes, or until the water is absorbed and the lentils are cooked, but not soft. If the lentils are old (I have been known to keep them till beyond their best-before date, though I don't advise it), you may need to give them longer. Season to taste and remove the bay leaves, then toss the lentils through with a little chopped parsley, or some chives, if wished, and sprinkle some more on top before serving.

I like to put a bottle of extra-virgin olive oil or chilli oil, or indeed both, for people to drizzle over the lentils as they eat, and I recommend you do, too. ■

IN *KITCHEN*, I CAME UP WITH THE IDEA of frying gnocchi to make near-instant mini roast potatoes, and I still immodestly exult in it. (To recap: just fry gnocchi, so long as they're fresh-packed rathen than frozen, in hot oil for about 4 minutes a side.) But I knew that there were other routes to be taken. Gnocchi are, after all, just potatoes and so it seemed that a dinner-party gratin that didn't involve more than 2 minutes' preparation could be possible. And I'm here to tell you now that it is indeed possible. And I don't know why I said just "dinner party". Yes, this recipe makes short work of any midweek entertaining, but I love this for everyday family suppers, too.

I make this gratin, for preference, only with the freshly made kind of gnocchi that can be found in the chill cabinet of the supermarket. They come (or do near me) in packets of 400g but, if you find them in packets of 500g, simply use two of those instead. I have even used three 400g-packets of gnocchi with the same amount of sauce without trouble.

As for the sauce: I mix the mascarpone and milk in a bowl first – otherwise I risk spraying my stove with everything – but if you're prepared to proceed more patiently and slowly, mix them in the casserole on the stove before you turn on the heat.

There would be nothing to stop you upping the cheese or adding some white truffle paste (or butter or oil) to the sauce as per the Mascarpone Mash overleaf, either.

GNOCCHI GRATIN

Preheat the oven to 200°C/gas mark 6, and put a pan of water on for the gnocchi.

Whisk the mascarpone in a bowl with the milk, then warm it in a shallow, flameproof casserole or gratin dish wide enough to fit the cooked gnocchi in later, in more or less a single layer.

Once the mascarpone mixture starts bubbling, turn off the heat, stir 3 tablespoons of the grated Parmesan into the sauce and then whisk till it melts. Add a good grinding of pepper and grate in some nutmeg, stir, then taste, and add salt only if you feel it needs it. Take the pan off the heat.

Salt the boiling water for the gnocchi and cook them according to packet instructions.

Drain the gnocchi and add to the sauce, turning them well, but gently, to coat, and once they are in an even layer in the dish, mix the remaining Parmesan with the breadcrumbs and sprinkle this on top.

Bake for 15 minutes, by which time the gratin should be bubbling and golden on top.

Remove from the oven and let it sit out for 5–10 minutes, to cool a little before serving. Don't let it stand for any longer than 15 minutes, or too much of the gloriously gooey sauce will be absorbed. ∎

SERVES 6, *AS A SIDE DISH*
250G MASCARPONE
60ML FULL-FAT MILK
4 X 15ML TABLESPOONS GRATED
   PARMESAN
FRESHLY GROUND PEPPER
FRESHLY GRATED NUTMEG
1 TEASPOON SEA SALT FLAKES OR
   ½ TEASPOON POURING SALT,
   OR TO TASTE
2 X 400G PACKETS GNOCCHI
2 X 15ML TABLESPOONS
   BREADCRUMBS

I JUST LOVE THIS MASH: it's gloriously rich, and yet fluffily light in texture. Normally, I like my mash plain, considering it a neutral starchy blanket and not an emphatic flavour-purveyor in its own right. I mean, obviously, I always load it up with butter and cream, but that doesn't counter my argument. Here I do without butter or cream, but before you rejoice in or scorn my supposed dietary restraint, let me tell you that mascarpone does the job of both. A sprinkling of Parmesan balances the creamy mellowness with spiky saltiness. Were I to leave it here, I think these mashed potatoes would still pass muster as plain. But I don't leave it here: I add white truffle paste or truffle butter. If you don't have either, use white truffle oil, though only a drop or two. The paste (which seems to last for yonks in my fridge) does have more of a natural truffle taste, but (unlike many) I don't absolutely condemn the use of white truffle oil. I have been known to use it myself.

Neither adding mascarpone nor truffle paste came as a revelation to me, but what *did* was this cooking method (courtesy of one of my favourite websites, food52.com), which involves steaming rather than boiling the potatoes. And because you're using a potato ricer later – I always do, incidentally – you don't even have to peel them. I should admit to simplifying their process from there on in.

When I have people over, I cook this slightly in advance, then trickle a film of full-fat milk over the top (as my mother taught me), cover with foil and keep it warm in a low oven, probably somewhere just below 100°C/gas mark ¼–½ for 45 minutes and no longer than 1 hour. The result: ultra-easeful pleasure all round. And should you be lucky enough to have a small amount left over, I recommend a gentle reheat with the addition of a little milk stirred in, to be eaten – for pure, private joy – with either a poached or soft boiled egg squished on top. You know it makes sense.

MASCARPONE MASH

SERVES 4–6 Ⓝ

1KG POTATOES (UNPEELED, IF YOU HAVE A RICER), CUT IN 5CM CHUNKS

125ML FULL-FAT MILK

3 X 15ML TABLESPOONS MASCARPONE, AT ROOM TEMPERATURE

1 TEASPOON SEA SALT FLAKES OR ½ TEASPOON POURING SALT, OR TO TASTE

▶

Put the unpeeled potato chunks in a steamer above a pan of boiling water, filled just about 8cm deep, and steam them until soft; I find this takes about 20 minutes. The scant amount of water will not boil dry in this time and the potatoes will not get too wet.

Remove the steamer part, pour out all the water from the pan, and then put the steamer with the cooked potato back on the now dry, hot pan, with the lid off, to stand for 10 minutes to dry out.

Then remove the top part and, in the bottom pan of the steamer, warm the milk but do not allow it to boil. Stir in the marscarpone and the salt.

Purée the potatoes using a ricer over the pan of warm milk, and give a good beat or two with a wooden spoon, whipping in some air as you do so.

When smooth, beat in the Parmesan and white truffle paste or truffle butter, tasting as you go: you may wish to add half the quantity of truffle paste, taste and then decide for yourself if you want to add the rest. And remember: if using truffle oil, add the merest drop or two and proceed with caution. Eat, however, with heady abandon. ∎

1½ X 15ML TABLESPOONS
GRATED PARMESAN
1 TEASPOON WHITE TRUFFLE
PASTE OR TRUFFLE BUTTER

THERE IS A REASON WHY THIS orzotto – think risotto, only made with barley, orzo in Italian – is huddling among the vegetables rather than being offered up with the pasta: I make it almost exclusively as a potato substitute, that's to say as a starchy accompaniment to a roast chicken or ham or bowl of meatballs and any number of stews.

It's incredibly simple to make, since, unlike risotto, there is almost no stirring involved, and it can easily be done ahead of time. On reheating, you may want to add a little more liquid first, and perhaps – to stir through at the end with the Parmesan – a couple of spoonfuls of mascarpone. In fact, if you would like a creamier texture, I suggest you add the mascarpone first time around.

My children are genetically predisposed to barley, but luckily this dish seems to win everyone over. It's just so charming to look at, as well as addictive to eat. The saffron-soused grains of barley positively ooze sunniness. I leave you with this thought: in my house there is a faction that insists on eating this with ultra-thin rashers of pancetta, fried to a crisp, crumbled on top.

SAFFRON ORZOTTO

SERVES 4, *AS A SIDE DISH* Ⓝ

750ML WEAK CHICKEN OR
  VEGETABLE STOCK
¼ TEASPOON SAFFRON THREADS
2 X 15ML TABLESPOONS
  GARLIC OIL
1 ECHALION OR BANANA SHALLOT,
  OR 1 SMALL ONION, PEELED AND
  FINELY CHOPPED
250G PEARL BARLEY
2 X 15ML TABLESPOONS DRY
  VERMOUTH OR WHITE WINE
2 X 15ML TABLESPOONS GRATED
  PARMESAN
SALT AND PEPPER, TO TASTE
2-3 X 15ML TABLESPOONS
  MASCARPONE (OPTIONAL)

First, make up the stock in a jug. (I don't use homemade, but just add good stock concentrate or bouillon powder to boiling water.) And use slightly less stock concentrate or powder to water than advised on the packet, to ensure that saltiness is kept at bay. Add the saffron, stir, and set aside for a moment.

In a shallow, heavy-based pan or flameproof casserole, about 26cm diameter and – importantly – that has lid, warm the garlic oil over a medium–low heat, then add the chopped shallot and cook for a couple of minutes, stirring. You don't want this to colour. If using an onion instead of a shallot, you may need to cook it for nearer 5 minutes.

Turn up the heat and add the barley, stirring it in the hot pan for a minute, then add the vermouth or wine and stir again.

Add the hot saffron stock, clamp the lid on, then turn the heat down to low and let the orzotto simmer gently for 20-30 minutes, or until the barley is cooked through and tender and most of the liquid absorbed. Do add a little extra boiling water if the liquid is absorbed before the barley is tender enough. Remove the lid, stir and take the pan off the heat; if you wanted, you could let it cool now, cover, refrigerate and leave it for a day or two (see Notes **p.265**). Otherwise, stir in the Parmesan and season to taste. Should you fancy adding the mascarpone, now would be the time to do it. ∎

ON THE ONE HAND, THIS IS an entirely non-Italian concept; on the other, its inspiration and derivation come hot-foot from Italy. Let me explain. I was making *gnocchi alla Romana* one day (think little round patties made with semolina) and before they'd been cut out, while I still had the mixture in front of me ready to cool, Lisa – who works with me and is Italian – walked past, dipped in a finger, tasted some and said "What lovely mashed potato!"

I went on, waited for the mixture to cool so that I could cut out my patties, laid them out like roof tiles, dusted with Parmesan and baked them. All good. But I couldn't help feeling afterwards that I could dispense with a major part of the activity: hence this, my mock mash. I know it sounds spooky – especially to those of us reared on semolina pudding at school, even those among us who have affection for the memory – but this is more wonderful than you could imagine. It's as fast as it is easy to whip up, so I wouldn't prepare it in advance. (Even with a little bit of standing, it does start to form a skin, but a quick stir – just with the serving utensils – gets rid of that.) I can't stop making it. I certainly can't stop eating it.

I know we can't get butter in tins here but, while we were shooting the photographs for this book, my sister gave me the tin, opposite, as a present from Italy and I couldn't *not* picture it.

MOCK MASH

SERVES 4–6, *AS A SIDE DISH* Ⓝ
1 LITRE FULL-FAT MILK
1 X 15ML TABLESPOON (15G)
 UNSALTED BUTTER
SEA SALT FLAKES OR POURING
 SALT, TO TASTE
FRESHLY GRATED NUTMEG
250G SEMOLINA
75G GRATED PARMESAN
PEPPER, TO TASTE

Heat the milk in a large, wide saucepan (you will need room to whisk later), then add the butter, a sprinkling of salt and a good grating of nutmeg.

When the milk is just coming to a boil, pour the semolina into the pan in a steady stream, whisking as you go.

Continue to whisk the mixture until it thickens, and big bubbles come to the surface with a gentle plopping sound. This should take 3–5 minutes.

Take the pan off the heat and beat in the grated cheese, check the seasoning, then tip the mash into a bowl, grating a little more nutmeg over it as you serve. ∎

CESARE CASELLA, A CHEF FROM LUCCA, whose family used to run the fabulous Vipore restaurant (from which the views over the Tuscan hills were more enchanting than I can say) and who is now cooking in New York, is the man who invented Tuscan Fries. Think French fries, but with garlic cloves and fresh herbs thrown into the hot oil towards the end of the cooking time.

Now, this would be too much for my nerves on a regular basis – deep-frying in anything other than small amounts, as per the Italian Tempura Prawns on **p.84**, say, isn't for me – were it not for the fact that the always compelling American magazine *Cook's Illustrated* introduced me to a radical, new and stress-free way of cooking chips.

It sounds crazy, but it works: you put the uncooked chips (or fries) into cold oil, then heat it up. It's revolutionary. You'd think it would make the chips unbearably greasy but in fact you end up with crisp, oil-free fries of utter fabulousness. That much you can tell by taste; but I have further proof in the fact that I once measured how much oil I had left when it had cooled down, and found that the potatoes had scarcely absorbed any. (If any of this gives you agita, use a jam or sugar thermometer.)

You do need, however, as I have found, to cut the potatoes more into the chunkier size of British chips than skinny French fries. That's no punishment, however.

Cesare's chips came on a plate lined with a chic and simple piece of brown paper, but I am happy to give them a quick sit on a baking tray lined with a double thickness of kitchen roll before letting them clatter out onto a platter or onto a newspaper (Italian, for preference), lined with greaseproof paper.

TUSCAN FRIES

SERVES 4–6

1KG WAXY POTATOES, SUCH AS MARIS PIPER

1.5 LITRES CORN OIL OR FLAVOURLESS VEGETABLE OIL, FOR FRYING

UNPEELED CLOVES FROM 1 HEAD GARLIC

8 TENDER TOP SPRIGS THYME, ROSEMARY AND SAGE, OR HERBS OF YOUR CHOICE

SEA SALT FLAKES, TO TASTE

Cut the short ends off each potato (but don't peel it) so that it can sit up vertically, and then slice it downwards into generous 1cm slices. Cut these slices into chips about 1cm thick; again, err on the generous side. Load up a clean tea towel with the chips as you cut them.

Put the oil into a wide, heavy-based pan (mine is approx. 28 cm diameter and 11cm deep), and add the freshly cut chipped potatoes. Then put the pan over a high heat and bring to a boil, which should take about 5 minutes. Keep a careful watch on the pan at all times.

Continue to cook the fries, without stirring them, for another 15 minutes. The pan will be bubbling vigorously. If the oil gets too hot or bubbles too hard, reduce the heat a little, and always keep a close eye on it. (If you're using a thermometer, once the oil temperature reaches 160°C, turn down the heat slightly and keep the fries cooking at between 150–160°C.)

Now you can very carefully give the chips a gentle stir with a pair of tongs held in an oven glove, moving any that have stuck away from the bottom or sides of the pan. Add the unpeeled cloves of garlic to the pan, stir gently again, and cook for another 5–10 minutes (watching the temperature and making sure the garlic doesn't look burnt or the fries too dark), before testing a chip for crispness on the outside and tenderness on the inside. Do not burn your mouth, though! You might need another 5 minutes or so beyond this, but stand by your pan: the chips can turn from a cooked gold to a burnt bronze quickly.

At the point when the chips are pale gold, but crisp, toss in the herbs, then after a minute or so scoop everything out – using a couple of perforated scoops for ease, and wearing oven gloves to protect your hands – onto a tray or platter lined with a double thickness of kitchen roll. Once any excess oil has been absorbed, tip the chips off the kitchen paper clatteringly onto the plate and sprinkle with sea salt flakes to taste, serving immediately. ■

SWEET THINGS

IN ITALY, IT'S NOT HARD TO GET FIGS that are so luscious it would be a sin to do anything more than pop them plumptiously into your mouth. I don't even hold with peeling. I suppose, though, even in Italy a disappointing fig cannot be unknown; here in Britain, it is sadly routine.

So, if you are unable to resist buying figs but then go home to discover that they are either bland or grittily tough, here's how to proceed.

I find 8 figs perfect for 4 people, but if they are small, then up quantities to 12 figs; the sauce quantities should be fine as they are. The idea is not to drown the figs in honey-scented cream, but to kiss them with it.

FIGS WITH HONEY-CREAM & PISTACHIOS

Preheat the oven to 220°C/gas mark 7.

Take a knife and cut into the figs as if you wanted to cut them into quarters, downwards, but do not cut right through to the bottom; you want to be able to open them like a flower. Arrange them in a small oven tin – I use a tarte Tatin tin – dribble the olive oil over them, then bake for 10 minutes (or a little less if the figs are small), until they are soft.

In a teeny-tiny saucepan, heat the cream and honey and let it bubble for about 1–1½ minutes so that it is slightly condensed and reduced. Keep an eye on it.

Remove the figs from the oven and arrange them on 1 large plate or 4 small plates, then pour the honeyed cream over them and scatter with the chopped pistachios. ■

SERVES 4
8 LARGE BLACK FIGS
2 TEASPOONS OLIVE OIL
60ML DOUBLE CREAM
2 TEASPOONS HONEY
2 X 15ML TABLESPOONS SHELLED, CHOPPED PISTACHIO NUTS

ICED BERRIES WITH LIMONCELLO WHITE CHOCOLATE SAUCE

THIS IS A CONTEMPORARY CLASSIC, INVENTED by the great British chef Mark Hix, but I have taken the liberty of speeding up the sauce-making process, and – crucially – adding limoncello for an Italian touch. It gives a real edge to the ultra-rich white chocolate and, besides, I have been longing to do something with this particular combo ever since I saw the winning Joanne Wheatley create her Limoncello and White Chocolate Croquembouche on BBC 2's *The Great British Bake Off.*

Now, white chocolate is much sneered at by those who take pride in their palate, considered – as the master baker Dan Lepard wrote in the *Guardian* – "the Big Mac of confectionery". Even if you take a similar line, and I'm afraid I have been known to do so myself, you are just going to have to believe me when I say that this recipe will challenge any prejudice you may be harbouring. This is elegant and punchy at the same time; the depth of the limoncello and the sharpness of the berries completely defuse the unsophisticated and otherwise one-note richness of the white chocolate. All the same, if in doubt, I advise telling people it's a limoncello sauce, with no mention of the white chocolate, to begin with.

I am too impatient to melt the chocolate in a double boiler, and I do like an element of risk, but heating any chocolate can be tricky and white chocolate especially so; I would totally understand it if you were to prefer to make the sauce sensibly in a heatproof bowl suspended over a pan of simmering water, but you must make sure the base of the bowl doesn't touch the bubbling water beneath.

I love to serve this on a rimmed cake stand, but it could make more sense to make up individual portions in saucers or side plates with a lip. I think it's important that, however you serve it, you try to keep the berries in a single layer, give or take.

What makes this fantastic for a last-minute, even impromptu, dinner-party pud (with interesting Christmas potential) is that you can keep the berries in the deep freeze until needed. I suppose you could, in summer, use fresh berries, though you would lose the contrast between warm rich sauce and sharp icy fruit.

Put the double cream and 2 tablespoons of the limoncello in a milk pan, and heat it until just about to come to the boil, but not actually boiling.

Take the pan off the heat and add the white chocolate, then swirl the pan about so that it is all submerged.

Take the berries out of the freezer and arrange them in a single layer in a dish or plate that has a small lip (so that the sauce doesn't drip off later). Sprinkle with the remaining 2 tablespoons of limoncello and leave for 5 minutes, during which time you can swirl your white chocolate pan about every now and again to help the chocolate melt into the lemony cream.

Using a rubber spatula, gently stir the chocolate-cream mixture, still off the heat, until it's smooth, then pour it over the berries and serve immediately. ■

SERVES 4–6

250ML DOUBLE CREAM
4 X 15ML TABLESPOONS
  LIMONCELLO (LEMON LIQUEUR)
200G WHITE CHOCOLATE,
  FINELY CHOPPED
500G FROZEN MIXED BERRIES
  (UNTHAWED), SOMETIMES
  LABELLED "SUMMER FRUITS"

WHITE CHOCOLATE MAY BE CONSIDERED an infra-dig ingredient, but for the self-styled tastemakers of the world, condensed milk is *really* beyond the pale. So how can you blame me for wanting to slip it into any recipe whenever possible? Not that I'm doing this simply to be kitsch: it is a strangely useful ingredient; see, too, the One-Step No-Churn Coffee Ice Cream on **p.170**. And, before you start wondering, there are many Italian recipes using *latte condensato*, but you tend to come across them in passed-down family recipe notebooks rather than in glamorous magazines or elegant books.

Not that I'm ashamed of using a tin of it myself – I always have one or two in the house – but I do feel obliged to say that no one would ever guess that this no-wait, egg-free mousse contained condensed milk. And when I made this for dinner recently, an Italian friend even asked me for the recipe. That's good enough for me.

As for that other key ingredient, the bitter orange liqueur, I only have to smell Aperol and I feel I'm in Italy. But if you can't find it, then use triple sec, Cointreau or Grand Marnier or any other orange liqueur in its place.

INSTANT CHOCOLATE-ORANGE MOUSSE

SERVES 6 Ⓝ
150G DARK CHOCOLATE (MIN.
  70% COCOA SOLIDS), FINELY
  CHOPPED
175G CONDENSED MILK
500ML DOUBLE CREAM
PINCH SALT
2 X 15ML TABLESPOONS APEROL,
  TRIPLE SEC, COINTREAU,
  GRAND MARNIER OR OTHER
  ORANGE LIQUEUR
2 X 15ML TABLESPOONS ORANGE
  JUICE AND ZEST ½ ORANGE

6 X APPROX. 150ML GLASSES

Melt the chocolate carefully either in an appropriate bowl in the microwave (following manufacturer's instructions) or over a pan of simmering water (making sure the bowl doesn't touch the water); when almost melted, stir with a rubber spatula, both to scrape down and to help the last solid bits of chocolate to melt. Take off the heat and leave to cool a little.

Pour the condensed milk and 250ml of the double cream into a bowl, add the salt, and whisk till thickened, but only just – when you lift the beaters, they should leave a trail of ribbons.

Stir about a third of the whipped cream mixture into the slightly cooled melted chocolate; you can be fairly brutal about this. Now, slowly – in 2 or 3 batches – fold the lightened chocolate mixture back into the rest of the whipped cream mixture. Then gently stir in the orange liqueur followed by the orange juice (having first zested the orange).

When all is combined, carefully fill 6 glasses of around 150ml capacity to about 1cm below the rim.

Put the chocolate mousses into the fridge for 1 hour (although you could serve them sooner, as they're edible straightaway); at the same time, whip the remaining 250ml double cream until thickened but still floppy, before peaks begin to form, and put this in the fridge, too (and see Notes **p.265**).

On serving, distribute the cream equally between the glasses of chocolate mousse and top these fluffy blobs with the orange zest. ■

I KNOW THERE ARE PEOPLE WHO, because of early over-indulgence in sambuca, maintain a shuddering revulsion for it now. Luckily, even those individuals seem to be won over by these, entirely salubrious sambuca kisses.

It's hard to explain the precise nature of these: they are light, almost like doughnuts, but made of scented, sweet air rather than batter. They are called kisses (baci) in Italy, as they seem to caress the mouth flutteringly as you eat them; think butterfly kiss rather than smooch.

Strictly speaking, you shouldn't leave them to stand, once they've been made. But pleasurable though it is to eat them as soon as you can – once they're out of the pan – I have found they're fine for a while in a low oven. The contrast between outside and inside is lost, rather, but not so much as you gain in the convenience of being able to make them ahead.

SAMBUCA KISSES

Put the egg and ricotta into a bowl and beat together until smooth.

Add the flour, baking powder, sambuca, sugar and grated orange zest. Beat the mixture again to make a smooth batter.

Pour about 2cm oil into a frying pan, and heat until a small piece of bread sizzles when you drop it into the pan and browns in about 40 seconds (the temperature should be at about 180°C). And keep your eye on the pan at all times.

Oil a teaspoon measure and gently drop rounded teaspoons of the ricotta batter into the pan; about 4 at a time is manageable.

The little kisses will puff up slightly and turn golden underneath, so flip them over carefully with an implement of your choice, to colour the other side. Watch out that the oil doesn't get too hot: turn the heat down if they are browning too quickly.

Once they are golden all over, lift them out with a slotted spoon and place them on a plate lined with 1 or 2 sheets of kitchen roll, to get rid of any excess oil. Carry on cooking until all the mixture is used up, then turn off the heat under the oil.

Once the kisses have cooled a bit, push the icing sugar through a small sieve to dust them thickly.

If you are not eating them straightaway, pop the pre-sugared, cooked kisses on a wire rack over a tin in a 150°C/gas mark 2 oven, and keep them warm for up to 1 hour.

If so inclined, serve with a shot of sambuca or an espresso. ■

MAKES 18–20

1 EGG
100G RICOTTA
40G PLAIN FLOUR
1 TEASPOON BAKING POWDER
2 TEASPOONS SAMBUCA LIQUEUR
1 TEASPOON SUGAR
1 TEASPOON GRATED ORANGE ZEST
FLAVOURLESS VEGETABLE OR CORN OIL, FOR FRYING
1–2 TEASPOONS ICING SUGAR, TO SERVE

LIQUORICE IS ONE OF THE SIGNATURE TASTES of Italy. As this is an ingredient that divides people viscerally, I've made it just for 2, or possibly 1 very greedy liquorice eater...

I use the tiny liquorice pellets that come, usually, from Calabria and are seen everywhere in Italy. Outside of Italy, you can find them in Italian delis and via the internet: for those who share my love for this almost vicious aniseed flavour, there is a whole world online for you.

This is a pudding in the Italian sense of *budino*, a word that Anna Del Conte explains in her *Gastronomy of Italy* (original edition) "though hard to define...suggests a dish of a round shape, a soft texture and a trembling consistency". This is an easy, almost-instant version (in terms of the cooking) that bypasses the bain-marie baking normally required, and is eaten from a glass rather than turned out. I melt the pellets in hot water, and don't mind at all if a few dark splodges are detectable in the finished, silky, buff-coloured cream.

I have expressed my passion for salted caramel elsewhere, but here I must declare my deep, almost deviant, love for salted liquorice. I don't want the two wholly mixed in here, but prefer to have some soft, sea salt flakes (the French *fleur de sel* is my choice here) to sprinkle on as I eat. I get a frisson just thinking of it.

LIQUORICE PUDDING

SERVES 2 Ⓝ
60ML WATER
1 TEASPOON PURE ITALIAN LIQUORICE PELLETS, SUCH AS AMARELLI ROSSANO
2 X 15ML TABLESPOONS LIGHT MUSCOVADO SUGAR
175ML DOUBLE CREAM
2 TEASPOONS CORNFLOUR
1 X 15ML TABLESPOON MILK
SOFT SEA SALT FLAKES, TO SERVE

Put the water and liquorice pellets in your smallest pan and bring to the boil, stirring or whisking frequently to help the liquorice melt. Once it starts bubbling, turn off the heat and leave for 5 minutes, stirring or whisking every now and again.

Turn the heat back on and whisk in the sugar, then the cream, and bring to a bubble. Remove from the heat.

Spoon the cornflour into a little bowl, cup or ramekin and slake it with the milk: which is to say, whisk in the milk until you have a smooth paste.

Pour this, whisking as you go, into the mixture in the saucepan. Still whisking, put the pan back on the heat and bring back to a bubble, whisking all the while, for 20–30 seconds, or until thickened.

Divide between 2 heatproof glasses or cups and – unless you want to eat this hot – cover, touching the surface of the puddings, with clingfilm or baking parchment that you've wet with cold water then wrung out (this is to prevent a skin forming, a thing I cannot tolerate), and put them in the fridge to chill for at least 2 hours or overnight.

Let the puddings come to room temperature before serving, and remove the clingfilm or baking parchment and smooth the tops with the back of a teaspoon. Put the soft sea salt on the table to sprinkle over as you eat, if wished. For those of us who love liquorice, this pudding is a sheer, spine-tingling joy. ∎

PANNA COTTA THREE-WAYS

I WROTE MY FIRST RECIPE FOR PANNA COTTA (admittedly, an anglicized version tagged Elderflower Cream) way back in my first book, *How To Eat*, published in 1998, but for me, this is a pud that never falls out of favour. Besides, flavour not fashion is what counts in food, and I can never tire of the perfect panna cotta. Custom cannot stale its infinite variety, although I have shown uncharacteristic restraint and confined myself to a mere trio of versions.

But I do say "the perfect panna cotta", and if real cooking is all about the palate, let me say that texture is the key issue here. Consistency is crucial: a panna cotta must have a voluptuous and quivering softness, as if trembling between solid and liquid. A panna cotta must never be overset; the trick is to add just enough gelatine to keep the unmoulded cream from collapsing, but it should still have just enough wibble about it to hint that it could, that its bulging form could break its borders and spill free. It won't, so don't worry. Because the point is I don't want you to feel that there is risk here, or that it is difficult to achieve the perfect set. Once you get it right, it's right. And so, so easy. You heat cream, dissolve gelatine, stir, pour, put in the fridge. That's taken about 5 minutes, max. And that's your work done. Now, you just leave it to set.

So here's the deal: I've worked out exactly how much gelatine is needed for this state of grace. Irritatingly, just when I'd truly perfected it, the makers of leaf gelatine changed the weight of the leaves and I had to start again. It is for this reason that when specifying how many leaves you need, I give the number and weight of total leaves in the pack sold. This is to make sure we're all using the same weight of gelatine. If the pack you've found differs, you will just have to dust off your quadratic equations to work out how many leaves you need.

And, although you can indeed flavour panna cotta freely (though Italian traditionalists may be reluctant to agree), it is important not to get too fanciful: this is a delicate creation, and an overwhelming flavour – anything too bold and shouty or attention-seekingly novel – will blow the balance. So my trio of flavours is simple: vanilla, coffee, Nutella. Served together, the slate-speckled ivory, manilla and hazelnut-coloured creams are beautifully harmonious, not just in terms of taste, but tonally, too. The reason that the Vanilla and Coffee Panna Cotta recipes each make 4 servings and the Nutella makes 6 is because I have found (especially, but not only, when children are eating) that this best reflects the likely take-up.

But it's only for a big party that I would really think of making these all together, so please read them as freestanding recipes. Accordingly, I repeat the instructions for each, even though the method doesn't change. It just makes life simpler: no fretful flicking back to check what you should be doing.

What I will state here, though, just to underscore its importance, is that you should use metal dariole moulds. There is any number of silicone panna cotta moulds on the market, but it is easiest by far to unmould from metal. It's not conventional but, if you prefer, you could always pour the panna cotta mixture into small glasses to set, and dispense with the unmoulding. Just an idea... ■

VANILLA PANNA COTTA

THIS IS THE PLAINEST OF THE TRIO, although it is still more emphatically flavoured than the original Piedmontese *Crema Cotta* (as it used to be called, and which I, with my appetite for alliteration, wish it were still called), which was often nothing more than cream, cooked and set. I like to use proper vanilla, rather than extract here, even though I have never managed to make the black seeds disperse themselves equally throughout the cream – they always seem to settle in a speckled layer at the top once the creams are unmoulded. Still, this doesn't bother me. (If it bothers you, I suggest you dispense with the seeds and, instead, use a vegetable peeler to shave off some strips of zest from an unwaxed lemon and add these to the cream while it's heating, then add a few drops of vanilla extract once you've heated the cream. Leave it to steep for 20 minutes, then remove the zest, reheat the cream a little and proceed from here with the gelatine.)

Traditionally, panna cotta is served without any accompaniment but, as in language so in cooking, usage dictates form, and it is now customary to add a berry or two or some sort of contrasting partner on the plate. For me, the choice is some finely diced strawberries, macerated in balsamic vinegar (same vintage as panna cotta, in terms of first modish moment), and for the amount of people I'm feeding here, I'd go for 200g of strawberries, dice them finely, put them in a bowl with ½ teaspoon each of caster sugar and of balsamic vinegar, cover with clingfilm and leave to steep for at least 15 minutes and up to 2 hours, out of the fridge, shaking the covered bowl to swirl the contents every now and again. This won't give you a lot of fruit, but you want only a spoonful or so on each plate. In winter, consider simply spooning some pomegranate seeds around, letting one or two drop on top. My son insists on a chocolate sauce (poured around the panna cotta, not over it) and if you feel so inclined, too, then make up half quantities of the Chocolate Sauce on **p.169**, but add a small espresso shot (about 2 tablespoonfuls) to the cream and chocolate in the pan when you kick off, and make sure the sauce is cool when you serve it.

SERVES 4 Ⓝ

75ML FULL-FAT MILK
425ML DOUBLE CREAM
50G CASTER SUGAR
1 VANILLA POD
2 LEAVES FINE-LEAF GELATINE
   (FROM PACK WHERE 15 LEAVES
   WEIGH 25G)

4 X 125ML METAL DARIOLE
   MOULDS

Pour the milk and cream into a saucepan and stir in the sugar. Remove the seeds from the vanilla pod (and see **p.164** for instructions should you want) and add them, plus the emptied-out pod, to the saucepan, and put it over a low heat.

While this is gently heating and coming to the boil, put the 2 leaves of gelatine into a shallow dish and cover them fully with cold water to soften. The softening should take about 3 minutes, so go back to the pan on the stove while the leaves sit and soak.

When the saucepan mixture is about to come to a boil – i.e. when it is beginning to bubble a little around the edges – take the pan off the heat, remove the vanilla pod (though rinse and dry it later to save for future use to flavour sugar) and pour about 1 breakfastcupful (approx. 250ml) of the mixture into a heatproof jug.

Check that the gelatine feels soft – it should feel a bit like a tissue made out of jellyfish – then squeeze out the leaves so that the excess cold water falls back into the soaking dish, and drop the squeezed-out leaves into the jug with its cupful of liquid, whisking as you go.

Once the gelatine has dissolved in the jug, pour the jugful back into the saucepan, which is still off the heat, whisking the pan as you do so, and then pour all of the mixture back into the jug, before pouring it into the pots, giving a gentle whisk to the jug's contents between each pour. Transfer to the fridge for at least 6 hours or preferably overnight, until set.

To unmould easily, dip the bottom of each pot into some just-boiled water, one at a time, and hold there for about 8 seconds and let them stand out of the water for another few seconds, before wiping off the water and putting a small side plate or saucer on top; then upturn the pot and let the panna cotta drop onto the plate. Do likewise with the remaining 3 pots and serve, with fruit or sauce as preferred. ■

COFFEE PANNA COTTA

I TRIED TO STOP MYSELF, BELIEVE ME, I did, as I realize that this book ain't light on coffee-flavoured confections, but this is my all-time favourite and it would have given me too much pain to leave it out.

The depth of the coffee flavour, combined with the treacliness of the sugar and the satiny richness of the cream, make this, for me, an unbeatable combination. It's startlingly, but simply, sensational.

I use a couple of proper espresso shots, since I've got a machine that makes this easy, but otherwise make up *very* strong coffee by other means. And if you fancy a chocolate sauce alongside, then make up half quantities of the recipe on **p.169**, adding a small espresso shot – about 2 tablespoons – to the pan at the beginning, and make sure the sauce is cool on serving; or make up the Frangelico cream on the facing page.

SERVES 4 Ⓝ

125ML ESPRESSO, FRESHLY MADE

50G LIGHT MUSCOVADO SUGAR

375ML DOUBLE CREAM

PINCH SALT

2 LEAVES FINE-LEAF GELATINE
  (FROM PACK WHERE 15 LEAVES
  WEIGH 25G)

4 X 125ML METAL DARIOLE
  MOULDS

Pour the hot strong espresso into a milk pan and stir in the light muscovado sugar until it has dissolved. Now stir in the cream and pinch of salt and put the saucepan on a low heat.

While this is gently heating and coming to the boil, put the 2 leaves of gelatine into a shallow dish and fully cover them with cold water to soften. The softening should take about 3 minutes, so go back to the pan on the stove while the leaves sit and soak.

When the cappuccino-scented mixture is about to come to a boil – i.e. when it is beginning to bubble a little around the edges – take the pan off the heat and pour about 1 breakfastcupful (approx. 250ml) of the mixture into a heatproof jug.

Check that the gelatine feels soft – it should feel a bit like a tissue made out of jellyfish – then squeeze out the leaves so that the excess cold water falls back into the soaking dish, and drop the squeezed-out leaves into the jug with its cupful of liquid, whisking as you go.

Once the gelatine has dissolved in the jug, pour the jugful back into the saucepan, whisking the pan as you go, and then pour all of the mixture back into the jug, before pouring it into the pots, giving the jug's contents a gentle whisk between each pour, then transfer to the fridge for at least 6 hours or preferably overnight, until set.

To unmould easily, dip the bottom of each pot into some just-boiled water, one at a time, and hold there for about 8 seconds and let them stand out of the water for another few seconds, before wiping off the water and putting a small side plate or saucer on top; then upturn the pot and let the panna cotta drop onto the plate. Do likewise with the remaining 3 pots and serve, as is, or with some cool chocolate sauce lapping around the edges. ■

NUTELLA PANNA COTTA

THIS CHEEKY LITTLE NUMBER COMES COURTESY of Angela Hartnett, a chef with, all jokiness aside, an exquisite palate and a sensibility that is utterly unsullied by the pretension natural to many of her profession.

My recipe is not quite hers, but I am grateful for the inspiration, though not nearly as grateful as my children are. By the way, don't be alarmed that I use the same number of gelatine leaves for this recipe as for the two others, despite the fact that the liquid content here is higher – the Nutella itself aids the set as it chills.

I like to serve this with some double cream poured around the panna cotta on the plate and, if the mood takes me, and I'm catering not for children but for adults with childish tastes, I splosh in some Frangelico hazelnut liqueur as well. Actually, you could also add a slug to the Nutella mixture in the pan as you cook, and put the bottle on the table with a clutch of shot glasses, on serving.

Pour the milk and cream into a saucepan and add the Nutella, stir to combine (adding a slug of hazelnut liqueur if the fancy takes you), then put the saucepan over a low heat.

While this is gently heating and coming to the boil, put the 2 leaves of gelatine into a shallow dish and cover them fully with cold water to soften. The softening should take about 3 minutes, so go back to the pan on the stove while the leaves sit and soak.

When the Nutella has melted in and the mixture is about to come to a boil – i.e. when it is beginning to bubble a little around the edges – take the pan off the heat, stir, then pour about 1 breakfastcupful (approx. 250ml) of the mixture into a heatproof jug.

Check that the gelatine feels soft – it should feel a bit like a tissue made out of jellyfish – and squeeze out the leaves so that the excess cold water falls back into the soaking dish, then drop the squeezed-out leaves into the jug with its cupful of liquid, whisking as you go.

Once the gelatine has dissolved, pour the jugful back into the saucepan, which is still off the heat, whisking the pan as you go, then pour all of the mixture back into the jug, before pouring it into the pots, giving a gentle whisk to the jug's contents between each pour. Sit the pots in the fridge for at least 6 hours or preferably overnight, until set.

To unmould easily, dip the bottom of each pot into some just-boiled water, one at a time, and hold there for about 8 seconds and let them stand out of the water for another few seconds, before wiping off the water and putting a small side plate or saucer on top; then upturn the pot and let the panna cotta drop onto the plate. Do likewise with the remaining 5 pots and serve. Put a jug of cream – spiked with Frangelico or not, as you wish – on the table to serve alongside. ◼

SERVES 6 Ⓝ

250ML FULL-FAT MILK

250ML DOUBLE CREAM

250G NUTELLA OR EQUIVALENT CHOCOLATE HAZELNUT SPREAD

2 LEAVES FINE-LEAF GELATINE (FROM PACK WHERE 15 LEAVES WEIGH 25G)

FRANGELICO CREAM, TO SERVE (OPTIONAL)

6 X 15ML TABLESPOONS DOUBLE CREAM

6 TEASPOONS FRANGELICO HAZELNUT LIQUEUR

6 X 125ML METAL DARIOLE MOULDS

THESE PANCAKES ARE – WITHOUT WISHING TO OFFEND ITALIANS – what we think of as French-style *crêpes*. For our purposes here, though, they are Italian-style *crespelle*. Be that as it may, as a quick supper party pud, I buy them readymade, to be turned easily into parcels, filled with mascarpone and ricotta, flavoured with lemon, vanilla and rum; once baked, these taste like soft, cheesecake-stuffed pancakes. The rum-soused confetti of strawberries that I dollop on top echoes the fruit toppings of retro cheesecakes; more importantly, the liqueur-heightened brightness of the berries undercuts the richness of the filling. One parcel per person would probably be fine, portion-wise, but I work on the principle that half those eating might have seconds. You could easily give each person 2 apiece if you preferred or, conversely, stretch them out to feed more if need be. Once cooked, they set and cut well, so you could even slice them into fingers or smaller squares.

MASCARPONE & RICOTTA PANCAKES WITH RUM-STEEPED STRAWBERRIES

Preheat the oven to 180°C/gas mark 4. Hull the strawberries and cut them into small dice, then put them in a bowl and sprinkle with the 2 tablespoons sugar and 2 tablespoons rum. Cover with clingfilm and leave to macerate – swirling once or twice – while you get on with the crêpes.

Lightly brush a swiss roll tin or similar lipped baking sheet with some of the melted butter or line with baking parchment, then stir the teaspoon of rum into the rest of the melted butter and set aside for a while.

Beat together the mascarpone and ricotta, until they are light and well combined, then beat in the egg, followed by the 50g sugar, the lemon zest, vanilla extract and the remaining tablespoon of rum.

Lay out a crêpe, pale-side up, and dollop about a third of a cup – think of an espresso cup filled brimmingly to the rim – of the mixture onto the middle, then fold the top and bottom of the pancake over, and do the same to the sides, to make a bulging parcel. Place, fold- or seam-side down, on your prepared swiss roll tin and proceed with the remaining 7 pancakes.

Brush the pancakes with the rum-butter and pop in the preheated oven for 20–25 minutes; when cooked, they will be puffed up and, although the filling will have oozed out a little, it will be safely set.

Let them stand a minute or so before carefully transferring to a serving plate (or serve straight from the tin), and spoon a gleaming sprinkle of rum-soaked strawberries over them as you serve. ∎

SERVES 6 *(MAKES 8 PANCAKES)*
FOR THE STRAWBERRIES:
500G STRAWBERRIES
2 X 15ML TABLESPOONS CASTER SUGAR
2 X 15ML TABLESPOONS RUM

FOR THE FILLED PANCAKES:
2 X 15ML TABLESPOONS (30G) UNSALTED BUTTER, MELTED
1 X 15ML TABLESPOON RUM, PLUS 1 TEASPOON
250G MASCARPONE, AT ROOM TEMPERATURE
250G RICOTTA, AT ROOM TEMPERATURE
1 EGG
50G CASTER SUGAR
ZEST 1 UNWAXED LEMON
½ TEASPOON VANILLA EXTRACT
8 CRÊPES, SHOP-BOUGHT

1 X SWISS ROLL TIN OR LIPPED BAKING SHEET

FOR SOMEONE WHO STARTED OFF as a tiramisu-scorner, I have turned out to be its most slavish proponent, finding any excuse to whip up a new one. From Anna Del Conte's all-white meringue version, and something more trad (and I say this being well aware that tiramisu as such came into being only in the latter half of the 20th century), to one made with Frangelico and another with Baileys.

Some say, challenging more generally accepted ideas about the provenance, that it was invented in a *casa chiusa* (a house of ill repute) to give the working girls a pick-me-up, as the name (*tira-mi-su*) suggests. Whatever its inception, this one reverts to the original formulation – although in dinkier format. This is not because I am a huge fan of the cute – you know that – but because it means you have a tiramisu worth making for fewer people (you don't need a partyful), and in less time. By which I mean very much less time, since, unlike the big, trifle-style tiramisu, these tiramisini – think coffee-soaked Savoiardi sponge fingers, topped with the familiar, whipped Marsala-spiked mascarpone in small-portioned martini glasses – don't even need to sit overnight before being ready to eat.

These are a tiny bit lighter, too, as I don't use the egg yolks – the mascarpone is plenty rich enough – but keep the whites to add moussiness and air. These I buy in a carton (pasteurized) and have always at the ready (and see Note to the Reader on **p.xiii** about eggs). I make sure the Savoiardi, mascarpone and Marsala are also to hand; and coffee is always in the house, as well as the liqueur that echoes it, but it's fine to leave out the coffee liqueur and just bump up the coffee quotient, if you prefer.

TIRAMISINI

SERVES 4

100ML ESPRESSO OR STRONG
   INSTANT COFFEE
2 X 15ML TABLESPOONS COFFEE
   LIQUEUR
4 SAVOIARDI BISCUITS (FINE
   SPONGE FINGERS)
2 EGG WHITES
250G MASCARPONE
2 X 15ML TABLESPOONS HONEY
2 X 15ML TABLESPOONS MARSALA
APPROX. 1 TEASPOON GOOD-
   QUALITY COCOA POWDER

4 X SMALL (APPROX. 125ML)
   MARTINI GLASSES

Make your espresso and pour it into a heatproof jug, adding the coffee liqueur, then leave it to cool. I find 10 minutes outside the window on a cool day does it!

Break each Savoiardi sponge finger into about 4 and drop the pieces into the martini glasses, then pour the cooled espresso mixture over them. Tamp down gently, making sure the biscuits are soaked all over.

Using an electric hand-held whisk for ease, beat the egg whites until they form soft peaks, and set aside for a moment.

Scrape the mascarpone into another bowl, adding the honey; I love the way its mellow sweetness marries with the Marsala, though sugar would be fine too. Beat with the whisk (no need to clean it out first) and, when smooth, slowly beat in the Marsala.

Fold in the egg whites, a third at a time, then dollop this mixture over the soused Savoiardi in each glass, using a spoon to whirl it into a swirly peak at the top.

Let these stand in the fridge for at least 20 minutes and up to 24 hours, then dust with cocoa, pushing it through a fine-mesh strainer, just before serving. ■

I DARE SAY THAT HAVING A TRICOLORE pud is not terribly original, when it comes to compiling a book of Italian recipes, but I just couldn't help myself. Besides, the sharpness of the berries and the aromatic rubble of pistachios provide contrast – of taste and texture – with the light, vanilla-flecked mousse. I say mousse, but this is a simple affair, consisting of no more than whisked egg whites, folded into double cream whipped with sugar and the seeds from a vanilla pod. To get the seeds out of the pod, I use the point of a small, sharp knife to make a lengthways incision all along the middle of the pod, and then use the point of the knife again to scoop and scrape all the damp black seeds out. And, if I can do that with what my TV director calls my "borderline dyspraxia", anyone can. Don't throw away the pod, by the way, but rinse and dry it later to put in a jar of caster sugar to flavour it for baking.

If you want to top these vanilla mousses with a fine dust of pistachio, then you'll need a coffee grinder; otherwise, chop the nuts finely by hand, and you'll probably need the extra spoonful for total coverage. As for the berries that go underneath, to keep to the *tricolore* theme, I like to use 50/50 raspberries (left whole) and strawberries (chopped to match the size of the raspberries) but, otherwise, a mixture of any berries that come your way would be fine and dandy.

I have so many recipes, as you may have noted, where I use only the egg whites that, these days, I make sure my fridge is always stocked with a pasteurized carton of them. In fact, I've got so used to this, I don't even find it strange that they do come in a carton. (And see Note to the Reader on **p.xiii** on using uncooked eggs.)

VANILLA MOUSSE WITH BERRIES & PISTACHIOS

SERVES 6

2 FREE-RANGE ORGANIC OR
  PASTEURIZED EGG WHITES
300ML DOUBLE CREAM
100G CASTER SUGAR
SEEDS FROM 1 VANILLA POD
200G RASPBERRIES
200G STRAWBERRIES, CHOPPED
1–2 X 15ML TABLESPOONS
  CHOPPED PISTACHIO NUTS

6 X APPROX. 175ML GLASSES

Whisk the egg whites in a clean, grease-free bowl until they form soft peaks.

Pour the cream into another bowl, add the sugar and vanilla seeds and whisk until this mixture, too, forms soft peaks. Fold the whisked egg whites gently into the vanilla cream to make your mousse.

Divide the berries between 6 glasses until just under half-full and dollop the vanilla mousse on top, until every glass is softly peaked.

Chill them in the fridge for 15–30 minutes. If keeping for longer (up to 4 hours), chill the fruit in the glasses and the mousse separately in its bowl, then assemble to serve.

On serving, dust the tops with the ground or finely chopped pistachios. ■

I FOUND THIS RECIPE FOR one of the world's easiest but most delicious desserts in a rather fabulous book, by chef and "culinary philosopher" Gioacchino Scognamiglio, called *Il Chichibio: ovvero poesia della cucina*, which translates as "The Gallant: or the Poetry of Cooking" (and Chichibio, I should also tell you, was a rakish Venetian cook in Boccaccio's *Decameron*). At Scognamiglio's instigation, I went to great lengths to acquire a bottle of Elisir San Marzano, which has a peculiarly Italian, chocolate-coffee-herbal hit. Feel free to use coffee liqueur or rum or, better still, a mixture of the two in its place.

This, like all the other ice creams in these pages, is a no-churn affair. You mix everything together, wodge it into a loaf tin, freeze and you're done.

I like this with a few raspberries to tumble around and a chocolate sauce to Jackson Pollock over it, the recipe for which is overleaf.

MERINGUE GELATO CAKE WITH CHOCOLATE SAUCE

SERVES 6–8 ◐

300ML DOUBLE CREAM

30G DARK CHOCOLATE (MIN. 70% COCOA SOLIDS)

1 X 15ML TABLESPOON ELISIR SAN MARZANO, OR COFFEE LIQUEUR AND/OR RUM

1 PACKET 8 MERINGUE NESTS (APPROX. 100G TOTAL)

TO SERVE (OPTIONAL):

1 BATCH CHOCOLATE SAUCE (SEE OVERLEAF)

250G RASPBERRIES

1 X 450G/1LB LOAF TIN (18 X 12 X 8.5CM OR SIMILAR CAPACITY)

Line your loaf tin with clingfilm, making sure you have enough overhang to cover the top later.

Whip the cream until thick but still soft.

Chop the chocolate very finely so that you have a pile of dark splinters, and fold them into the cream, along with the liqueur.

Now, using brute force, crumble the meringue nests and fold these in, too.

Pack this mixture into the prepared loaf tin, pressing it down with a spatula as you go, and bring the clingfilm up and over to seal the top, then get out more clingfilm to wrap around the whole tin. Freeze until solid, which should take around 8 hours, or overnight.

To serve, unwrap the outer layer of plastic wrap, then unpeel the top and use these bits of long overhanging wrap to lift out the ice-cream brick. Unwrap and unmould it onto a board and cut the frozen meringue cake into slabs to serve. I like to zig-zag a little chocolate sauce (see opposite and overleaf) over each slice, and sprinkle a few raspberries alongside on each plate. ■

THIS IS A USEFUL BLUEPRINT FOR a chocolate sauce; it is gloopily thick, but intentionally so. If pouring over an ice cream, as here or on **pp.170** or **254**, you want to leave this until only subtly warm; if to accompany panna cotta (and see **pp.155–159**), then leave it to cool to room temperature. In either case, whisk well before bringing to the table. If you feel that the sauce has become too solid, then stand the jug in a bowl of warm water for a few minutes, whisking frequently, before pouring. Or I whisk in a small shot – about 2 tablespoons – of hot espresso to make it a little more fluid.

CHOCOLATE SAUCE

Pour the cream into a saucepan and add the tiny bits of chocolate.

Put over a gentle heat and whisk as the chocolate melts, taking the pan off the heat once the chocolate is almost all melted. If the mixture gets too hot, the chocolate will seize, whereas it will happily continue melting in the warm cream off the heat.

Add the liqueur, still off the heat, and whisk again to amalgamate the sauce completely. Pour into a jug, whisking every now and again until it cools to the desired temperature. ◼

MAKES APPROX. 300ML Ⓝ
250ML DOUBLE CREAM
125G DARK CHOCOLATE (MIN. 70% COCOA SOLIDS), FINELY CHOPPED OR IN BUTTONS MADE FOR MELTING
2 X 15ML TABLESPOONS ELISIR SAN MARZANO, OR COFFEE LIQUEUR AND/OR RUM

I'M ALMOST EMBARRASSED AT HOW EASY this is but, as you will find out, simple though it is to make, its flavour is deep, complex and utterly compelling.

So, here's how it goes: you don't make a custard and you don't need an ice-cream maker. You could (and I often do) serve it with a chocolate sauce (see previous page) but my absolute favourite way of eating this is by squidging it into little brioches, like sweet burger buns, as they do in the south of Italy. Luckily, I live near an Italian *caffè* that will sell them to me, but I am also searching dutifully for an online source.

I use Illy espresso liqueur here, but any coffee liqueur would do, even if it weren't quite as strong. I have never tried using regular instant coffee granules in place of the instant espresso powder stipulated, though I dare say if you boosted quantities and dissolved the granules in a little boiling water first, you could make it work for you.

But this works so perfectly for me, that I have no desire to meddle. And I whip up this ice cream so often, it makes comforting sense for me to keep the key ingredients in stock.

Maybe I don't have to add this but, as a security measure, let me remind you that 1 tablespoon in cooking is a precise 15ml measurement; my instant espresso powder comes with a 5ml teaspoon inside, so, if it helps, use 6 of those to make sure you're adding the correct amount.

ONE-STEP NO-CHURN COFFEE ICE CREAM

MAKES 800ML Ⓝ
300ML DOUBLE CREAM
175G CONDENSED MILK
2 X 15ML TABLESPOONS INSTANT
   ESPRESSO POWDER
2 X 15ML TABLESPOONS
   ESPRESSO LIQUEUR

2 X 500ML AIRTIGHT TUBS OR
   CONTAINERS

Whisk all the ingredients together until soft peaks form, and you have a gorgeous, caffè-latte-coloured airy mixture, and then fill airtight containers, and freeze for 6 hours or overnight. Serve straight from the freezer. ∎

THE "DOUBLE AMARETTO" PART OF THE title refers to the fact that both amaretti biscuits and amaretto liqueur are included; "*semifreddo*", which simply means "semicold", indicates that although this is an ice cream, it has a soft rather than frozen-solid texture. (Please take note that the biscuits are the crunchy amaretti, not those labelled "*morbidi*" or soft; and see Note to the Reader on **p.xiii** about eggs.)

This is very much a shortcut semifreddo, incidentally; I have given recipes before that – divine though they are – involve much beating of egg yolks and sugar in a heatproof bowl suspended over a pan of simmering water. And as far as ice creams go, this is a double-doddle: no effort to whip up and no machine to churn it. You just fill some dainty dariole moulds (not really me, generally speaking, though see also Panna Cotta Three-Ways **p.155**) and stash them in the deep freeze for at least 6 hours or overnight.

To unmould, dip the bottom of the dariole moulds into a cup or bowl of hot water for 30 seconds, then clamp a small plate or saucer over the top, upend and turn out. But you could simply line the moulds with clingfilm (leaving an overhang for pulling out the semifreddo later), if you prefer. The apricot amaretto sauce is for pouring over each little semifreddo, as you serve. You don't need much sauce, so don't worry about the scant quantity below. Also, the sauce must not be hot, so make it early doors. I like to get it done at the same time as the semifreddi go into the freezer, and then leave it in a milk jug, clingfilmed and out of the fridge until required.

I know smart Italians consider amaretto to be too frightfully déclassé for words, but surely that is part of its charm?

DOUBLE AMARETTO SEMIFREDDO WITH GOLDEN-GLEAMING SAUCE

SERVES 6 Ⓝ

50G AMARETTI BISCUITS (CRUNCHY NOT "MORBIDI")

250ML DOUBLE CREAM

1 EGG WHITE

2 X 15ML TABLESPOONS ICING SUGAR

3 X 15ML TABLESPOONS AMARETTO LIQUEUR

▶

Put the amaretti biscuits into a freezer bag and bash them with a rolling pin until you have crumbs: you should end up with a mixture of coarse and fine crumbs but don't be so brutal that you end up with sand.

Put the cream and egg white into a mixing bowl and whisk together until soft peaks form; for speed, use an electric whisk.

Whisk in the icing sugar and amaretto liqueur, then fold in the amaretti biscuit crumbs.

Fill 6 dariole moulds, packing in the mixture, tamping it down and smoothing the top. Then cover each one with clingfilm and place in the freezer, leaving for at least 6 hours or overnight (and not longer than 1 week).

To make the sauce, put the jam and amaretto liqueur into a small saucepan and bring to a boil, whisking together.

Boil for 1 minute, then take off the heat and cool slightly before pouring into a small milk- or cream-jug. Leave to cool, then cover and set aside.

When you are ready to serve the semifreddo, sit the bottom of each dariole mould, one at a time, in a bowl of just boiled water for a brief 30-second dip, wipe off the water, then put a small plate or saucer on top, upturn the mould and turn out the semifreddo (dip again if it won't come out first time) and spoon a little of the golden, gleaming sauce over it. I'd put the bottle of amaretto and 6 shot glasses on the table, too. ■

FOR THE SAUCE:
50G APRICOT JAM
60ML AMARETTO LIQUEUR

6 X 125ML METAL DARIOLE
  MOULDS

I DON'T KNOW IF I SHOULD apologize for this or boast about it. Either way, I feel you will thank me for it. The thing is that it's embarrassingly easy and, although I first started making it last Christmas – a lot – reckoning that it was just the sort of count-no-calorie indulgence that the season demands, I have since decided that something this good, and this speedily simple to conjure into being, needs to be in our lives all year round.

Don't be tempted to let the cheesecake come to room temperature before serving. It slices and eats better with a bit of fridge-chill on it.

However, you must have both Nutella and cream cheese at room temperature before making it. To simplify your life a little, you can buy the hazelnuts ready chopped and toasted.

CHOCOLATE HAZELNUT CHEESECAKE

Break the biscuits into the bowl of a food processor, then add the butter and 1 x 15ml tablespoon of Nutella and blitz until the mixture starts to clump. Add 25g of the toasted hazelnuts, and continue to pulse until you have a damp, sandy mixture.

Tip this into your springform tin and press it into the base, using either your hands or the back of a spoon. Place in the fridge to chill while you get on with the filling.

Beat together the cream cheese and icing sugar until smooth and soft, then patiently scrape the rest of the Nutella out of its jar and into the cream cheese mixture and continue beating until combined.

Take the springform tin out of the fridge. Carefully scrape and smooth the Nutella mixture over the biscuit base and scatter the remaining chopped hazelnuts on top to cover. Place the tin in the fridge for at least 4 hours or overnight.

Serve straight from the fridge for best results, unspringing the cake from the tin, still on its base, just before you eat. To cut it, dip a sharp knife in cold water, wiping it and dipping again between each cut. And don't worry: it may look disappointingly flat when whole, but when sliced, its dark depths are revealed. ■

SERVES 8–12 Ⓝ

250G DIGESTIVE BISCUITS

75G SOFT UNSALTED BUTTER

1 X 400G JAR NUTELLA OR EQUIVALENT CHOCOLATE HAZELNUT SPREAD, AT ROOM TEMPERATURE

100G CHOPPED TOASTED HAZELNUTS

500G CREAM CHEESE, AT ROOM TEMPERATURE

60G ICING SUGAR, SIFTED

1 X 22 OR 23CM SPRINGFORM CAKE TIN

THERE IS SOMETHING SO COSY-MAKING ABOUT the way new technology recreates the recipe-sharing traditions of older communities. This recipe is a case in point. Francesca Petracca, one of my Italian Twitter followers, tweeted a picture of her family's *Torta di Mele* and I asked her to post the recipe on my website. She did, I made it – or a version of it – and here we are.

The English title Francesca gave to her *Torta di Mele* was Italian Apple Pie, and I have stayed faithful to it, although the finished product is really more of a cake. Whatever it is, it is just wonderful: simple to make, and alluringly rustic. I like it best served still warm, as a kind of pudding-cake, with custard, mascarpone or double cream (whipped or runny), but *la famiglia* Petracca prefer to eat slices as an accompaniment to a cup of tea or an espresso "in the company of lovely friends". Who can argue with that?

I used Pink Lady apples here, as I don't peel the slices that go on top of the cake, and a firm, red-skinned apple works well and looks pretty. But it's not worth going for a red-skinned apple that won't hold its shape – such as a Red Delicious – so bear that in mind while shopping; the colour of the skin is not the crucial factor here. Perhaps I should mention that the original recipe, as posted on my website, stipulates that all the apples be peeled; what follows is my lazy version...

As ever with baking, all the ingredients should, of course, be at room temperature.

ITALIAN APPLE PIE

SERVES 8 Ⓝ

100G SOFT UNSALTED BUTTER, PLUS MORE FOR GREASING

250G PLAIN FLOUR

2 TEASPOONS BAKING POWDER

PINCH SALT

150G CASTER SUGAR

2 EGGS

ZEST 1 UNWAXED LEMON

1 TEASPOON VANILLA EXTRACT

75ML FULL-FAT MILK, AT ROOM TEMPERATURE

3 PINK LADY APPLES, OR ANY CRISP EATING APPLES (APPROX. 500G TOTAL)

▶

Preheat the oven to 200°C/gas mark 6. Butter your springform tin and line the bottom with baking parchment.

Into a food processor, put the flour, baking powder, pinch of salt, 100g soft butter, caster sugar, eggs, lemon zest and vanilla extract, and blitz till it forms a thick, smooth batter. Then, with the motor still running, pour the milk gradually down the funnel to lighten the mixture.

To do this by hand, if you prefer, beat the butter and sugar together until pale and creamy, then beat in the eggs, followed by the flour, baking powder, salt, vanilla, lemon zest and milk, till you have a batter with a soft, dropping consistency.

Halve 1 of the apples, then peel, core and chop one half into approx. 1cm cubes, add these to the batter and either pulse to mix, or beat in. Pour your batter into the springform tin.

Quarter and core the remaining apples (including the unused half apple, above), leaving the skin on, then finely slice them and arrange in pleasing concentric circles on top of the cake batter.

Mix together the brown sugar and cinnamon and sprinkle this over the apples, then bake for 40–45 minutes, by which time the cake should be risen and golden. Pierce with a cake tester, which should have only a few crumbs sticking to it when removed.

Leave to cool for 1 hour, before springing it out of the tin to cut and serve warm, or leave to cool completely once out of the tin. ■

1 TEASPOON SOFT LIGHT
  BROWN OR DEMERARA SUGAR
½ TEASPOON GROUND
  CINNAMON

1 X 22 OR 23CM SPRINGFORM
  CAKE TIN

THE BEST WAY TO DESCRIBE CROSTATA is to say that it's like a giant jam tart, only instead of having to roll out pastry, you can make a dense sponge. This, anyway, is the homestyle *crostata*; shop-bought ones tend to involve the more labour-intensive pastry process, with a lattice-weave effect on top.

I find that some ground almonds added to the mixture stop the sponge casing from being too dry; you cannot, of course, make too damp a batter, as it needs to be firm enough to hold its shape on baking – not too firm, however. Gratifyingly, it does still have a tender, marzipanny centre beneath the jam. Talking of which: once I'd added almonds, the apricot jam seemed an obvious pairing, but use any jam you please. I have a hankering after a filling of gleaming ruby blackcurrant jam: I think it would have a charming, but still majestic, queen of tarts look to it. Whatever jam you use, it's important that it's not too sweet. Failing that, there's always the juice from the lemon, whose zest has given up its ultra-Italian aroma in the sponge, so squeeze some in if you want to sour it up. As with most sponges, this really should be eaten on the day it's made.

APRICOT & ALMOND CROSTATA

SERVES 6–8

100G SOFT UNSALTED BUTTER, PLUS MORE FOR GREASING
150G CASTER SUGAR
2 EGGS
ZEST 1 UNWAXED LEMON, PLUS (OPTIONAL) JUICE
150G PLAIN FLOUR
50G GROUND ALMONDS
PINCH SALT
1 TEASPOON BAKING POWDER
300G GOOD-QUALITY APRICOT JAM

1 X 25CM FLUTED TART TIN WITH LOOSE BASE (MEASURE FROM THE FLUTED EDGES)

Preheat the oven to 180°C/gas mark 4. Butter the tart tin, getting into all the crevices, or use a specially made baking spray.

Beat together the butter and sugar until pale and fluffy. Add the eggs, one at a time, continuing to beat the mixture as you go, then beat in the lemon zest.

Mix together the flour, ground almonds, salt and baking powder and fold these dry ingredients into the mixture.

Pour or scrape the batter into the tart tin, and spread it with a silicone spatula to make an even layer, pushing the batter into the sides. Then, using a smaller metal spatula or the back of a spoon, make a shallow circular indentation in the middle of your batter – for the jam – leaving a thicker raised border about 3cm wide all around it.

Measure the jam into a bowl and whisk to make it looser, squeezing in some lemon juice now, if you want to offset the sweetness. Then spread the jam into the indentation in the middle of the tart base, leaving the raised edge clear all round.

Bake for 25–30 minutes, until the sponge round the edges is risen and golden-brown and firm to the touch and a cake tester comes out clean when inserted into the edge. Remove with care from the oven.

Let it cool in its tin on a wire rack for about 15 minutes or so, then very carefully ease the tart out of the fluted sides, still on its base. If you leave it to get too cold, it will be harder to get out of the tin. Do not even attempt to get it off the base.

Slip a cake slicer between the bottom of the *crostata* and the tin base to loosen it, then slice it still on the base and eat it warm with ice cream, whipped cream or mascarpone, as pudding, or cold with a cup of tea or coffee. ■

ALONG WITH A LOT OF NOT traditionally Italian baking, the good old English crumble has seemed to be gaining popularity – even modishness – in Italy. *"Il crumble"*, as it is called there, is described as fruit covered with *briciole croccanti* or crunchy crumbs, and I have added to the crunch-factor here by incorporating – in the spirit of harmony between our two great nations – crushed-up amaretti biscuits, letting some fall into the stove-softened fruit first, to bring a little thickness to the ruby juices without adding cornflour.

By all means, use other-coloured plums – or indeed any other fruit you feel like – but be prepared to modify lemon and sugar content accordingly. You should also know that I like the fruit beneath the sweet crunchy crumbs to have a tanginess that could, for some people, be thought to verge on the sharp. For me, contrast is key; but if you want to keep sourness in stricter check, add more sugar to taste.

RUBY-RED PLUM & AMARETTI CRUMBLE

Preheat the oven to 190°C/gas mark 5, and slip in a baking sheet at the same time. Put the amaretti into a freezer bag and bash with a rolling pin or similar, until reduced to coarse crumbs, then decant them into a bowl.

Melt the 2 tablespoons of butter in a large pan (that comes with a lid), add the prepared plums, sprinkle in the 2 tablespoons of sugar, add the lemon zest and juice and shake the pan over the heat, cooking for 2 minutes without a lid and 2 further minutes with the lid on. These timings are based on having plums that are ripe; if the fruit is disappointingly unyielding, be prepared to cook for longer with the lid on, checking frequently. You may need to add the juice of the remaining half lemon – and more sugar – if cooking for much longer.

Pour the plums (with care – they're hot), into your pie dish and set to one side. Already the red skins will have made a gorgeous garnet gravy. Sprinkle in 2 tablespoons of your amaretti crumbs.

To make the crumble the easy way, put the flour and baking powder into the bowl of a freestanding mixer, shake to mix, then add the small, cold butter cubes and beat, not too fast, with the flat paddle until you have a mixture rather like large-flaked oatmeal. Or you can do this by hand, just by rubbing the butter into the flour with your fingers.

Add the sugar and mix with a fork, then tip in the rest of the amaretti crumbs and fork to mix again. Pour the mixture over the waiting fruit in its pie dish, making sure you cover right to the edges to stop too much leakage; although for me, some of the rich-hued syrup spurting out over the crumble topping is essential.

Place on the baking sheet in the oven and bake for about 30 minutes; by which time you should see some ruby bubbling at the edges, and the top will be scorched gold in places. If you can bear it, let this stand for 10–15 minutes before eating, with ice cream, whipped cream or mascarpone. ■

SERVES 6–8 Ⓝ
100G AMARETTI BISCUITS
 (CRUNCHY NOT "MORBIDI")
2 X 15ML TABLESPOONS (30G)
 UNSALTED BUTTER
1KG RED PLUMS, QUARTERED
 IF LARGE, HALVED IF SMALL,
 STONES REMOVED
2 X 15ML TABLESPOONS CASTER
 SUGAR
ZEST AND JUICE ½ UNWAXED
 LEMON

FOR THE CRUMBLE TOPPING:
150G PLAIN FLOUR
1 TEASPOON BAKING POWDER
100G COLD UNSALTED BUTTER,
 CUT INTO SMALL DICE
3 X 15ML TABLESPOONS CASTER
 SUGAR

1 X APPROX. 23CM X 6CM DEEP
 OVENPROOF PIE DISH

YOGURT POT CAKE

IF THERE'S A FAMILY IN ITALY that doesn't have a recipe for yogurt pot cake, then I've yet to meet them. And I love this plain cake with perhaps disproportionate intensity. There is something so quintessentially Italian about its scent – as it bakes, I think I'm in a kitchen in Italy – and its taste – that combination of lemon and vanilla – and even the old-fashioned charm of its method.

This is it: your yogurt pot is your unit of measurement. And even though I saw from the original recipe that I copied down (from some scrawled piece of paper in the kitchen of a house I'd rented one summer), that the specified yogurt pot had a 125ml capacity, I have kept the same number of eggs for my 150ml yogurt pot. I work on the principle that eggs these days are larger than when the cake first came into being. Anyway, it works, and that's the main thing. And this is the way it works: for 1 cake, you need 1 pot of yogurt, 2 pots of sugar, 1 pot of oil, 1 pot of potato starch or cornflour and 2 pots of flour. In keeping with this style of measuring, you will see that I have even stipulated 2 capfuls of vanilla extract.

Although potato starch is the norm in Italy, it isn't easily available in Britain, which is why I have substituted cornflour. Bear in mind that potato starch is denser, or rather weighs more per pot than cornflour does. Which is to say, if you're using potato starch, it will weigh in as 100g, whereas the same volume of cornflour is 75g. I've specified actual weights in the ingredients list, not only so that you can make this even if you're working from a jumbo carton of yogurt, but also because I feel the ingredients list should double as a shopping list, too.

I know this cake best in a ring shape, *ciambella* (pronounced "chambella") as it's known in Italy, and a 22cm savarin or ring mould is a fairly standard baking tin here in the UK, too, but do use a 22 or 23cm springform tin if that's easier for you: the cake won't be as high, but don't use a smaller diameter because, without the hole in the middle, the cake wouldn't cook properly in the centre if the tin were any deeper.

Finally, I'm aware it may sound a bit of a bore having to whisk the egg whites, but it only *sounds* it; in the days of electric whisks, it really isn't any trouble.

This is my favourite weekend breakfast, or – indeed – anytime treat.

Preheat the oven to 180°C/gas mark 4, and grease your ring mould (or springform tin); you can use vegetable oil for this or a special baking spray.

Separate the eggs and put the whites in one bowl and the yolks in another. Whisk the whites until you have firm peaks, then set aside while you get on with the rest of the cake.

Scrape the yogurt out of its pot and on to the egg yolks, then use the emptied yogurt pot to measure out your other ingredients – so, next, add 2 pots (just) of sugar and whisk with the egg yolks and yogurt until airy and light.

Now fill your yogurt pot up with vegetable oil and, beating all the while, slowly add this to the egg yolk mixture. Then beat in 2 capfuls of vanilla extract and the zest of half a lemon.

Still beating, add 2 yogurt potfuls of flour followed by 1 yogurt potful of cornflour or potato starch, then scrape down and fold in with a rubber or silicone spatula. Now, with a large metal spoon, dollop in the whisked egg whites, and fold them in with the spatula.

Fill the prepared ring mould with the smooth, soft batter – it will come right to the top – and bake in the oven for 30–35 minutes; when cooked, the sides will be coming away at the edges and a cake tester will come out clean.

Remove it from the oven to a wire rack, letting the cake sit in the tin for 10 minutes before turning it out.

Once cooled (although I love this still slightly warm), transfer it to a serving plate or stand and dust with icing sugar. Traditionally, this cake would be placed on the plate with the smooth side uppermost, but I rather like it turned back up the way it was baked, with its rustic cracks and uneven surface visible. ■

CUTS INTO 16 SLICES, *BUT IT WOULD BE EASY TO EAT 3 OR 4 AT A SITTING* Ⓝ

150G PLAIN YOGURT

150ML FLAVOURLESS VEGETABLE OIL, PLUS SOME FOR GREASING

3 EGGS

250G CASTER SUGAR

2 CAPFULS (1½ TEASPOONS) VANILLA EXTRACT

ZEST ½ UNWAXED LEMON

175G PLAIN FLOUR

75G CORNFLOUR

1 TEASPOON ICING SUGAR, TO SERVE

1 X 22CM SAVARIN OR RING MOULD (OR 22 OR 23CM SPRINGFORM CAKE TIN)

ALTHOUGH I FIRST CAME UP WITH THIS RECIPE because I had someone coming for supper who – genuinely – couldn't eat wheat or dairy, it is so meltingly good, I now make it all the time for those whose life and diet are not so unfairly constrained, myself included.

It is slightly heavier with the almonds – though not in a bad way – so if you want a lighter crumb, rather than a squidgy interior, and are not making the cake for the gluten-intolerant, then replace the 150g ground almonds with 125g plain flour. This has the built-in bonus of making it perhaps more suitable for an everyday cake.

Made with the almonds, it has more of supper-party pudding feel about it and I love it still a bit warm, with some raspberries or some such on the side, as well as a dollop of mascarpone or ice cream.

CHOCOLATE OLIVE OIL CAKE

CUTS INTO 8–12 SLICES Ⓝ

150ML REGULAR OLIVE OIL, PLUS
 MORE FOR GREASING
50G GOOD-QUALITY COCOA
 POWDER, SIFTED
125ML BOILING WATER
2 TEASPOONS BEST VANILLA
 EXTRACT
150G GROUND ALMONDS OR
 125G PLAIN FLOUR
½ TEASPOON BICARBONATE OF
 SODA
PINCH SALT
200G CASTER SUGAR
3 EGGS

1 X 22 OR 23CM SPRINGFORM
 CAKE TIN

Preheat your oven to 170°C/gas mark 3. Grease your springform tin with a little oil and line the base with baking parchment.

Measure and sift the cocoa powder into a bowl or jug and whisk in the boiling water until you have a smooth, chocolatey, still runny (but only just) paste. Whisk in the vanilla extract, then set aside to cool a little.

In another smallish bowl, combine the ground almonds (or flour) with the bicarbonate of soda and pinch of salt.

Put the sugar, olive oil and eggs into the bowl of a freestanding mixer with the paddle attachment (or other bowl and whisk arrangement of your choice) and beat together vigorously for about 3 minutes until you have a pale-primrose, aerated and thickened cream.

Turn the speed down a little and pour in the cocoa mixture, beating as you go, and when all is scraped in you can slowly tip in the ground almond (or flour) mixture.

Scrape down, and stir a little with a spatula, then pour this dark, liquid batter into the prepared tin. Bake for 40–45 minutes or until the sides are set and the very centre, on top, still looks slightly damp. A cake tester should come up mainly clean but with a few sticky chocolate crumbs clinging to it.

Let it cool for 10 minutes on a wire rack, still in its tin, and then ease the sides of the cake with a small metal spatula and spring it out of the tin. Leave to cool completely or eat while still warm with some ice cream, as a pudding. ∎

YOU MIGHT THINK THAT BANANA BREAD was not an Italian recipe and you'd be right, of course. It is, however, hugely popular in Italy right now, as are many recipes that emanate from the baking canon of North America and the UK. Still, I wanted to introduce an Italian element (ironic, as Italians are keener not to) and I've done that by adding some instant espresso powder. And, even though I add quite a bit, the flavour doesn't overwhelm at all: it's there, but as a hint, and the subtle bitterness of the coffee undercuts, most elegantly, the creamy sweetness of the banana.

The Italians like something sweet for breakfast, which is more than I do, so this is only mutedly so. But feel free to smooth some chocolatey spread – or mascarpone dusted with cinnamon – over a damp slice or two.

This banana bread is best if you can bear to let it stand a day after baking. Actually, I find this makes life easier: you can throw it together on Sunday, say (and it is the work of moments to make the batter), and then you have a delicious stash of breakfast slices waiting for you in the week. But, please, just because it says "breakfast" in the title, don't disregard it for any other time of the day; it's perfect for a teatime treat – and is my stepdaughter's perennial favourite.

You can also make 12 muffins out of this mixture: they will need 20 minutes in a 200°C/ gas mark 6 oven.

ITALIAN BREAKFAST BANANA BREAD

CUTS INTO 8–10 SLICES Ⓥ
150ML FLAVOURLESS VEGETABLE OIL, PLUS SOME FOR GREASING
3 MEDIUM BANANAS, VERY RIPE INDEED (APPROX. 400G TOTAL WITH SKIN ON, 300G WITHOUT)
2 TEASPOONS VANILLA EXTRACT
PINCH SALT
2 EGGS
150G CASTER SUGAR
175G PLAIN FLOUR
½ TEASPOON BICARBONATE OF SODA
4 TEASPOONS INSTANT ESPRESSO POWDER

1 X 450G/1LB DEEP LOAF TIN OR
1 X 12-BUN MUFFIN TIN

Slip a baking sheet into the oven, and preheat to 170°C/gas mark 3. Get out a loaf tin, and line it with baking paper or a loaf tin liner, or lightly oil it. I find that the bananas create a non-stick bouncy surface, though, rather like prunes do on baking, so don't fret if you don't have a liner.

Mash the bananas with the vanilla extract and salt and then beat in the oil. Here, I use a 1/3 American cup measure for ease, as 150ml is two-thirds of a cup. And after I've used the 1/3 cup (twice!), I use any residue in the cup measure to grease my loaf tin.

Now, beat in the eggs, one by one, followed by the sugar.

Mix the flour with the bicarb and espresso powder, and beat these dry ingredients into the runny batter.

Pour the batter into your prepared loaf tin, and pop it into the oven, on the baking sheet, and bake for 50–60 minutes, or until slightly coming away at the sides and bulgingly risen: a cake tester should come out clean, barring the odd crumb. I urge you exercise restraint and wait for a day or at least half a day before slicing into it. If I can do that, so can you. ∎

THE WARM SCENT OF ANISEED in the air is, for me, the smell of Italian baking. And while I willingly concede that liquorice is one of those love-it-or-loathe-it tastes (those on the positive side of the divide can turn briskly to **p.152**), for some reason this anise-flavoured shortbread has even made greedy conquests of those who have promised me in advance that they don't like anything aniseedy or liquorice-linked. It's true to say that I wouldn't have minded in the least had they insistently resisted; all the more for those of us who are grateful for the offering in the first place. Still, it is useful to know that this recipe does not rely on a niche-market following. I'd rather hope it could be considered a safe bet all round: perfect for elevenses, teatime, or to be brought out with after-dinner coffee. But for those closest to my heart, the hard-core liquorice-lovers: can I just plead with you to consider this as an accompaniment to that pudding on **p.152**?

Do make sure you buy aniseeds or anise seeds, i.e. the seeds themselves, and if you have trouble finding them locally, look online.

ANISEED SHORTBREAD

Preheat the oven to 160°C/gas mark 3, and get out your sandwich tin. Line the base with baking parchment or liner.

Put the flour, cornflour, icing sugar and butter in a food processor and blitz till combined and just clumping into a pale dough.

Remove the lid, add the aniseeds, then put the lid back on and pulse until the aromatic seeds are well mixed in.

Tip the mixture into the sandwich tin and press it out smoothly and patiently until you have an even layer at the bottom of the tin. (Yes, I do know that the aniseeds are indistinguishable from mouse droppings, but I really don't know what can profitably be said on the matter; so ignore it.)

Put it in the oven and bake for 20–25 minutes, until the shortbread is cooked through, slightly gold at the edges but still pale on top.

Remove to a wire rack, and if you want that familiar dotty-patterned shortbread look, gently use the tines of a fork to dimple the surface straight after it comes out of the oven (taking care – the tin is hot); then leave it in the tin for 10 minutes before cutting into 16 slender wedges, still in its tin. Cool for another 20–30 minutes, before lifting out the base of the tin and gently transferring the shortbread wedges to a wire rack or plate. Serve cool, or eat as warm as you like. ■

MAKES 16 SLICES Ⓝ
85G PLAIN FLOUR
65G CORNFLOUR
50G ICING SUGAR
125G SOFT UNSALTED BUTTER
2 X 5ML TEASPOONS ANISEEDS

1 X 20CM SANDWICH CAKE TIN
   WITH LOOSE BASE

NOT LONG AGO ANNA DEL CONTE, who for me represents authentic Italy in England, emailed me a recipe – for chocolate tagliatelle – that she'd made with her granddaughter, Coco (and this is where I must interrupt myself to tell you that Anna's *Cooking with Coco* is not only a contemporary classic but an absolute must-have, though without her chocolate pasta recipe which came after). "So," she said in her email: "I am become a Britalian cook, too". I took this as permission to make a chocolate pudding pasta. This is really Anna's recipe, only I in slovenly fashion use shop-bought chocolate pasta. Well, this is a book that emphasizes speed and simplicity, so it would seem not in the spirit of things to instruct you to make homemade cocoa pasta. The ready-made stuff is not available everywhere, but it is worth tracking down (and can be found online) for this unconventional but intriguing sweet treat.

CHOCOLATE PASTA WITH PECANS & CARAMEL

SERVES 2

100G COCOA OR CHOCOLATE
   PASTA, SUCH AS COCOA FUSILLI
PINCH OR TWO OF SALT
50G UNSALTED PECAN NUTS,
   ROUGHLY BROKEN UP
50G SOFT UNSALTED BUTTER
50G DARK BROWN SUGAR
100ML DOUBLE CREAM, PLUS
   MORE (OPTIONAL), TO SERVE

Put water on to boil for the pasta and, when it's boiling, add a pinch of salt and cook the pasta, setting a timer for 2 minutes before the packet instructions say it will be ready.

Put a medium-sized, non-stick frying pan on the stove and tumble in the pecans, then toast them over a medium heat. Once you can smell their scent wafting up from the pan, remove them to a cold plate.

Now stir the butter and sugar together in the frying pan over a low heat, until you have a hot, treacly syrup. Carefully, pour in the cream, stir and let the caramel mixture bubble up, add the toasted pecans and a pinch of salt, then turn off the heat.

Just before draining the pasta, lower in a cup to remove a little pasta-cooking water, then toss the drained pasta back into the frying pan with the dark and nutty caramel sauce, adding a tablespoon or two of the cooking water, if needed, to help coat the pasta. Stir to combine before dividing between 2 bowls. Serve with a little double cream in a small jug to pour over as you eat, if wished. ■

AN ITALIAN-INSPIRED CHRISTMAS

THIS MAY SEEM A MODEST RECIPE with which to open the great celebratory Christmas chapter – more exuberantly expansive than all those preceding it – but it is indicative of the approach I recommend throughout the season: low-effort yet uplifting. Even in festive mood, I prefer an informal approach.

Actually, I blush to call this a recipe, but it is too useful a part of my repertoire for me to exclude it. Think, rather, of this as a blueprint for the perfect, no-cook pre-dinner or party *cicchetti*. The word "*cicchetti*" is the Venetian term for little snacky nibbles, only so much more glamorous and enticing than any English term.

All you have to know about my wrapped grissini is this: you need equal weights of Parma ham (or my preferred version, prosciutto di San Daniele from the Friuli-Venezia Giulia region) and of the chunkier Italian breadsticks, often labelled "grissini rustici". Should you be using the more industrial-looking, streamlined grissini, then you'll probably need slightly less ham.

And by the way, if you're interested, when we see a tall, skinny model-type person, we might call them a stick insect; an Italian would label them a "grissino". Not that this will ever overly concern me. Besides, I think that the grissini rustici I use are rather more plus-size.

PROSCIUTTO-WRAPPED GRISSINI

Get out your grissini and break them into irregular lengths, then wrap strips or pieces (depending on how the ham comes out as you unpeel the slices) of pink prosciutto around each breadstick bit and arrange them on plates for people to pick at. ◼

SERVES 10
250G GRISSINI RUSTICI OR OTHER ITALIAN BREADSTICKS
250G PROSCIUTTO DI SAN DANIELE, OR PARMA HAM, DELI-SLICED VERY FINE

CRAB CROSTINI

IN MY VERY FIRST BOOK, *How To Eat*, I dedicated many, many pages (well, it was a very long book) to crostini, and I still can't stop with them. If you're new to the crostini caper, let me fill you in briefly: get baguette or slim stick of bread, slice it, toast it in oven till pale gold, let it cool and then spread with toppings of your choice. It's that simple. As you may know, I am not a great starter person, but a plate of these with drinks has kicked off many a supper of mine.

Crab, chilli, lemon: three ingredients; one deep joy. Toss them in spaghetti or linguine for the ultimate no-cook sauce (a recipe I've given before, which is why it doesn't feature here) or into creamy rice for a dreamy risotto (see **p.40**). Here, they are garnered together for just about the most low-effort antipasti possible. And I do mean low-effort: now that I have discovered you can get the fabulous Italian crackers, *lingue di suocera*, in the UK – they translate as mother-in-law's tongues – I buy a packet, break them into pieces and smear them, just before serving, with the spicy crab. For more traditional crostini, cut a baguette or ficelle (so called because it is thinner, like "string", and I know both terms are French, but there it is) into slices about 1cm thick, leaving both "elbows" out (cook's treat: eat immediately or they'll stale), and brush them with garlic oil; then arrange them on a wire rack above an oven tray, bake in an oven preheated to 200°C/gas mark 6 for 5–7 minutes a side, and leave to cool. I keep bags of these plain bread slices in the deep freeze (or they will keep in an airtight box for 2–3 days) so that I have them ready to be oiled and toasted without notice.

Now for the chilli-crab topping: I use a 50/50 mix of white and brown crabmeat. And I'm not expecting you to start cooking and picking over crabs yourself. I go to Rex my fishmonger for this, or even the supermarket, as I now find little tubs of fresh crabmeat, either all white, half-white and half-brown, or all brown. Actually, I'd really love these made with nothing but the rich, almost offally, brown meat but I know this is strong medicine for most people. Half and half works perfectly, not least because the soft brown meat helps you spread the crab topping on the bread and helps it to stick. If you won't eat brown crabmeat or can't find it, then you will have to think of some other fixative for the sweet, white flakes. I am presuming a spoonful or so of mayonnaise would do it, but I am not enough of a (shop-bought) mayonnaise person myself to champion this tack.

Be that as it may, the amount here is enough to cover 35 little slices or biscuit pieces.

If you are using bread rather than crackers, see the introduction to this recipe and proceed as directed.

Check the white crabmeat for stray pieces of shell, then put all the crabmeat into a bowl, and add the finely grated zest and juice of 1 lemon.

Tip in the chopped red chilli and the chopped parsley, and stir to mix thoroughly. You can mix this up, cover it and sit it in the fridge for up to 24 hours, then stir before using.

Spread onto the toasts (prepared as suggested in the intro) or crackers: a scant teaspoon on each one is enough, as the brown meat provides richness and the chilli, fire. ■

MAKES 35

1 BAGUETTE OR FICELLE LOAF, OR 1 PACKET LINGUE DI SUOCERA BISCUITS OR OTHER CRACKERS

200G CRABMEAT, HALF-WHITE AND HALF-BROWN, FOR CHOICE

ZEST AND JUICE 1 UNWAXED LEMON

1 RED CHILLI, DE-SEEDED AND FINELY CHOPPED

1 X 15ML TABLESPOON CHOPPED FRESH PARSLEY

GORGONZOLA & CANNELLINI DIP WITH A TRICOLORE FLOURISH

I LOVE THIS COMBINATION OF BLUE CHEESE AND WHITE BEANS, but I have to say its gorgeousness is due in no small part to the mascarpone and Marsala that add creaminess of texture and smoky depth of tone respectively.

I like this dip to have real tang: I need to feel that burning, blue-cheese buzz. If you want something milder and maybe with more universal appeal, simply reduce the amount of cheese. I started with 150g (rindless weight), and bumped it up until I felt its fierceness, which made me end up with double that amount; you could stop anywhere along the route.

The dip itself does have a corpse-like grey-blue pallor, I don't deny it, but not for long: I cover it with a sprinkling of finely chopped spring onion – chives would do as well – and de-seeded red chilli and then, with a further flourish, serve it with a platter of *tricolore* crudités. For the amount of dip below, I'd core, de-seed and slice up 2 red bell peppers, take the florets from a small head of cauliflower and tumble these alongside, then add about 300g of raw sugar snaps. (Talking of which: apologies to all Italians for picturing your flag at the wrong angle here.) But I do also add some breadsticks and crackers, mainly the mother-in-law's tongues I used for the Crab Crostini on the previous page, for dipping in, as well as and sometimes instead of the raw veg.

When I halve this (as I often do) I still use the whole can of beans, as having half an empty can sitting around would be too annoying.

MAKES 800ML *(SERVES AT LEAST 12 PEOPLE AS STARTER, MANY MORE AS PART OF A BUFFET)* ◐

1 X 400G CAN CANNELLINI BEANS, DRAINED AND RINSED

300G GORGONZOLA PICCANTE (RINDLESS WEIGHT)

125G MASCARPONE

150ML PLAIN YOGURT

3 X 15ML TABLESPOONS GRATED PARMESAN

FRESHLY GROUND PEPPER

2 X 15ML TABLESPOONS MARSALA

2 X 15ML TABLESPOONS EXTRA-VIRGIN OLIVE OIL, OR TO TASTE

TO SERVE:

1 RED CHILLI

1 SPRING ONION (GREEN PART ONLY), OR 1 X 15ML TABLESPOON CHOPPED CHIVES

Put the beans, drained and rinsed, into a food processor (or you could mash everything by hand or with a stick blender) and drop in the Gorgonzola, broken loosely into chunks. Add the mascarpone, yogurt and Parmesan and grind in some pepper enthusiastically. Put on the lid and blitz to mix.

When it's a stiff purée, still slightly grainy, blitz again, pouring the Marsala and then the olive oil down the funnel. Taste for seasoning (remembering that the top is to be sprinkled with chilli) and texture; you may want to add extra oil for a more fluid, dressing-like, smoothness.

Remove the blade carefully, then scrape the dip into a bowl or divide between as many little bowls as you want (and see Notes **p.266** if you want to pause here).

Just before serving, de-seed and finely chop a shiny red chilli and slice the green part of a spring onion into teeny-tiny pieces (or just finely slice some chives), and sprinkle both red and green dip-decorations over the waiting dip. Serve with the crudités and other accompaniments mooted in the introduction, or with whatever takes your fancy. ■

I HAVE WRITTEN A RECIPE FOR PANETTONE STUFFING BEFORE: the sweet seasonal fruit bread was cubed, toasted and mixed with Italian sausage; this is very different, not least because I see it not as an accompaniment to the turkey on **p.221** (which has its own interior stuffing) but to be served, at parties or over drinks, in small squares, like savoury brownies.

As ever, feel free to substitute the plainer pandoro if you wish, though I do think the rich fruitiness is part of this unconventional canapé's charm.

PANETTONE STUFFING SQUARES

Peel and halve the shallots (or peel and quarter the onions) and quarter and core the apples, and roughly cut up the pancetta (or bacon). Drop the shallot or onion and the apple pieces into the bowl of a food processor along with the celery sticks, snapped in half, and the sage leaves, and process in a short burst to start the chopping, before adding the roughly cut pancetta (or bacon), and then blitz at full pelt until finely chopped. Don't worry about the mixture's wetness; mush is what I expect. You can chop everything by hand, though; in which case, don't expect to get everything as minced as it would in the processor. Anything goes.

Heat the garlic oil in a wide, heavy-bottomed pan and fry this mixture, stirring every now and again, for 10–15 minutes, until the vegetables et al. have softened.

Remove the fried mixture to a large bowl, crumble in the chestnuts, grate in the lemon zest and squeeze in the juice, then tear and crumble in the panettone, and – I use my hands for this – combine everything into a squidgy, fragrant paste. (If you're making this in advance, leave it to cool at this stage, then cover and transfer to the fridge where it can stand for up to 2 days – and see Notes **p.266** if you want to freeze it).

When you are ready to cook this, preheat the oven to 200°C/gas mark 6 and let the stuffing come to room temperature. Uncover the bowl, beat the eggs and mix them in, then spread the mixture into a foil tray or lightly greased ovenproof dish, and bake for 25–30 minutes, until the edges brown and begin to come away from the tray or dish and a cake tester comes out clean.

For canapés, let the tray cool for 30 minutes and then cut into 48 little bite-sized squares – or into 24 larger pieces to accompany a roast, if you'd prefer. ∎

MAKES 48 LITTLE SQUARES Ⓝ

4 ECHALION OR BANANA SHALLOTS, OR 2 ONIONS (APPROX. 250G TOTAL)

2 EATING APPLES (APPROX. 250G TOTAL)

375G PANCETTA SLICES OR RINDLESS STREAKY BACON

2 STICKS CELERY

4 LARGE FRESH SAGE LEAVES

3 X 15ML TABLESPOONS GARLIC OIL

200G VACUUM-PACKED CHESTNUTS

ZEST AND JUICE 1 UNWAXED LEMON

500G PANETTONE (OR PANDORO), SLIGHTLY STALED, SLICED

2 EGGS

OLIVE OIL, FOR GREASING

1 X FOIL TRAY OR OVENPROOF DISH APPROX. 30 X 20CM

THIS IS AN ITALIAN-INSPIRED RECIPE that comes to me from Australia via Brazil. To explain: a Brazilian friend, and the best cook I know, Helio Fenerich made it for me, and I had to keep (rudely) asking him to carry on making it for me. Eventually, I begged him for the recipe, which he told me he'd found in Australia. The journey was certainly worthwhile: it is a complete winner; I go into auto-Parmesan-shortbread mode whenever I have friends coming for supper, as not only is it perfect with drinks, but it can be made in advance.

Indeed, you can make the dough, wrap it and then leave in the fridge for up to 3 days before slicing and baking it as instructed below, although you will need to let these cheese-scented cylinders sit out on a kitchen surface just long enough to get the fridge-chill off them before slicing. Sometimes, I freeze a cylinder for later use (and see Notes **p.266**).

PARMESAN SHORTBREADS

MAKES 35–40 Ⓝ
150G PLAIN FLOUR
75G GRATED PARMESAN
100G SOFT UNSALTED BUTTER
1 EGG YOLK

Mix all the ingredients together – using bowl and spoon, electric mixer or food processor as wished – until a golden dough begins to form a clump.

Turn it out onto a surface and knead for about 30 seconds until smooth, then divide into two.

Take the first half and, using your hands, roll it into a cylinder, as uniform as possible without stressing over it, about 3cm in diameter. Make sure the ends are flat, too, so that the cylinder resembles a roll of coins. Now roll this up in a piece of clingfilm, twisting the clingfilm at the ends, like a Christmas cracker, and put the roll in the fridge, then proceed in the same way with the remaining half of the dough.

Preheat the oven to 180°C/gas mark 4 while the wrapped cylinders of dough rest in the fridge for about 45 minutes, by which time you should be able to cut them into thick slices easily: aim for about 1cm; think fat £1 coins, or similar.

Arrange on a baking sheet lined with baking parchment, and put in the oven for 15–20 minutes, when they should be just beginning to turn a pale gold at the edges.

Remove from the oven, then leave to cool (if you can) before eating. ∎

ALTHOUGH THESE CHEESE-INFUSED, CRISP AND GOLDEN polenta triangles with their tangy tomato dipping sauce are perfect for party picking, I have to say that in Casa Mia we like them mighty fine, too, at breakfast time as an Italianate version of hash browns or fried slice, depending on where you're coming from.

I've given a range of cheese quantity to add: if I'm eating the polenta triangles as either a breakfast add-on or supper accompaniment, I stir in 50g of Parmesan; when I'm treating the triangles as antipasti to be eaten alone or, rather, dipped into the tomato sauce, I add 75g of the cheese. To make the polenta is not exactly hard, since the polenta I use here is the instant or quick-cook kind. All packets come with instructions, but bear in mind – should you want to fiddle with amounts – that you should use 4 times the weight of water to polenta: e.g., for 100g instant polenta, you need 400ml water.

This is a real party pleaser: cosy but with the glamour of the not-entirely familiar.

POLENTA TRIANGLES WITH CHILLI TOMATO SAUCE

MAKES 30 TRIANGLES Ⓝ
600ML WATER
1 TEASPOON SEA SALT FLAKES OR
  ½ TEASPOON POURING SALT,
  OR TO TASTE
150G INSTANT OR QUICK-COOK
  POLENTA
50–75G PARMESAN, GRATED
OLIVE OIL, FOR COOKING THE
  TRIANGLES

1 X FOIL TRAY OR BROWNIE TIN
  APPROX. 30 X 20CM

TO SERVE:
CHILLI TOMATO SAUCE
  (SEE OVERLEAF)

Put 600ml water in a large saucepan and bring to the boil. Add the salt and then whisk in the polenta in a steady stream. Cook the polenta, stirring constantly, for 1–3 minutes, until it is thick. When it is the required consistency it should take 3–4 seconds to flow back when you pull a wooden spoon through the polenta.

Once it is thickened and has cooked for the required time, take off the heat, then beat in the Parmesan and check the seasoning.

Dampen a foil tray or brownie tin, by letting some water from the cold tap splash it a bit, and then spread the polenta out in an even layer in the tray or tin, smoothing the top with a wet spatula.

Leave to cool and set, which should take about 1 hour. Once the polenta is cold, cut the trayful into 15 squares (3 columns long ways by 5 columns short ways). Then cut each square into triangles, i.e. halved diagonally.

When you are ready to cook the triangles, preheat the oven to 220°C/gas mark 7 or heat the grill.

Arrange the triangles on a baking sheet, lined with foil or baking parchment, and drizzle each triangle with about ½ a teaspoon olive oil, then cook for 10–15 minutes, until hot through and a deeper gold in parts; or cook under the grill for 5 minutes until they begin to crisp – and don't leave the grill.

Allow to cool slightly, then arrange on a plate ready to serve with the tomato dipping sauce overleaf. ■

I LIKE A LOT OF TANG in my tomato sauce, but if you feel that you need to make it more universally appealing you may want to reduce, or even eliminate, the chilli.

Don't take alarm at the 2 cloves of garlic: they are left whole and then removed, so that they infuse the sauce rather than stomp all over it.

Although this amount of sauce is – provided no double dipping, of course – enough for the Polenta Triangles on the previous page, I like to dot a couple, or more, of bowls around for people to dip in, so I sometimes make a double batch. This is also a quick and simple, piquant sauce for pasta, when hot; cold, it is an accompaniment well worth considering for the butterflied lamb on **p.58** and many other meats besides.

CHILLI TOMATO SAUCE

Put the oil and garlic cloves into a small saucepan that has a lid and heat until the garlic becomes golden, at which point remove the pan from the heat, stir in the chilli flakes and let the oil cool slightly.

Now – standing well back in case of spitting – add the white wine or vermouth.

When any spitting has died down, put the pan back on the heat and add the canned tomatoes and the salt.

Let everything come to the boil, then turn the heat to the lowest possible setting, put the lid on and leave to cook for 10 minutes.

Pour the sauce into a heatproof bowl and let it cool, at which point remove the garlic cloves and check for seasoning. If you wish to serve this warm, by all means do of course. Similarly, should you want a smooth, rather than rustically chunky sauce, get out a stick blender and blitz or push through a vegetable mill. ■

MAKES ENOUGH FOR 30 POLENTA TRIANGLES Ⓝ

2 X 15ML TABLESPOONS OLIVE OIL

2 CLOVES GARLIC, PEELED BUT LEFT WHOLE

½ TEASPOON DRIED CHILLI FLAKES

2 X 15ML TABLESPOONS DRY WHITE WINE OR VERMOUTH

1 X 400G CAN CHOPPED TOMATOES

½ TEASPOON SEA SALT FLAKES OR ¼ TEASPOON POURING SALT, OR TO TASTE

BECAUSE OF THE TIME OF YEAR I first made this, I think of it as my Christmas Caprese, but I didn't want its title to shackle it seasonally. Not least, you could argue, because nobody's really got any business buying cherry tomatoes in December. But, frankly, if you live in the UK, the tomatoes you buy in August are not necessarily any sweeter or juicier than those bought in the bleak midwinter. Anyway, I can't start apologizing for my unseasonal and unlocal approach now. I buy the tomatoes from my local greengrocer's and that's good enough for me. I mean, do I want to be eating nothing but cabbage and parsnips all winter?

I had thought that this approach to the simple tomato, mozzarella and basil salad would not have much currency in Italy, but I hear that Italian supermarkets now stock tomatoes in winter, even if their greengrocers – quite rightly – won't. So, for anyone who buys tomatoes when they shouldn't, and wants to help them up their game: this is the recipe for you. But you have to know that if I didn't feel it was a bonus in its own right, I wouldn't include it here.

In short, I roast the tomatoes to intensify their flavour, let them cool and then dot these sweet and sticky heat-wilted blobs of red around some of the best mozzarella I can get my hands on. Instead of strewing basil leaves (also unseasonal) around, I blend a cupful of them to a snooker-baize green purée with a little olive oil; you'll need a stick blender for this, or at least I do.

TOMATOES, MOZZARELLA & BASIL, MY WAY

Preheat the oven to 220°C/gas mark 7.

In a small baking tin in which the tomatoes will fit snugly (I use a tarte Tatin tin) arrange the tomatoes cut-side up. Going over each tomato half, one by one, grind a little pepper and sprinkle on a little salt and the oregano, then dribble the tablespoon of olive oil over and transfer the tin to the oven to cook for 25 minutes, though check at 20 just in case they are softened and heat-wilted by then. Remove and leave to cool to room temperature or just above. (They can be left at room temperature for about 4 hours.)

To make the sauce, put the basil leaves and 2 tablespoons extra-virgin olive oil and 1 teaspoon vinegar and a small sprinkle of salt into a suitable bowl or cup, and blend to a deep-green purée with a stick blender. Add another 1–2 tablespoons extra-virgin olive oil as needed to form a not-entirely-smooth brilliant green paste that can be poured; taste to see if you want the remaining ½ teaspoon vinegar or more salt, and blend in if you do.

Take the mozzarella balls out of their liquid, drain, tear into pieces and, on a platter, arrange the mozzarella blossoms and the cooked, cooled tomato halves, then drizzle the basil dressing over them, and your beautiful creation is ready to be served, preferably with bread. ∎

SERVES 6, *OR MORE AS PART OF AN ANTIPASTI TABLE OR BUFFET*
300G CHERRY TOMATOES, HALVED
½ TEASPOON DRIED OREGANO
1 X 15ML TABLESPOON REGULAR OLIVE OIL
SEA SALT FLAKES AND GROUND PEPPER, TO TASTE
APPROX. 20G BASIL LEAVES
4–5 X 15ML TABLESPOONS EXTRA-VIRGIN OLIVE OIL
1–1½ TEASPOONS GOOD RED WINE VINEGAR
2 X 125G (DRAINED WEIGHT) BALLS MOZZARELLA (PREFERABLY BUFFALO)

THIS IS A WARMLY BUT NONETHELESS ELEGANTLY ROBUST winter pasta, salty with the bacon and grainily sweet with chestnuts, bound in a scant and glossy sauce infused with the mellow, musky grapiness of Marsala. It is not a starter – though of course it could be – but a relaxed main course, both for those cooking and those eating: an ideal state of affairs all round, and a comforting showcase for the seasonal chestnuts, even if they do come out of a vacuum pack. You can get the pancetta out of a packet, too, but for this festive special, I do try and get a slab of pancetta and chunk it up generously myself: pre-cut pancetta tends to come in tiny dice – they're not called *cubetti* for nothing.

PAPPARDELLE WITH CHESTNUTS & PANCETTA

SERVES 8, *DEPENDING ON AGE AND APPETITE*
500G EGG PAPPARDELLE
SALT FOR PASTA WATER, TO TASTE
2 TEASPOONS GARLIC OIL
400G SLAB PANCETTA, CUT INTO APPROX. 1CM DICE
50G BUTTER, PLUS MORE ON SERVING, AS DESIRED
200G VACUUM-PACKED COOKED CHESTNUTS
100ML MARSALA
2 X 15ML TABLESPOONS FINELY SNIPPED CHIVES
2 X 15ML TABLESPOONS FINELY CHOPPED FRESH PARSLEY

Put a large pan, filled abundantly with water, on the stove to heat for the pasta, and when it comes to a boil, salt generously and confidently.

Meanwhile, in a wok or large flameproof casserole, heat the garlic oil, then tip in the pancetta cubes and cook over a high heat until they are bronzed and crisp.

At the appropriate moment, according to how long the pasta needs (egg pappardelle is quick), add the pasta to the bubbling salted water and cook according to packet instructions, but make sure to start testing a minute or so before it should be ready.

Returning to the pancetta pan, add the butter and, when it has melted, tumble in the chestnuts, released from their vacuum-packed captivity, then, using a wooden spoon or other implement of your choice, squish them down so each chestnut crumbles into a good 4 pieces, and stir everything to mix.

Pour in the Marsala, letting it bubble up, then, just before you drain the pasta, lower in a ladle or measuring jug to remove a cupful of the starchy cooking water and tip about half of it – aim for 125ml or think 1 small wineglassful – into the pancetta and chestnut pan and stir well, letting it bubble and reduce down a little.

Drain the pasta and add it to the wok or casserole of sauce, followed by just under half the prepared chives and parsley, then mix gently but firmly together so that all ingredients are equally dispersed and the light sauce is clinging to the thick ribbons. You may need to stir in some more of the pasta-cooking water, and a little extra butter if you like.

If you're not serving from the pan you cooked it in, transfer the pasta to a warmed bowl, sprinkle with the remaining herbs, and serve. If you're dishing out from the pan, just sprinkle and serve. ∎

HEARTY WHOLEWHEAT PASTA WITH BRUSSELS SPROUTS, CHEESE & POTATO

IT IS NOT QUITE NORMAL TO FEEL AS JOYOUS as I do when saying the words "Brussels sprouts", but this recipe does not merely use said much-denigrated ingredient, it also celebrates it. Sprouts are nutty, fresh, gorgeous, and I regard this recipe as their seasonal showcase. Not Italian, you might say. Well, my inspiration for it is the one authentically defining dish of Valtellina, in Lombardy, up towards the Swiss border. That dish is *pizzoccheri*, a traditional winter-warmer hotchpotch of homemade buckwheat tagliatelle, potatoes, Savoy cabbage and Taleggio or fontina cheese, baked and flavoured with sage, garlic and Parmesan. You can buy *pizzoccheri* in boxes, with dried short lengths of buckwheat pasta, but for me it is too gummy and tastes nothing like the *pizzoccheri* I've eaten in Italy. I thought it better to do an Anglo version and very happy I am with it indeed. This is no self-aggrandizing boast: it's a tribute to the ingredients, rather than the cook (as all food should be).

I do understand that Gruyère cheese is not English but its nuttiness matches that of the sprouts – if you avoid picking ones that have moved towards blowsiness – and the sweet richness appeals. Feel free to use a mild Cheddar, if the spirit – or appetite – moves you.

Don't be modishly alarmed by the double-carb combo; it can be an alcohol-sopping salve, much appreciated at this time of year. Besides, it is important to remember that the original predates central heating.

SERVES 8 AS A MAIN COURSE, *OR MORE AS PART OF A BUFFET*

750G BRUSSELS SPROUTS, TRIMMED AND HALVED

250G (1) BAKING POTATO, PEELED AND IN 2–3CM DICE

500G WHOLEWHEAT OR SPELT TORTIGLIONI OR PENNE

SALT FOR VEGETABLE AND PASTA WATER, TO TASTE

100G RICOTTA

250G GRUYÈRE, IN 1CM DICE

50G SOFT UNSALTED BUTTER

1 X 15ML TABLESPOON GARLIC OIL

4 SAGE LEAVES, SHREDDED

50G GRATED PARMESAN

1 X ROASTING TIN APPROX. 25 X 36CM OR 1 X LASAGNE DISH APPROX. 23 X 34CM

Preheat the oven to 200°C/gas mark 6, and fill a large pot with water to cook the sprouts, potato and pasta.

When the water boils, salt it generously, tip in the prepared sprouts, the potato dice and the pasta and let the water come back to the boil, then cook for about 8–10 minutes, or until the potato is tender and the pasta al dente. Just before draining, remove 2 cupfuls of the cooking liquid and put to one side.

Tip the drained pasta, sprouts and potato pieces into a roasting tin (or a lasagne dish), then add the ricotta and diced Gruyère and a cupful of cooking water, and toss well to combine. Add more liquid if you feel the pasta is too dry.

Warm the butter and garlic oil in a small saucepan and, when melted and beginning to sizzle gently, add the shredded sage and fry for about 30 seconds before spooning or dribbling the butter and crisp sage over the pasta bake. Sprinkle with the Parmesan and bake in the oven for 20 minutes, by which time the surface will be scorched a light gold. I like this best if it's left to stand for at least 15 minutes before eating. ∎

ASTUTE READERS WILL BE ABLE TO SPOT straightaway that the pasta I have used is not macaroni but, in fact, penne. But Mountain Macaroni is the name of this dish, partly due to the alliterative allure, but more pointedly because it is adapted (in much-simplified fashion) from the Alpen Magrone recipe I found in the quite beautiful and altogether inspiring book, *Winter in the Alps*, by Swiss-born cook and food writer Manuela Darling-Gansser.

I have specified pancetta below, as it's easier to come by than the speck that I think would be more commonly used in the region. Jamon Serrano would be good here, too. Similarly, you can use the more accessible corrugated penne (*rigate*), if you can't find the smooth penne (*lisce*). Or, of course, just use macaroni.

By the way, my children love this best – and it is one of their top favourites in this book of mine – when it's cooked ahead and (once cooled) left to stand for a day or so in the fridge before being brought to room temperature and blitzed in a hot oven.

MOUNTAIN MACARONI

SERVES 6–8

500G (2) BAKING POTATOES, PEELED AND CUT INTO APPROX. 4CM CUBES

2 TEASPOONS SEA SALT FLAKES OR 1 TEASPOON POURING SALT, OR TO TASTE

500G PENNE LISCE OR PENNE RIGATE

2 TEASPOONS GARLIC OIL

350G PANCETTA CUBES

2 ECHALION OR BANANA SHALLOTS, PEELED AND CHOPPED

1½ TEASPOONS DRIED THYME

100ML DRY WHITE WINE OR VERMOUTH

300ML DOUBLE CREAM

FRESH NUTMEG

200G GRUYÈRE, GRATED

Preheat the oven to 220°C/gas mark 7, unless you are making this up ahead.

Fill a large pan of water to cook the pasta in and add the potato cubes and salt and put it on to boil. When it's come to the boil, leave it to bubble away for 5 minutes to help cook the potatoes a bit more before the pasta goes in. Once the pasta is in, cook for a little less time than it says on the packet; my penne stipulated 12 minutes, so I set my timer to 10. You need the pasta slightly more *al dente* than you would otherwise eat it.

On the hob, heat the garlic oil in an ovenproof pan that can later take all the cooked pasta and other ingredients, and add the pancetta cubes.

Cook for 4–5 minutes, stirring frequently, until the fat begins to render, although the pancetta will be far from crisp, and add the chopped shallots and thyme.

Stirring the pan every now and again, cook the shallots and pancetta together for another 4–5 minutes, or until the pancetta is crisping up and the shallots are soft. You can take the pan off the heat at this stage, and keep it to one side until the pasta is nearly ready.

When you're a couple of minutes away from draining the pasta, put the pancetta pan back on the heat and when it begins to sizzle again, add the wine or vermouth and let it bubble away in the heat. Now add the cream and a good grating of nutmeg and stir well. Take off the heat.

Check that the potatoes are just tender and the pasta still slightly *al dente*, then remove and reserve a good cupful of the cooking water. Drain the pasta and the potatoes and put them back in the pan they were cooked in.

Pour the creamy pancetta–shallot mixture over the pasta and toss well together, adding about half your cup of pasta-cooking liquid as you go. Keep the rest in case you need more; I tend to use it all. The sauce should be quite runny at this point – the pasta will soak it up as it bakes.

Now add half the cheese and toss again, and when it is pretty well incorporated add most of the remaining cheese, leaving just enough to sprinkle on top before the assembled dish goes into the oven.

Toss again and tip everything into the tin that the pancetta and shallots were cooked in. (If you're making this up ahead, you can let it cool now and leave it to stand, covered in the fridge, for up to 2 days, bringing it to room temperature before cooking.)

Now sprinkle with the remaining cheese and pop it straight into the preheated oven for 20 minutes or until the top is a pale gold. (If the pasta is cold when you put it in the oven – but winter room temperature, please, not fridge cold – it will probably need 30 minutes, and check that it is piping hot all the way through.) Once cooked, let it stand out of the oven for 10 minutes or so before serving. If you can wait... ■

IT'S ALWAYS WISE, WHEN HAVING PEOPLE OVER for drinks, to make sure there is something to absorb excess alcohol at the end of the evening. I don't mind if this be a phoned-in pizza but I'd much prefer it to be this rich plate of pork belly, cut into slices, then slow-roasted with that familiar southern Italian pairing of fennel seeds and chilli.

All you need to do, frankly, is put these slices in the oven. Once they're cooked, drain off most of the fat, and serve them with hunks of bread and, should vegetable accompaniment be required, some thinly sliced fresh fennel.

As far as I know, you need to go to a butcher to get the pork belly cut into slices. Do request that the rind be scored and the rib bones be left attached. It's up to you whether you ask for them by weight or by number of pieces; any way you slice it, it's a bit of a lottery as to how big each piece is, as pigs are not necessarily uniform in size.

PORK BELLY SLICES WITH CHILLI & FENNEL SEEDS

SERVES 6–8 *(MAKES 12 SLICES)*
60ML GARLIC OIL
2 X 15ML TABLESPOONS FENNEL SEEDS
2 TEASPOONS DRIED CHILLI FLAKES
1 X 15ML TABLESPOON SEA SALT FLAKES OR ½ TABLESPOON POURING SALT, OR TO TASTE
2.25KG (12) BELLY PORK SLICES

Preheat the oven to 170°C/gas mark 3.

Put the garlic oil, fennel seeds, dried chilli flakes and salt into a wide, shallow dish, and stir to mix.

Rub all the belly slices in this mixture on both sides, and then sit them in a roasting tin, with the rind uppermost, leaning the slices against each other snugly like a line of fallen dominoes. If it works in your tin, then do 2 lines of pork slices, even if the second line might have to be at a slight angle. I prefer doing it this way rather than using 2 tins.

Roast the belly slices for 2 hours, turning the tin, though not the slices, around halfway through. If they have not crisped up completely then give them another 30 minutes.

Take the belly slices out of the tin carefully: I use tongs and apply more care than is characteristic; the pork belly may have given out a lot of fat as it cooked, and caution is needed with the hot pan.

When the belly slices are arranged to your satisfaction – on a platter or a wooden board – then take them to the table, breathing in the warming and heady aroma, and dig right in. ◼

TURKEY BREAST STUFFED WITH ITALIAN SAUSAGE & MARSALA-STEEPED CRANBERRIES

AS WITH THE BISCOTTI on **p.238**, there is an undeniable American-Italian influence at play here but, once again, I embrace this. Actually, though, American-Italian food has had its own influence on the cooking of the Old Country: these days, I am reliably informed by my Italian publisher and celebrated food writer, Csaba dalla Zorza, you can find dried cranberries with relative ease in Italy.

The true Italian Christmas dinner is very much about the capon. Yes, you can find capons in Britain, although not everyone can quite cope with the idea of eating a castrated cockerel. Actually, old-school caponization is illegal in the UK, although it is considered ethically acceptable if the rooster has been chemically rather than surgically castrated. I don't know about you, but the idea of eating meat that has been flooded with the types of hormones necessarily involved here gives me the willies.

Besides, my Christmas Dinner is my Christmas Dinner: unchanging, ritualistic, an intrinsic part of me. When in Rome, and all that, but if I'm cooking at home, I don't fiddle with my time-honoured menu. I'm not going to give an evangelical tub-thump about my turkey brining techniques, as I've done enough of that in the past, but I am still open to other ways of celebrating the Big Bird and this recipe is a case in point. For me, it is perfect for any sort of seasonal supper party, but really comes into its own on a buffet table, as it carves fantastically and is as good (maybe even better) cold than hot, so you can make it in advance and then be the world's most unharried host on the night.

You need to go to a butcher to get a whole breast joint and you need to ask for it to be butterflied and boned and make sure the skin is left on.

I know it might sound a bit of a faff, but take it from me that stuffing a whole double breast joint is very much easier than stuffing and rolling a single breast joint, as is more commonly found in supermarkets. Basically, all you're doing here is opening out your boneless turkey joint, smothering it with stuffing and folding it over. What you end up with, for all the ease of its creation, is nothing short of a showstopper.

SERVES 12, *OR MANY MORE AS*
PART OF A BUFFET ◐
FOR THE STUFFING:
100G DRIED CRANBERRIES
100ML MARSALA
2 X 15ML TABLESPOONS
    OLIVE OIL
2 ECHALION OR BANANA
    SHALLOTS, PEELED AND FINELY
    CHOPPED
¼ TEASPOON GROUND CLOVES
½ TEASPOON GROUND ALLSPICE
2 TEASPOONS CHOPPED FRESH
    SAGE
1KG ITALIAN SAUSAGES
2 EGGS, BEATEN
APPROX. 50G GRATED PARMESAN
APPROX. 60G BREADCRUMBS

FOR THE TURKEY JOINT:
5KG DOUBLE BREAST TURKEY
    JOINT, BONED, BUTTERFLIED,
    WITH SKIN LEFT ON
4 X 15ML TABLESPOONS DUCK OR
    GOOSE FAT

Put the cranberries and Marsala into a small saucepan and bring to a boil, then take off the heat and leave to one side.

Put the oil into a large frying pan or similar heavy-based pan, and fry the shallots for a minute or so, then add the spices and shredded sage, turning them in the soft shallots.

Squeeze the sausagemeat out of its skins, add to the pan and break it up – using a wooden fork and spatula for ease – turning it in the hot pan until it loses its pinkness. This will take about 5 minutes.

Take the frying pan off the heat and turn the contents into a large bowl, mixing in the steeped cranberries and any Marsala clinging to them, and leave to cool. You can cover with clingfilm and put in the fridge for up to 2 days at this stage.

When you are ready to stuff the turkey breast, take the bowl of sausagemeat out of the fridge.

Preheat the oven to 200°C/gas mark 6.

Uncover the bowl of sausagemeat, add the eggs, Parmesan and breadcrumbs and – I use my hands for this – mix well.

Lay the butterflied turkey joint out in front of you. It really does look like a butterfly, though admittedly a fleshy one. Spread the stuffing out first in the slight cavity in the centre of the butterfly and then outwards onto the wings though not going right up to the edge (or it will squodge out when cooking) but as evenly as possible over the whole joint.

Carefully, in one swift but steady movement, fold one "wing" over the other to close the joint, and then sit the turkey on a large roasting tin, breast bone (or where the breast bone would be) uppermost as it would look were it the whole bird, with the pointier bit furthest away from you. Thread 2 skewers through the base – i.e., the widest part that is nearer you – to keep it closed, and smear it all over with the duck or goose fat.

Roast the turkey breast for 2–2½ hours, then check it is cooked with a turkey or meat thermometer. When cooked, it should read 75°C in the centre. (If you're leaving it to rest, as you should, or to cool, you could take it out at 73°C – it will retain heat and continue to cook for a short while once out of the oven.)

Flex your muscles, then lift out onto a carving board, and leave to rest for at least 20 minutes. Or leave to get cold if you are eating it as part of a cook-ahead buffet.

Cut through the whole joint in wide slices right across; they will need to be quite thick, at least 1cm maybe 2cm, to keep the stuffing intact within the slice.

As you place it on table or sideboard, dot around it the condiments of your choice: I revert to Christmas in Italy here by putting a lusciously extravagant pot or two of Italian *mostarda di Cremona* on the table alongside: this is a hot and sweet preserve of mustardy candied fruits that gleam beautifully and taste both festive and fabulous. ■

THIS IS SUCH A BASIC RECIPE of mine, but I still felt it had a place here. A roast potato is always celebratory but often labour-intensive; here, life's easy as I don't go in for peeling and I don't turn the potatoes over as they cook. Actually, it's better that way as they've really had time to crisp up on the bottom and therefore don't stick to the tin as you take them out.

I have a very large roasting tin, so can fit all the potatoes in, but it would be fine to use 2 tins; just cook them for 15–30 minutes longer and swap the tins over halfway through. In which case, too, you may as well bump the spuds up to 2kg.

I love serving these on platters lined with my favourite lettuce, escarole, thus providing potatoes and salad on one easy-serving dish.

ITALIAN ROAST POTATOES

Preheat the oven to 220°C/gas mark 7.

Dice the potatoes, with their skins on, roughly into about 2–3cm chunks, and then spread them out on a large but shallow roasting tin or lipped baking sheet.

Break up the garlic heads into cloves, keeping their skins on too, but discarding the loose papery outside layers. Arrange the garlic among the potato pieces.

Sprinkle with the chopped rosemary and then drizzle the oil over, turning everything in the tin to coat well.

Cook in the hot oven for 1 hour, by which time the potatoes should be golden on the outside and tender within. Lift or scrape the potatoes off the tray with the implement of your choice, and put onto a couple of salad-lined plates or a warmed platter, sprinkling with sea salt flakes to taste, then serve. ∎

SERVES 8, *OR 10 IF MIXED WITH LETTUCE*
1.75KG WAXY POTATOES, SUCH AS DESIREE OR MARIS PIPER
2 HEADS GARLIC
2 TEASPOONS CHOPPED FRESH ROSEMARY NEEDLES
150ML OLIVE OIL
1 HEAD ESCAROLE LETTUCE (OPTIONAL), TO SERVE
SEA SALT FLAKES, TO TASTE

IN MY HEAD – AND IN MY HOME – this recipe is known as Fir-Tree Romanesco. Admittedly, the epithet "fir-tree" is a seasonally induced fantasy; I came across a beautiful display of Romanesco last Christmas and it seemed to me that, once dismembered, this dazzling, bright-green vegetable had the look of fir trees in tiny, squat form. Actually, as you can see from the still life on **p.195**, it more closely resembles the cartoonily sci-fi landscape of the film *Avatar*. There is something about the whirls and whorls of its orderly design that could make you think it was a new-fangled, genetically engineered breed of vegetation altogether, but in fact Romanesco predates broccoli and cauliflower (to both of which it is related) having been established in Italy in the 16th century. I call it (as do the greengrocers who stock it) by its majestic Italian name, but I have seen references to it both as caulibroc and broccoflower.

I like best to eat this nuttily flavoursome Romanesco at room temperature (which makes life easier when staggering your cooking for seasonal meals) but it is good – of course – when hot, too, and I know that not everyone shares my taste (acquired from living in Italy) for room-temp veg.

ROMANESCO WITH ROSEMARY, GARLIC, LEMON & PECORINO

SERVES 4–6, *OR MORE AS PART OF A BUFFET*
1 HEAD ROMANESCO
SEA SALT FLAKES OR POURING SALT, TO TASTE
60ML EXTRA-VIRGIN OLIVE OIL
1 X 15ML TABLESPOON FINELY CHOPPED FRESH ROSEMARY NEEDLES
1 CLOVE GARLIC, PEELED
ZEST AND JUICE 1 UNWAXED LEMON
2–3 X 15ML TABLESPOONS GRATED PECORINO (OR PARMESAN) CHEESE

Fill a large pan with water and put on to boil.

Remove the top floret/fir tree of the Romanesco in its entirety, and the larger of the remaining florets, and when the water comes to the boil add salt according to your taste, then drop in (gently) the big central floret and cook for 2 minutes.

Now add the other large florets and cook for another 2 minutes. Meanwhile, cut off all the remaining Romanesco florets. Add all these to the pan and bring back to the boil. Let everything bubble for a final 3–5 minutes until the florets are tender, but still with a bit of crispness about them, then drain and tip gently into a shallow serving bowl.

In a very small saucepan, heat the olive oil, then add the chopped rosemary needles and let them sizzle for a few seconds. Then grate in (or mince and add) the garlic, stir it in and turn off the heat.

Add the lemon zest and now take the pan away from the stove altogether and let the contents cool slightly before whisking in the lemon juice and salt to taste (remembering that you are adding salty cheese in a moment), then pour this over the Romanesco in its bowl. Toss again gently and then, as soon as it's all touchable, turn the little florets of Romanesco to stand up so they look like a bowlful of small fir trees (as best you can!).

Grate a "snow" of pecorino (or Parmesan) over them and serve – although I love this best once it's all stood together for a while (30–60 minutes) and is at room temperature. ∎

RENAISSANCE SALAD

IN OLD-FASHIONED WOMEN'S MAGAZINES, writers used to advise their readers to create a signature vinaigrette to charm their guests and polish their hostessly credentials. I'm not sure about any of that, but if I don't have a signature dressing, I most certainly have a signature salad, and it's this.

I hesitate even to give a recipe, I throw it together in so – intentionally – slapdash a fashion, but I have no doubt at all that I need to tell you about it. I call it my Renaissance Salad, sometimes my Red Renaissance Salad, quite simply because the deep, garnet tones of the ivory-veined Treviso and tardivo radicchio have something of the glorious colours in the paintings that line the walls of the Uffizi; though, really, I should have called this Late Renaissance Salad, as the glowing dark reds bring to my mind even more vividly the Caravaggio paintings I remember seeing in Rome. Though I should tell you that actually these beauteous lettuces come from around Venice.

I ought to mention, too, that if you don't come across the beautifully bitter Treviso or the sweeter tardivo, simply use a couple of the more accessible round radicchio, instead. I sometimes add some blushing spears of red chicory, too.

Radicchio, Treviso and tardivo are the names these red lettuces are sold by in British greengrocers. In Italy, they'd be identified as – going from top to bottom (see left) – *radicchio di Chioggia, radicchio precoce di Treviso* and *radicchio tardivo di Treviso*. These days, both early (*precoce*) and late (*tardivo*) Treviso varieties can be found together for an overlapping period.

I use a ludicrously vast platter for this – about 40cm in diameter – which means I can get all the red leaves in a single layer, with a frame of plate around them, before I sprinkle sprouts and seeds over, but you can use a regular salad bowl and toss everything together if you prefer.

Tear the Treviso into ragged rough pieces and pull the tardivo off its stalk into fronds, then strew a large platter with them. Leaves from round radicchio can be left whole or treated like the Treviso.

Sprinkle with salt, then drizzle with the oil and vinegar, in a roughly zig-zag fashion, and scatter the pomegranate seeds on top. And that is that. Just beautiful! ∎

SERVES 8–10

1 HEAD TREVISO RADICCHIO
AND 1 HEAD TARDIVO
AND 1 HEAD ROUND RADICCHIO
OR 3 HEADS ROUND RADICCHIO
SCANT TEASPOON SEA
   SALT FLAKES OR SCANT ½
   TEASPOON POURING SALT, OR
   TO TASTE
2 X 15ML TABLESPOONS EXTRA-
   VIRGIN OLIVE OIL
2 TEASPOONS BALSAMIC
   VINEGAR
75G POMEGRANATE SEEDS

FIG & OLIVE CHUTNEY

THE SCRAWL ON MY KITCHEN NOTEBOOK under this recipe reads: Ancient Italian flavours, English recipe; that just about sums it up.

I often give homemade chutneys to Italian friends when I visit, as I'm proud of our traditional recipes and know that an English chutney can pair magnificently with an Italian cheese. Italians themselves are not averse to a condiment or two of their own, either. But I love bringing the two strands of our differing cultures together – and this fig and olive chutney is a marriage made in *paradiso*.

The quantities below are modest, but then this is not a chutney that can be kept for long, so I don't make a lot at a time. Plus, it is so quick and easy that there is no need for old-school "putting down", as preserving used to be known in the kitchen, or even for sterilizing your jars (unless you especially want to make a longer-life version described just below).

I cannot cope without a few jars of pitted dry-packed black olives in the cupboard; you don't find them everywhere so it's worth getting a stash in when you do come across them. And if you don't have these, then you will need 300g of black olives with stones in – the kind that are stored in oil – and will have to pit them yourself. Do not use cans of pitted olives in brine, please, as you won't get the depth of flavour or the right consistency.

Should you be inclined to store this chutney for longer, up to 3 months or thereabouts (in which case you'll need sterilized jars – see Notes **p.267**), then you should return the processed chutney to the saucepan, put it over a medium heat and bring it back up to a boil; it will bubble at the edges and be steaming slightly. Transfer it to warm, sterilized jars, seal and leave them to cool, then store in a cool, dark place. I tend not to bother with this fandango but warn friends who are the recipients of my chutney as a gift that they must keep it in the fridge and eat within the month; they don't find this problematic at all. Nor will you.

I use the amount below to fill 3 preserving jars of 250ml or 6 tinier ones.

MAKES APPROX. 750ML Ⓝ

325G SOFT DRIED FIGS, SNIPPED
   IN HALF
2 X 110G JARS PITTED DRY-
   PACKED BLACK OLIVES
100G DARK MUSCOVADO SUGAR
1 TEASPOON FENNEL SEEDS
1 TEASPOON GROUND
   CINNAMON
PINCH GROUND CLOVES
60ML MARSALA
150ML RED WINE VINEGAR
100ML WATER

3 X 250ML OR 6 X APPROX. 125ML
   SEALABLE JARS WITH VINEGAR-
   PROOF LIDS

Put all the ingredients into a smallish (approx. 17–18cm diameter), heavy-based saucepan that has a lid, bring to a bubble and when it starts boiling, clamp on the lid, turn down the heat and simmer for 15 minutes.

Remove from the heat, take off the lid and let it stand to cool a little for 5 or so minutes, then tip into a food processor and blitz until finely chopped: this does not take long.

Spoon the chutney into clean, warm jars, then seal with their lids and leave to cool for about 3 hours before transferring to the fridge. ■

WHENEVER I'M IN ITALY, I buy and bring back bulging cellophane parcels of herb mixes to keep in a cupboard at home so I can turn some plain pasta into an instant Italian-scented supper. All of them contain dried parsley, chilli flakes, garlic granules, and salt, though others add oregano and crumbled dried tomato, too. I thought I'd stick to the simpler version myself, as it makes it actually more versatile.

The reason I give the recipe – more of a blueprint – for it here is that I find a small jar makes for a charming present. I attach a label to the jar, with instructions for use, namely that for each 100g of spaghetti (uncooked weight), 2 teaspoons of the mix should be sprinkled in a tablespoonful of olive oil in the still-hot pan once the pasta's drained, then the spaghetti should be tossed back in, along with 30–60ml of starchy cooking water.

I have given precise weights below in an effort to be helpful, but basically you need to think of using – in weight not volume – 1 part dried parsley and garlic to 2 parts chilli flakes and 3 parts sea salt flakes. I know this sounds as if the chilli will dominate but remember that the chilli flakes weigh more, as it were, than the dried parsley, so that even though you have double the weight of chilli flakes, the volume of parsley is greater.

It goes without saying – or ought to – that you should try to get the best-quality dried herbs that you can find.

SPAGHETTI SPICE

Mix the ingredients in a bowl and then, when you're happy everything's thoroughly combined, fill your waiting containers, close tightly and attach instructions for use, if so desired. ■

**MAKES ENOUGH TO FILL
4 X 110ML JARS Ⓝ**
15G DRIED PARSLEY
15G GARLIC GRANULES
30G DRIED CHILLI FLAKES
45G SEA SALT FLAKES

4 X 110ML AIRTIGHT JARS

WHILE I WAS TEMPTED TO CALL THIS ITALIAN TOAST, rather than the almost tactless Panettone French Toast, I felt the latter title had the benefit of conveying to you exactly what this is. You can certainly make it with plainer golden pandoro, but it may also be useful to know that should you have made, or be making, the Italian Christmas Pudding Cake on **p.250**, the amount of panettone specified below is pretty much what you'll have left over if you started with a 1kg panettone. Besides, the panettone with its spicy studding of sweet fruits does make this feel like a fully festive breakfast. Dried and candied fruit phobes should obviously take the pandoro path.

Either way, you don't really need to start measuring and weighing, though: I just cut 4 slices, cutting each in half so I end up with 8 small-loaf-sized slices. If need be, and with a lot of extra fruit about, you could easily stretch this to feed 8 for breakfast. Especially if you give in to requests (as I have done) for some crisp-cooked, wafer-thin rashers of pancetta on top. For me, though, this needs no more than a scant sprinkling of sharp, fragrant, festive pomegranate seeds.

If you cook these, as I do, for 1 minute a side, the egg will be soft inside, so some eaters may want them cooked longer (and see also Note to the Reader about eggs on **p.xiii**).

PANETTONE FRENCH TOAST

In a dish that will take half the panettone pieces easily – I use a 24cm square glass dish – whisk the eggs together with the mascarpone and milk; you will have to be a bit patient to smooth out the mascarpone – not that a normal person would register this, but my impatience colours my judgement.

Dunk 4 of the panettone slices in the egg mixture and leave to soak for 1 minute.

Put 25g butter and ½ a teaspoon oil in a large frying pan, and set over a low heat to melt. Turn the panettone slices in the egg mixture, and soak the other side for another minute, by which time the bread should have soaked up enough to soften it and the butter should have melted in the pan.

Turn up the heat, then add the soaked slices to the frying pan and cook for 1 minute each side, so that their egg-soaked surfaces are golden, and browned in part. Meanwhile, soak the remaining 4 slices in the egg mixture for their 1 minute a side.

Remove the first batch of Panettone French Toast from the pan to a large plate, add the remaining butter and oil to the pan, and cook the second batch as you did the first.

When all the pieces are cooked and on the platter, scatter with pomegranate seeds, then dust thickly with the icing sugar pressed through a tea strainer, letting the "snow" fall mostly on the golden sweet-bread slices rather than on the fruit. ∎

SERVES 4–6

4 EGGS
2 X 15ML TABLESPOONS
  MASCARPONE
125ML MILK
300G PANETTONE (OR
  PANDORO), SLIGHTLY STALED,
  CUT INTO 8 EQUAL PIECES
50G UNSALTED BUTTER
1 TEASPOON FLAVOURLESS
  VEGETABLE OIL

TO SERVE:
APPROX. 50G POMEGRANATE
  SEEDS
1 TEASPOON ICING SUGAR

I READILY CONCEDE that, what with the addition of dried cranberries, this is rather more of an Italo-American recipe than an Italian one, but this is not a bad thing: Italian-Americans bring a lot of vigour and expressiveness to the traditional canon. In any event, the story of Italian food is inextricable from the history and mores of the Italian diaspora.

Biscotti, so named because they are cooked (*cotti*) twice (*bis*) are not tricky to make, but it's not a fast job. Still, you need do nothing while they get their double-baking in the oven, and this kind of cooking can be very calming.

The method below follows traditional lines, and brings you bold, golden biscotti, gorgeous wrapped or in a jar for a Christmas present.

But even if I do like to give these as presents (in which case it may be simpler to make more than one batch at a time) I certainly keep some back for PU. And just as I embrace the American influence behind this recipe, so I like to bring a little Anglo-touch to the table when I eat them. The Italians dip their biscotti into the sweet dessert wine, vin santo; I dip my cranberry-studded ones in a glass of colour-coordinated ruby port.

CRANBERRY & PISTACHIO BISCOTTI

MAKES 15, *EXCLUDING THE END PIECES* Ⓝ

1 EGG
75G CASTER SUGAR
2 TEASPOONS FINELY GRATED ORANGE ZEST
125G PLAIN FLOUR, PLUS MORE FOR ROLLING
½ TEASPOON BAKING POWDER
FRESH NUTMEG
75G PISTACHIO NUTS
50G DRIED CRANBERRIES

Preheat the oven to 180°C/gas mark 4.

Whisk the egg and sugar until pale and moussy: the mixture should leave a ribbon-like trail when you lift the beater. Beat in the orange zest, and then slowly fold in the flour, baking powder and a good grating of nutmeg.

Fold in the whole pistachios and dried cranberries, then flour your work surface well, and you may find it helpful to dust your hands lightly with flour, too, as the dough is quite sticky. Now form the dough into a flattish, oval ciabatta-like loaf, approx. 25 x 5cm, tapering the ends slightly.

Lay the biscotti dough loaf onto a piece of baking parchment on a baking sheet and cook for 25–30 minutes, or until it is a pale brown colour. It may help to rotate the baking sheet halfway through the cooking time, as the base can brown quickly; this reduces the risk of the base scorching at one end.

Transfer to a wire rack and leave for 5 minutes to harden slightly, and then – using a bread knife or similar stout serrated-edged knife – cut the baked loaf diagonally into fingers about 1cm thick.

Put these back onto the baking-parchment-covered sheet and cook again for another 10 minutes, then turn the biscotti over and cook for yet another 5 minutes. Let the golden-brown biscotti cool on a rack and then store them in an airtight container. ◼

CHRISTMAS IN ITALY WOULD NOT BE COMPLETE without *torrone*, that slab of dentist-defying chewiness made with egg white, honey, toasted nuts and, often, orange blossom, that we know by the French word *nougat*. I considered making some, I really did, but I came to the conclusion that it involved too much precision-heat measuring and a degree of patience that eludes me at any time of year, but most specifically at Christmas. (You should know that most Italians buy rather than make their own *torrone*, too, no shame attached.) One day I hope to overcome my visceral anxiety and become a serene if – by necessity – energetic *torrone*-maker, but until then I wanted a way to incorporate the shop-bought version into my own seasonal festivities. This is what I present to you here and now.

Before I felt I could go public with it, I tested it on a number of Italians – a small sample, I concede, but not an irrelevant one – and was gratified, or rather relieved, by the enthusiastic response. It's always a risk playing about with time-honoured traditions. But Italians are, as I've mentioned elsewhere in these pages, embracing the Anglo-American baking tradition and are cupcakes and cookies a-go-go right now, so this recipe seems a timely marriage of kitchen customs. In fact, it was an Italian friend, admittedly one who's been resident in London for over a decade, who gave me the idea in the first place.

If you're cooking for those who can't or won't (that's my children, actually) eat nuts, then you will have to give up any aspiration towards Italianness and use a 170g packet of white chocolate chips, instead. This is how my daughter loves these cookies, and has insisted they be part of her birthday (which is around Christmas) celebrations from now on. When I make them with chocolate chips, I think they should be eaten still warm; if using nougat, then they are best cold, as the firmness of the cooled cookies contrasts best with the still chewy chunks of *torrone*. And to cut up the sticky nougat first (if you're including it) into the required 1–2cm pieces, it helps to use a heavy knife, spraying the blade with baking spray, or you could dip it in cold water every so often.

CHOCOLATE NOUGAT COOKIES

MAKES 25 Ⓝ
125G SOFT UNSALTED BUTTER
100G CASTER SUGAR
75G SOFT LIGHT BROWN SUGAR
1 EGG
200G PLAIN FLOUR
30G BEST-QUALITY COCOA
  POWDER, SIFTED
½ TEASPOON BICARBONATE OF
  SODA
▶

Preheat the oven to 180°C/gas mark 4, and line a baking sheet.

Beat together the soft butter and white and brown sugars until creamy, then add the egg, beating quickly to incorporate it well.

In another bowl, mix together the flour, cocoa, bicarb, salt and coffee. Then slowly add the dry ingredients to the wet ingredients in a couple of batches, tossing the chopped nougat pieces into the second batch of flour before you add it. Mix to combine, but don't overbeat as it will make the mixture too sticky.

Using a lightly oiled rounded tablespoon measure, take out a scoop of the cookie mixture, flatten off the top, and ease out the round dome of cookie dough onto a tray you can fit in your fridge. Repeat until all the dough is used. Let the cookie dough mounds chill in the fridge for 30 minutes. This is not crucial but it helps keep the inside of the cookies chewy; if you like yours crisp, go straight to oven. You could always freeze them at this stage, too (see Notes **p.267**).

When you are ready to bake the cookies, gently transfer them to your lined baking sheet, spacing them about 4cm apart. Bake in the oven for 12–15 minutes, then carefully move the cookies to a cooling rack – they will be firm on the outside but still soft inside. Allow to cool. Push the teaspoon of icing sugar through a fine sieve to decorate the cookies before serving proudly on a stand or platter. ■

¼ TEASPOON SEA SALT FLAKES OR SMALL PINCH POURING SALT

2½ TEASPOONS ESPRESSO POWDER

200G NOUGAT, CHOPPED INTO 1–2CM PIECES

FLAVOURLESS VEGETABLE OIL, FOR GREASING SPOON

1 TEASPOON ICING SUGAR, FOR DUSTING

1 X ROUNDED TABLESPOON MEASURE

1 X BAKING SHEET

I'VE ENCOUNTERED QUITE A FEW VERSIONS of chocolate salame in Italy – coming to the conclusion that it's really an Italian version of our chocolate refrigerator cake – and although I am not normally a huge fan of the culinary pun, this does seem the right time of year for such whimsical enterprises. And, I admit, the chocolate salame does have a certain charm, especially when dusted with icing sugar, tied like a proper salame with string. (I am grateful here to Jacob Kenedy for his instructions on how to string up a *finocchiona* in the *Bocca Cookbook*.) If I can do the stringing up, then you can, honestly, but if you prefer, you can just dust the unstrung salame with icing sugar and leave it picturesquely on a board. (And please see Note to the Reader on **p.xiii** about eggs.)

CHOCOLATE SALAME

In the microwave (following manufacturer's instructions), or in a heatproof bowl suspended over a saucepan of simmering water (but not touching the water), melt the chocolate until smooth. While the chocolate's melting, put the biscuits into a large freezer bag, seal and bash them with a rolling pin until you have a bag of rubble – not dust. When the chocolate's melted, remove it to a cold place (not the fridge) and set aside to cool.

Cream the butter and sugar together; I do this in a freestanding mixer, but you don't have to. You just need to use a large bowl and make sure the mixture is soft and superlight.

Gradually, and one by one, beat in the eggs. (Don't worry if the mixture looks curdled at this stage: all manner of ills will be righted once the chocolate is added later.) Then beat in the amaretto liqueur.

Push the cocoa powder through a little sieve or tea strainer into the cooled chocolate and, with a small rubber spatula, stir till combined, then beat this into the egg mixture, too.

When you have a smooth chocolate mixture in front of you, tip in the chopped nuts and crushed biscuits. Fold these in firmly but patiently to make sure everything is chocolate-covered. Transfer this mixture, still in its bowl, to the fridge to firm up a bit for 20–30 minutes. Don't leave it for much longer than this or it will be difficult to get out of the bowl to shape.

Unroll and slice off 2 large pieces of clingfilm, overlapping them, so that you have a large cling-covered surface to roll the chocolate salame out on. Tip the chocolate mixture out in the middle of this and – using your hands, messy though this is – mould the mixture into a fat salame-like log, approx. 30cm long.

Cover the chocolate log completely with the clingfilm, and then firmly roll it, as if it were a rolling pin, to create a smooth, rounded cylinder from the rough log you started with. Twist the ends by grasping both ends of the clingfilm and rolling the sausage-log towards you

MAKES APPROX. 20 GENEROUS SLICES Ⓝ

250G GOOD-QUALITY DARK CHOCOLATE (MIN. 70% COCOA SOLIDS), ROUGHLY CHOPPED

250G AMARETTI (CRUNCHY NOT "MORBIDI") OR RICH TEA BISCUITS

100G SOFT UNSALTED BUTTER

150G CASTER SUGAR

3 LARGE EGGS

2 X 15ML TABLESPOONS AMARETTO LIQUEUR

2 X 15ML TABLESPOONS UNSWEETENED COCOA POWDER

75G NATURAL ALMONDS (UNSKINNED), ROUGHLY CHOPPED

75G HAZELNUTS, ROUGHLY CHOPPED

50G PISTACHIO NUTS, ROUGHLY CHOPPED

1–2 X 15ML TABLESPOONS ICING SUGAR, TO DECORATE

several times. Then put it in the fridge for at least 6 hours – though preferably overnight – to set.

Now – once it's set – for the exciting bit: tear off a large piece of greaseproof paper and lay it on a clear kitchen surface. Take the salame out of the fridge and sit it on the paper. Measure out a piece of string at least 6 times longer than the length of the salame, and tie one end of the string firmly round the twisted knot of clingfilm at one end of the salame. Then trim away as much clingfilm as you can, but without cutting either of the tapered, nose ends, so that you can attach the string to these.

Dust your hands with a little icing sugar and then rub 2 tablespoons of icing sugar (more if needed) over the unwrapped salame to stop it getting sticky as you string it up. Plus it makes it look more like a salame!

Make a loop with the string, a little wider than the salame, and feed it over the end of the salame, close to where it is tied on. Pull on the trailing end to tighten (but not too tightly) and form another loop of string as before. Work this second loop around the sausage, 4cm or so further along from the first, tighten again and repeat until you reach the far end of the salame, then tie the string firmly round the other twisted nose of clingfilm.

With your remaining length of string, start to feed it back along the salame, twisting it around the encircling string each time it crosses a loop, then tie it again when you come to the end. Repeat these lengths as many times as you want, to make the authentic-looking pattern, but two or three times would be enough to get the effect.

Transfer it to a wooden board, and cut some slices, fanning them out as if they were indeed slices of salame, leaving a knife on the board, too, for people to cut further slices, as they wish. Obviously, when you cut the salame, you will cut through the string, but the many knots and twists keep it securely tied. Serve fridge cold, or very near to it. ■

THIS TIME OF YEAR IS SO FILLED with rich confections, fruited and larded and celebratory (not that this is a bad thing), that I am drawn to the underplayed hand of this only deceptively plain cake. It is not one of those high-rise spectaculars, but rather a modest shallow cake; at least insofar as appearances go. To taste, it is meltingly damp, and fragrantly redolent of marzipan – not surprising, since it is made with ground almonds. So, yes, it's a plain cake, but it has a restrained richness of its own: small cinnamon-scented slices suffice.

Although a grating of clementine (or orange) zest and a sprinkling of ground cinnamon confer Christmas status, and the icing sugar dusted on top makes it look seasonally snowy, I do make it all the year round and it's wonderful in summer with fresh, sharp raspberries. Also in its favour, for any time of year, is that it is gluten- and dairy-free, though not in a special-pleading kind of way.

Normally, when using olive oil in cakes, I am happy to use regular, non-extra-virgin, but for this cake, which has only egg whites rather than the rounded fullness of yolks, I feel it's better to go for olive oil specifically labelled "mild and light". Also, I use free-range pasteurized egg whites out of a carton, rather than leaving myself with 8 egg yolks gazing reproachfully from the fridge afterwards.

CINNAMON ALMOND CAKE

CUTS INTO 8–12 SLICES Ⓝ

8 EGG WHITES
150G CASTER SUGAR
FEW DROPS ALMOND ESSENCE
ZEST 1 CLEMENTINE OR ½
   ORANGE
125ML MILD AND LIGHT OLIVE OIL,
   PLUS MORE FOR GREASING TIN
150G GROUND ALMONDS
1 TEASPOON BAKING POWDER
100G FLAKED ALMONDS
1 TEASPOON GROUND
   CINNAMON
APPROX. 2 TEASPOONS ICING
   SUGAR, TO DECORATE

1 X 22 OR 23CM SPRINGFORM
   CAKE TIN

Preheat the oven to 180°C/gas mark 4, and grease a springform cake tin (or use a special baking spray) and line the base with baking parchment.

In a clean, grease-free bowl, whisk the egg whites until they are opaque and start to hold their shape, then slowly add the sugar, whisking until it's all incorporated and the mixture is thick and shiny.

Add the almond essence and the clementine or orange zest. Then, in about 3 goes each, alternately whisk in the oil and the ground almonds (mixed with the baking powder) until they are both smoothly incorporated into the meringue.

Pour the mixture into the prepared tin, then mix together the flaked almonds and cinnamon and sprinkle them over the top of the cake.

Bake for 35–40 minutes (though start checking at 30), by which time the top should have risen and be set and the almonds become golden, and a cake tester should come out clean, barring the odd almondy crumb.

Remove from the oven and let the cake cool, in its tin, on a wire rack. Once it is no longer hot, spring open the sides of the tin, but don't try to remove the cake from the base until properly cool.

When you are ready to serve, push the icing sugar through a small sieve and over the cake to create a snowy effect, and take to the table. ■

I AM INORDINATELY PROUD OF THIS, and am not ashamed to say so. I have long been a Pavaholic but this is my first venture into a fruit-free, though far from fruitless, version. The instant espresso powder (do not use regular instant coffee granules) gives bitter oomph to the sweet, marshmallowy meringue, which (as with the Cinnamon Almond Cake on the previous page) I make with free-range pasteurized egg whites from a carton. I saw Monica use these on *MasterChef: The Professionals* on TV, and if it's good enough for her, it's more than good enough for me.

I feel disinclined to labour any Italian *bona fides* here, but the cappuccino element – in flavour and form – is self-explanatory and we could always think of it not as a Cap Pav (as it's known in my house) but as *meringa al caffè con panna montata*. Not that I feel the need: I declare its inspiration, not its identity, to be authentically Italian.

CAPPUCCINO PAVLOVA

Preheat the oven to 180°C/gas mark 4, and line a flat oven tray with baking parchment and – if it helps – using a 23cm cake tin as a guide – draw a circle on it with a pencil.

In a smallish bowl, mix the sugar with the instant espresso powder, and set aside for the moment.

In a clean, grease-free bowl, preferably metal (and wipe the inside with a piece of kitchen roll dipped in vinegar first, if you want) whisk the egg whites with a pinch of salt until they are holding soft peaks and keep whisking while you gradually add the sugar-coffee mixture, 1 tablespoon at a time.

When all this mixture is incorporated and you have a firm, gleaming écru-coloured meringue, fold in – using a grease-free metal spoon – the cornflour and vinegar.

Dollop large spoonfuls of the meringue mixture inside the drawn circle (or make a circle shape freehand if you prefer) on the baking parchment, and smooth and shape it with a spatula so that it looks rather like the crown of a straw boater: it must be flat on top.

Put this in the oven and *immediately* turn the oven down to 150°C/gas mark 2, and cook for 1 hour. The meringue's outer shell should be crisp, but only just. When it's ready, turn off the oven and leave the Pavlova base inside it until it's cool.

Once the Pavlova base is cool, lift it carefully in its paper and place it, top-side down, on a large, flat plate, then gently peel off the paper.

Whip the double cream until thickened and airy, but still soft, and spread this delicately over the top (which previously was the bottom) of the meringue. With a teaspoon, push the cocoa powder through a fine sieve or tea strainer to decorate – cappuccino-style – the top. ■

SERVES 8 Ⓝ
250G CASTER SUGAR
4 TEASPOONS INSTANT ESPRESSO POWDER (*NOT* INSTANT COFFEE GRANULES)
4 EGG WHITES
PINCH SALT
2 TEASPOONS CORNFLOUR
1 TEASPOON WHITE WINE VINEGAR
300ML DOUBLE CREAM
1 TEASPOON GOOD-QUALITY COCOA POWDER

ITALIAN CHRISTMAS PUDDING CAKE

THIS RECIPE IS MY OWN BUT at the same time a conflation of a couple of Italian Christmas must-haves: the glorious, fruit-studded panettone and *crema di mascarpone*, which is best described as tiramisu without the Savoiardi biscuit layer, and sometimes with pieces of chocolate stirred through the mascarpone mixture. I have brought in a cassata element, which means I add, along with the chocolate, some crumbled *marrons glacés* (though any candied or dried fruits could do) and chopped pistachios. The pomegranate seeds I tumble over the top at the end are there for their beauty as well as to add a further seasonal touch but, importantly, are (according to my Italian publisher) thought to bring luck and should therefore be an indispensable part of the Christmas table.

With all the liqueur, chocolate, mascarpone and other sweetmeats involved here, you'd think it would be unbearably rich: instead, it is curiously elegant. If sophisticated weren't such an unsophisticated term, I'd be tempted to use it to describe this glorious creation.

I've called it Italian Christmas Pudding Cake because, while it does possess very much the elements of an Italian Christmas and is presented in cake form, for me it also invokes the liqueur-laden fruitiness – in lighter guise – of our own traditional Christmas pudding.

I use Tuaca to soak the panettone slices, as this Italian vanilla liqueur with its citrus essences and brandied undertones has always seemed to me to be panettone in alcohol form (and I also tend to put a splosh of it in Prosecco to create an aromatic and festive cup of seasonal cheer), but really you can use rum, brandy or Grand Marnier in its place. Indeed, if you don't want to splash out on more than one bottle for this pudding, simply use the Marsala that's in the mascarpone mixture.

Naturally, you can substitute pandoro for the panettone if you want to do away with the dried-fruit element, and you can also dispense with the *marrons glacés* – the beautiful ones overleaf are from the venerable Giovanni Galli in Milan – not by replacing them with other candied fruits, but by upping the quantities of chocolate and nuts instead. Talking of which, I found some adorable mini chocolate chips in America (and have sourced them near home) and they are my chocolate of choice here, but regular chocolate chips, or finely chopped chocolate – dark, milk or white – can be used without anxiety. Still on the chocolate theme: although this magnificent pudding cake needs absolutely no accompaniment, if you have an excess of chocolates that people have given you at Christmas you can chop them up (crumble them into the cream if they're chocolate liqueurs) and use them in place of the chopped chocolate in the sauce on **p.169**; it must be at room temperature when serving.

I've written at length about the cake, and there may seem to be many steps to the recipe overleaf. This conceals the fact that it is ludicrously, dazzlingly easy to make: it doesn't require cooking or technical brilliance; it is merely an assembly job. Not that you need to be advertising this fact to appreciative eaters.

One thing I must be strict about, is that the eggs, mascarpone and cream be at room temperature. (And, as the eggs are not cooked, see Note to the Reader on **p.xiii**.)

Using a serrated knife, cut the panettone roughly into 1cm slices, then use about a third of these to line the bottom of the springform tin. Tear off pieces to fit so that there are no gaps; panettone is fabulously soft and mouldable, so this isn't a hard job. Drizzle 2 tablespoons of the Tuaca (or other liqueur of choice) over it so that the panettone lining is dampened. It looks like a beautiful golden patchwork made out of cake.

Now get on with the luscious filling. Whisk - using a freestanding electric mixer for ease - the eggs and sugar until very frothy and increased in volume and lightness.

More slowly, whisk in the mascarpone and double cream, then gradually whisk in the Marsala and carry on whisking until the mixture is thick and spreadable. Remove 250ml (a good cupful) to a bowl or other container, cover and put in the fridge; this is for the top layer, which is not added until you serve the cake.

Crumble the *marrons glacés* into the big bowl of mascarpone cream mixture, followed by 100g of the chocolate chips and 75g of the chopped pistachios, and fold in. Use half of this creamy filling to top the panettone layer that is lining the cake tin.

Use another third (approx.) of the panettone slices to cover the cream filling, again leaving no holes for the cream to escape through. Dampen with another 2 tablespoons of liqueur.

Spoon on the other half of the cream mixture and spread it evenly. Then top with a third and final layer of panettone, covering the cream as before, and drizzle over it the last 2 tablespoons of liqueur.

Cover tightly with clingfilm, pressing down on the top a little, and put in the fridge overnight or for up to 2 days.

When you are ready to serve, take the cake out of the fridge, unmould and sit it on a flat plate or cake stand, then spread with the reserved mascarpone mixture. Don't try to lift the cake off the base, as the panettone slices at the bottom are too delectably damp.

Scatter the top - and all around the cake, if wished - with the remaining chocolate chips and chopped pistachios and your pomegranate "jewels". These sprinklings also provide beauteous camouflage for any less than aesthetically uplifting edges of the springform base which may be visible. ∎

CUTS INTO 12–14 SLICES Ⓝ

APPROX. 625G PANETTONE (OR PANDORO)

6 X 15ML TABLESPOONS TUACA LIQUEUR (SEE INTRO FOR OTHER OPTIONS)

2 EGGS, AT ROOM TEMPERATURE

75G CASTER SUGAR

500G MASCARPONE, AT ROOM TEMPERATURE

250ML DOUBLE CREAM, AT ROOM TEMPERATURE

125ML MARSALA

75G PIECES MARRONS GLACÉS

125G MINI (OR REGULAR) CHOCOLATE CHIPS, OR FINELY CHOPPED CHOCOLATE

100G PISTACHIO NUTS, CHOPPED

2 X 15ML TABLESPOONS POMEGRANATE SEEDS

1 X 22 OR 23CM SPRINGFORM CAKE TIN

I ADORE ALL CHRISTMAS AND WINTRY FOODS but my chief joy is the chestnut. In my view, there is no bad way to eat chestnuts, ever: my greatest – and exquisitely extravagant treat – is a *marron glacé*, as dispersed prodigally and festively within the mascarpone cream that is layered with panettone in the Italian Christmas Pudding Cake on **p.250**; but I adore them just as much when, unglacéd, they add their waxen sweetness to savoury pasta or stuffing (see **pp.212** and **203**). Nothing, though, gives me quite the same frisson of intense, sugary delight as a can or jar of sweetened chestnut purée. I know I've told you about my Ma's Quickly-Scaled Mont Blancs before, but I need to tell you how to make them again here. Get out 6 smallish glasses, with a capacity of about 125ml each, and into them drop a layer of chopped dark chocolate (you'll need a 100g bar altogether); on top of the rubbly shards of chocolate, dollop some sweetened chestnut purée from a can (a 500g can is more than generous); then whip 500ml double cream until thick but still soft, fold in one crumbled meringue nest (about 10cm in diameter) from a packet and spoon this on top of the chocolate and chestnut layers; finally, crumble another meringue in a snowy layer on top.

Frankly, I wouldn't complain about having to eat the sweet grainy purée from a spoon straight out of the can, but this ice cream is perhaps a more elegant showcase for it. If you have any *marrons glacés* (and this is a particularly good use for broken pieces) you could crumble some as you serve; otherwise make the chocolate sauce from **p.169**, using rum as your liqueur of choice. I couldn't resist the chocolate spoon, pictured, though it's better to eat than to eat with.

NO-CHURN CHESTNUT ICE CREAM

MAKES ENOUGH FOR 2 X 500ML TUBS, *FILLED JUST UNDER CAPACITY* Ⓝ

250G SWEETENED CHESTNUT PURÉE, FROM A CAN OR JAR

2 X 15ML TABLESPOONS DARK RUM

300ML DOUBLE CREAM

50G ICING SUGAR

2 X 500ML AIRTIGHT TUBS OR CONTAINERS

Mix the chestnut purée and rum together until gloopily smooth.

Whip the cream with the icing sugar until it forms soft peaks, then fold into the chestnut mixture, or pour the chestnut mixture into the cream and fold to combine. Either way works.

Spoon into an airtight tub or container, cover and freeze for 12 hours or overnight. Serve straight from the freezer. ∎

STRUFFOLI

IF YOU'VE NEVER ENCOUNTERED *STRUFFOLI* BEFORE, they are best described – visually at any rate – as the *croquembouche* of southern Italy: small dough balls, and I mean really small, the size of marbles, that are deep-fried and then rolled in honey before being assembled into a cone – as in the French piled-up profiteroles model – or a bulging wreath. Since I was taught the recipe by a pair of Calabrian sisters, I make mine as their *mamma* makes hers; and this takes the wreath form.

I'll be honest: you don't make these because you're seeking some exquisite taste sensation; *struffoli* are about custom, celebration and sweetness. This, in effect, is *the* festive centrepiece of Christmas in the south of Italy.

You get a very real sense of this if you make the *struffoli* not alone, but in company, with other hands to roll out the dough with you. Children love doing this, by the way, and their little hands are much better suited for rolling the small marble-sized dough balls you need. Obviously, children are best kept away from the deep-frying part of the operation.

As for the decoration, I've seen not only the regular cake-decorating sprinkles used but also candied fruit, glacé cherries, almond *dragées* and cinnamony-preserved pumpkin pieces. It's the former, solely, for me. And although I've seen only the multicoloured ones in Italy, I go for the festive and flag-resonant Christmas sprinkles in red, white and green. The *struffoli* would look more beautiful, perhaps, left burnished but otherwise unadorned, although gaudiness not elegant restraint – I'm firmly told – is in order here; I have tried to maintain some balance between the two.

Get out a large, rimmed baking tray and shake the semolina over the base. And get out another tray (it doesn't have to be a baking one) and line it with a double layer of kitchen roll. Set both aside while you get on with the dough.

Beat the eggs, sugar, finely grated lemon zest and 2 tablespoons of olive oil until frothy.

Gradually add about 400g of the flour and the baking powder, and mix to a dough. If it is too sticky, then add more flour and keep kneading, using either your hands or a freestanding mixer fitted with a dough hook, until you have a smooth, pliable dough. This doesn't take very long: probably around 3 minutes or 5 by hand.

Flour your work surface and turn out your dough. Then divide the dough into 10 roughly equal pieces, each about the size of a golf ball. Take 1 ball and roll it into a rope approx. 1.5cm thick, then with floury hands divide this into about 20 small pieces, and roll each piece between your hands (flouring them again if this helps) to make marble-sized balls. Place the formed balls of dough on the semolina-sprinkled baking tray, as you shape them. Repeat the process with the remaining golf-ball-sized portions of dough: you should make a staggering 200 of the tiny balls!

Heat the vegetable oil in a wide, heavy-based pan – about 28cm diameter and at least 11cm deep – and then when the oil is at 190°C but no higher (you can leave a preserving or sugar thermometer in, if you want), or a piece of bread sizzles and browns immediately when dropped in the pan, you can begin to cook the dough balls. Regulate the temperature and keep a careful eye on the pan and the oil all the time.

Gently lower in, using a mesh scoop or perforated spoon, about 15 little dough balls at a time. At first they will sink and then, as they cook, they'll float to the surface and begin to turn golden brown. This will take up to about 1 minute depending on how many you have in at a time, but be ready to fish them out with your mesh scoop or perforated spoon onto the kitchen-paper-lined tray as soon as they become the right golden colour. And keep watching your pan.

Continue to cook them in batches – making sure the oil returns to the correct temperature but doesn't get too hot or bubble too vigorously – until they are all fried; you can pile them up on the tray without harm. Now turn off the heat under the oil pan, and move on to the adhesive and assembly stage.

Pour the honey into a roasting tin that can go on the hob, and heat very gently until it becomes runny – a matter of moments, so do not leave the tin – then take it off the heat.

Tip all of the fried dough balls into the warmed honey and, using a soft spatula, turn them gently to coat them. Get out a large plate or cake stand with a slight lip or rim and, with wet hands, check the balls are not too hot then pick up the sticky balls and arrange them around the outer edge of the plate in the shape of a bobbly wreath, leaving just a small empty circle in the middle. Do not worry about symmetry or perfection or counting dough balls here, please.

Wash the honey from your hands and shake your chosen sprinkles over the sticky wreath, then stand back and admire, before placing your creation where others can do likewise. These struffoli are best, to my mind, eaten on the day they're made. Use a scoop or spoon and fork to serve. It will be a sticky affair, but that's part of their charm. ∎

SERVES 10 OR UP TO 16;
ESSENTIALLY A CHRISTMAS CENTREPIECE

2 X 15ML TABLESPOONS SEMOLINA

6 EGGS

1 X 15ML TABLESPOON SUGAR

ZEST 1 UNWAXED LEMON, FINELY GRATED

2 X 15ML TABLESPOONS OLIVE OIL

450–500G FLOUR, PLUS MORE FOR ROLLING

½ TEASPOON BAKING POWDER

2½–3 LITRES FLAVOURLESS VEGETABLE OIL, FOR FRYING

450G HONEY

APPROX. 2 TEASPOONS CHRISTMAS SPRINKLES, TO DECORATE

...TO START THE NEW YEAR

EGGS IN PURGATORY

...OR WHAT TO EAT WHEN YOU'RE FEELING LIKE HELL.

I'm not saying that New Year's Day has to mean you have a hangover, but after that evening of almost-enforced carousing, this dish of eggs cooked in a fiery tomato sauce can feel like heaven.

I feel I should address this recipe's name, but I have nothing conclusive to offer you. The heat of the chilli and the red of the tomato might more plausibly have led this to be called *uova in inferno* rather than *in Purgatorio*. Purgatory is the place where those who die in a state of grace but are not ready for ascension into Heaven must wait, in a long-suffering limbo. This, I do appreciate, is a simplistic categorization, but please: I'm writing an introduction to an egg recipe, here, not a work of doctrinal history. Besides, not being Catholic, all I know about Purgatory I learned from reading Dante. So I particularly liked the hopeful literary attribution which suggests that said dish of golden egg yolks rising out of Parmesan-hazy tomatoes might be a reference to Dante's having reached Purgatory at dawn, and later hailing the advancing sun as the "cheeks of beautiful Aurora...changing into orange". Yes, I know, I wouldn't push it too far either, but you can't blame a person for trying.

Let's put questions of attribution and whimsical theories aside, for we have the pure and pleasurable physicality of the dish to consider. Now, normally I have an almost hysterically inflexible no-red-with-egg rule: I can't bear to see so much as a blob of ketchup or grilled tomato near (let alone mixed with) an egg on someone's plate. But these heavenly Eggs in Purgatory utterly challenge and overturn my previously rigid prejudice.

To the cooking itself: if I use my little cast-iron skillet, only 16cm diameter, there is really only room for 1 egg; but generally, a small frying pan tends to come in at about 20cm diameter, in which case you can easily fit 2 eggs in. Or you could always do 1 egg and drop the yolk of the second egg on the white of the first... Either way, this is so easy and speedy to make, I can find time to rustle it up for breakfast, brunch, lunch, supper or late-night snack, whatever state I'm in.

If solo salvation turns into brunch for a roomful of people, obviously use a bigger pan and I would think 2 cans of tomatoes could provide enough liquid – if there's room in the pan – for up to 8 eggs (but do see Note to the Reader on **p.xiii** about eggs).

Pour the olive oil into a frying pan, then grate in (or mince and add) the garlic, scatter in the chilli flakes and put the pan over a medium heat, stirring, for 1 minute.

Tip in the tomatoes, stir in the salt, and let it come to a bubble. It's got to be hot enough to poach an egg in.

Crack in the egg (or eggs), sprinkle the Parmesan over it, leaving some of the yellow yolk still exposed, and partially cover with a lid. Let it bubble for 5 minutes, by which time the white should be set and the yolk still runny, but keep an eye on it.

Remove from the heat and serve – if so wished – sprinkled with a little more Parmesan and some chilli oil, and some bread to dunk in. ■

SERVES 1

1 X 15ML TABLESPOON OLIVE OIL
1 SMALL CLOVE GARLIC, PEELED
¼ TEASPOON DRIED CHILLI
   FLAKES
1 X 400G CAN CHOPPED
   TOMATOES
½ TEASPOON SEA SALT FLAKES
   OR ¼ TEASPOON POURING
   SALT, OR TO TASTE
1–2 EGGS
2–3 TEASPOONS GRATED
   PARMESAN

TO SERVE:
GRATED PARMESAN (OPTIONAL)
CHILLI OIL (OPTIONAL)
BREAD (MANDATORY)

THIS IS EITHER A LENTIL SOUP WITH PASTA, or a dish of pasta with lentils, depending on where you are in Italy. And when I say that, I don't mean so much where you are geographically: this differs from house to house, family to family, day to day. My version is on the soupy side, or at least it is on its first outing; any leftover soup will thicken on cooling.

This recipe does double-duty for the New Year: on the one hand, it is carbohydrate-dense and well-suited to sopping up seasonal excess; on the other, lentils are customarily eaten on New Year's Day in Italy as their coin-like shape is thought to bring prosperity for the year ahead. Since I have given a recipe for a New Year's Day lunch of lentils and sausage before, this recipe simply begged to be included here in its stead.

PASTA & LENTILS

Put the onion, bacon or pancetta, parsley and garlic into the bowl of a food processor and chop finely.

Heat the oil in a casserole that has a lid (I use an enamelled cast-iron one measuring 26cm in diameter and 10cm deep). Add the contents of the processor and stir to cook over a medium heat for 5–7 minutes, or until softened.

Stir in the lentils and then the tomatoes, then fill the emptied tomato can with cold water and add this, too. Throw in the bay leaves.

Stir again and pour in the stock and bring to the boil, then turn down the heat, cover and let the lentils simmer, with the lid on, for 30 minutes, by which time they should be soft.

Remove the lid, turn up the heat so that you've got a bubble, then add the pasta and cook it in the casserole, with the lid off, for 10 minutes, until the pasta is al dente. Season to taste, then put the lid on, turn off the heat and leave to stand for 10 minutes.

Serve with chilli oil, or some extra-virgin olive oil, for people to drizzle over each bowl as they eat. ∎

SERVES 8–10 Ⓝ

1 ONION, PEELED AND
    QUARTERED
150G RINDLESS STREAKY BACON
    OR PANCETTA
SMALL HANDFUL FRESH PARSLEY
1 CLOVE GARLIC, PEELED
2 X 15ML TABLESPOONS
    OLIVE OIL
500G LENTILS, BROWN OR
    GREEN, RINSED
1 X 400G CAN CHOPPED
    TOMATOES, PLUS 400ML COLD
    WATER TO RINSE OUT
2 BAY LEAVES
2.5 LITRES CHICKEN OR
    VEGETABLE STOCK
250G PASTA *MISTA* (MIXED), OR
    ANY BROKEN OR SMALL PASTA
    SHAPES
SALT AND PEPPER, TO TASTE
CHILLI OIL, OR EXTRA-VIRGIN
    OLIVE OIL, TO SERVE

NOTES

Make ahead dishes and leftovers (except cakes) should be cooled and refrigerated as quickly as possible, and always within 2 hours of making. Foods should be stored in the fridge in airtight containers, or tightly covered or wrapped with clingfilm, as appropriate.

PASTA

SICILIAN PASTA WITH TOMATOES, GARLIC & ALMONDS

Refrigerate leftovers as soon as possible. Will keep in the fridge for up to 3 days.

MINI MACARONI CHEESE ALL'ITALIANA

You can also cook all of the pasta in a larger dish (approx. 24 x 17 x 6cm/1.25L). Bake for 20–25 minutes in an oven preheated to 200°C/gas mark 6, until golden brown on top and bubbling around the edges.

TORTELLONI MINESTRONE

Refrigerate leftovers as soon as possible. Will keep in the fridge for up to 3 days. Reheat gently in a saucepan until piping hot.

SQUID SPAGHETTI

Tomato sauce can be made ahead up to the end of step 4. Cool and refrigerate, or freeze, as quickly as possible. Will keep for 3 days in the fridge or 3 months in the freezer (defrost overnight in the fridge before using). Reheat gently until just boiling then add squid and continue as directed in the recipe.

CHILLI CRAB RISOTTO

It is not advisable to reheat leftovers of crabmeat or rice.

FARRO RISOTTO WITH MUSHROOMS

Can be made ahead up to the end of step 7. Cool and refrigerate as quickly as possible. Will keep in the fridge for up to 2 days. Return to the pan, cover and reheat gently until piping hot, stirring occasionally and adding a splash of extra water or stock if needed. Continue as directed in the recipe. Leftovers should be refrigerated as quickly as possible, will keep in the fridge for up to 3 days and are best eaten as a salad. It is not advisable to keep leftovers from reheated farro risotto.

FLESH, FISH & FOWL

BUTTERFLIED LEG OF LAMB WITH BAY LEAVES & BALSAMIC VINEGAR

Refrigerate or freeze leftovers as quickly as possible, wrapped tightly in foil. Will keep for 2 days in the fridge or 2 months in the freezer (defrost overnight in the fridge before using).

ITALIAN TRAYBAKE

This is an easy recipe to scale up for a large crowd, if you have enough baking trays and oven space – just make sure you swap the trays and turn them around in the oven at half-time.

VEGETABLES & SIDES

CHERRY TOMATOES WITH OLIVES

Can be made ahead up to the end of step 3. Cool and refrigerate as quickly as possible. Will keep in fridge for up to 2 days. Return to pan and reheat gently until piping hot, then continue as directed in the recipe. Leftovers should be refrigerated as quickly as possible, will keep in the fridge for up to 2 days and are best eaten as a pasta sauce. It is not advisable to keep leftovers from reheated tomatoes.

PEAS WITH PANCETTA

Can be made ahead up to the end of step 4. Cool and refrigerate as quickly as possible. Will keep in fridge for up to 2 days. Return to pan and reheat gently until piping hot, then continue as directed in the recipe. Leftovers should be refrigerated as quickly as possible and will keep in the fridge for up to 2 days. It is not advisable to keep leftovers of reheated peas.

BRAISED BROAD BEANS, PEAS & ARTICHOKES WITH THYME & MINT

Can be made ahead up to the end of step 3. Cool and refrigerate as quickly as possible. Will keep in fridge for up to 2 days. Return to pan and reheat gently until piping hot adding a splash of extra water if needed, then continue as directed in the recipe. Leftovers should be refrigerated as quickly as possible and will keep in the fridge for up to 2 days. It is not advisable to keep leftovers of reheated beans.

ROAST RED ONIONS WITH BASIL

Can be made ahead up to the end of step 3. Cool and refrigerate as quickly as possible. Will keep in fridge for up to 2 days. Remove the onions from the fridge about 1 hour before serving, to allow to come to room temperature, then continue as directed in the recipe.

SAVOY CABBAGE WITH POTATOES, FENNEL SEEDS & TALEGGIO

Leftovers should be refrigerated as quickly as possible and stored in a non-metallic container. Will keep in the fridge for up to 2 days.

SICILIAN CAULIFLOWER SALAD

Can be made ahead up to the end of step 6. Cool and refrigerate as quickly as possible. Will keep in fridge for up to 3 days. Remove the cauliflower from the fridge about 1 hour before serving to allow to come to room temperature, or leave chilled, and continue as directed in the recipe. Leftovers should be refrigerated as quickly as possible and will keep in the fridge for up to 3 days from day of making.

CANNELLINI BEANS WITH ROSEMARY

Leftovers should be refrigerated as quickly as possible and will keep in the fridge for up to 2 days. Eat at room temperature or

return to the pan and reheat gently until piping hot.

ITALIAN GOLDEN LENTILS

Can be made ahead, omitting chopped herbs. Cool and refrigerate as quickly as possible. Will keep in fridge for up to 2 days. Return to pan and reheat gently until piping hot then add herbs; or remove from fridge about 1 hour before serving, to allow to come to room temperature, and add herbs. Leftovers should be refrigerated as quickly as possible and will keep in the fridge for up to 2 days and are best eaten cold. It is not advisable to keep leftovers of reheated lentils.

MASCARPONE MASH

Leftovers should be refrigerated as quickly as possible and will keep in the fridge for up to 2 days. Reheat gently in a small saucepan until piping hot, adding a splash of extra milk if needed. Can also be reheated in a microwave, following the manufacturer's instructions.

SAFFRON ORZOTTO

Can be made ahead omitting Parmesan. Cool and refrigerate as quickly as possible. Will keep in the fridge for up to 2 days. Return to the pan, cover and reheat gently until piping hot, stirring occasionally and adding extra water or stock as needed to loosen the orzotto. Add Parmesan and continue as directed in the recipe.

MOCK MASH

Leftovers should be refrigerated as quickly as possible and will keep in the fridge for up to 2 days. To reheat transfer to an ovenproof dish, dot with butter, grate some Parmesan on top and cook in an oven preheated to 200°C/gas mark 6 oven for 20–30 minutes, until piping hot in the centre and golden brown on top.

SWEET THINGS

INSTANT CHOCOLATE-ORANGE MOUSSE

Can be made ahead up to the end of step 4. Cover and refrigerate. Will keep for up to 2 days in fridge. Remove from fridge about 30 minutes before serving to take some of the chill off. Continue as directed in the recipe.

LIQUORICE PUDDING

Can be made ahead to the end of step 5. Will keep for up to 3 days in fridge. Serve as directed in the recipe.

PANNA COTTA THREE-WAYS

Can be made ahead. Will keep for up to 3 days in the fridge. Serve as directed in the recipe.

MERINGUE GELATO CAKE WITH CHOCOLATE SAUCE

Cake can be made ahead. Best if eaten within 1 week but can be kept for up to 1 month in the freezer. Sauce can be made ahead. Cool and refrigerate as quickly as possible. Will keep in fridge for up to 3 days. Remove the sauce from the fridge 1 hour before serving to allow it to come back to room temperature; if necessary rewarm as directed in the recipe.

ONE-STEP NO-CHURN COFFEE ICE CREAM

Can be made ahead. Best if eaten within 1 week but can be kept up to 1 month in the freezer.

DOUBLE AMARETTO SEMIFREDDO WITH GOLDEN-GLEAMING SAUCE

Semifreddo can be made ahead. Best if eaten within 1 week but can be kept up to

1 month in the freezer. Sauce can be made ahead. Cool and refrigerate as quickly as possible. Will keep in fridge up to 1 week. Remove sauce from fridge about 1 hour before serving to allow it to come back to room temperature.

CHOCOLATE HAZELNUT CHEESECAKE

Can be made ahead. Will keep for up to 4 days in fridge. Leftovers should be kept refrigerated and eaten within 4 days of making.

ITALIAN APPLE PIE

Can be made ahead. Cool and freeze on day of making, wrapped tightly in a double layer of clingfilm and a layer of foil. Unwrap and defrost at room temperature for 4 hours. Best on day of making or as soon as defrosted. Leftovers will keep for up to 1 day in the fridge, tightly wrapped in clingfilm.

RUBY-RED PLUM & AMARETTI CRUMBLE

Crumble topping can be made ahead. Store in the fridge for up to 3 days or freeze in a plastic bag and use directly from frozen. Leftovers should be refrigerated as quickly as possible and will keep in the fridge for up to 2 days.

YOGURT POT CAKE

Can be made ahead. Store in an airtight container in a cool place for 2–3 days or freeze for up to 3 months, wrapped in a double layer of clingfilm, followed by a layer of foil. Unwrap and defrost at room temperature for about 2 hours.

CHOCOLATE OLIVE OIL CAKE

Can be made ahead. Store in an airtight container in a cool place for 2–3 days or freeze for up to 3 months, wrapped in a double layer of clingfilm, followed by a layer of foil. Unwrap and defrost at room temperature for about 3 hours.

ITALIAN BREAKFAST BANANA BREAD

Can be made ahead. Store in an airtight container in a cool place for up to 5 days or freeze for up to 3 months, wrapped in a double layer of clingfilm, followed by a layer of foil. Unwrap and defrost at room temperature for about 4 hours. If the bread is to be toasted it is best to store it in the fridge.

ANISEED SHORTBREAD

Baked shortbread will keep in an airtight container for up to 5 days.

AN ITALIAN-INSPIRED CHRISTMAS

GORGONZOLA & CANNELLINI DIP WITH A TRICOLORE FLOURISH

Can be made ahead to end of step 3. Refrigerate for up to 1 day and serve as directed in the recipe.

PANETTONE STUFFING SQUARES

Can be made ahead to end of step 3. Cool and refrigerate as quickly as possible, or freeze. Will keep for up to 2 days in the fridge or 3 months in the freezer (defrost overnight in the fridge before using). Continue as directed in the recipe. Leftovers should be refrigerated as quickly as possible and will keep in the fridge for up to 2 days.

PARMESAN SHORTBREADS

Can be made ahead to end of step 3 and kept in the fridge for up to 3 days or frozen, wrapped in a double layer of clingfilm and a layer of foil, for up to 3 months (defrost overnight in the fridge). Bake as directed in the recipe. Sliced dough can also be frozen on parchment-lined baking sheets until solid, then transferred to plastic bags and kept in the freezer for up to 3 months. Bake from frozen as directed in the recipe. Baked shortbreads will keep in an airtight container for up to 5 days.

POLENTA TRIANGLES

Can be made ahead. Cool and refrigerate triangles as quickly as possible, or freeze on parchment-lined baking sheets until solid, then transfer to plastic bags and keep in the freezer for up to 3 months and bake from frozen. Chilled and frozen triangles should be baked as directed in the recipe, but add an extra 5–10 minutes to the baking time.

CHILLI TOMATO SAUCE

Can be made ahead. Cool and refrigerate, or freeze, as quickly as possible. Will keep for 3 days in the fridge or 3 months in the freezer (defrost overnight in the fridge before using). If serving warm, return to saucepan and reheat gently until piping hot then cool slightly before serving.

TURKEY BREAST STUFFED WITH ITALIAN SAUSAGE & MARSALA-STEEPED CRANBERRIES

Can be made ahead to end of step 4. Cool and refrigerate as quickly as possible. Will keep in fridge for up to 2 days. Continue as directed in the recipe.

Cooked breast should be cooled and

refrigerated, or frozen, as quickly as possible, wrapped in a double layer of clingfilm and a layer of foil (defrost overnight in the fridge and make sure it is thoroughly defrosted before serving). Cooked breast will keep in fridge for up to 2 days and in freezer for up to 3 months.

FIG & OLIVE CHUTNEY

The chutney will keep for up to 1 month in the fridge, or for up to 3 months if prepared as described in the recipe's introduction. For the longer-life version I consider a jar straight from a dishwasher (as long as I don't touch the inside) to be a sterilized jar, but those with higher standards should wash their jars in warm, soapy water before rinsing and letting them dry in a cool (140°C/gas mark 1) oven for 10 minutes. After opening, the chutney keeps for up to 1 month in the fridge.

SPAGHETTI SPICE

The spice mix will keep for up to 1 year if stored in a cool, dry place.

CRANBERRY & PISTACHIO BISCOTTI

The biscotti will keep for up to 1 month in an airtight container. If baking 2 batches on different shelves of the oven at the same time, switch the baking trays about halfway through each of the cooking times; they may take a minute or two longer to bake.

CHOCOLATE NOUGAT COOKIES

Can be made ahead to the end of step 5 and stored in the fridge for 24 hours. Bake as directed in the recipe. Unbaked cookies can also be frozen on parchment-lined baking sheets until solid, then transferred to plastic bags and kept in the freezer for up to 3 months. Bake from frozen as directed in the recipe, adding an extra 1–2 minutes to the cooking time. Baked cookies will keep for up to 5 days in an airtight container in a cool place.

CHOCOLATE SALAME

Can be made ahead, wrapped in the clingfilm, then tied with string just before serving. Store in fridge and eat within 4 days of making. Can also be frozen on day of making, wrapped in a double layer of clingfilm and a layer of foil, for up to 1 month (defrost overnight in the fridge, remove foil and tie with string before serving. Eat within 2 days).

CINNAMON ALMOND CAKE

Can be made ahead. Store in an airtight container in a cool place for 2–3 days or freeze for up to 3 months, wrapped in a double layer of clingfilm, followed by a layer of foil. Unwrap and defrost at room temperature for about 3 hours.

CAPPUCCINO PAVLOVA

The Pavlova base can be made ahead to end of step 7. Keep in an airtight container for up to 2 days and serve as directed in the recipe. Leftovers should be kept refrigerated and eaten within 2 days.

ITALIAN CHRISTMAS PUDDING CAKE

Can be made ahead to the end of step 7. Will keep in fridge for 2 days. Serve as directed in recipe. The cake can also be frozen for up to 3 months. Spread the reserved layer of mascarpone cream on top of the cake and chill for 6 hours. Unmould the cake, leaving it on its base, and open-freeze until solid. Wrap in a double layer of clingfilm and a layer of foil then return it to the freezer. Unwrap and defrost on a serving dish overnight in the fridge, sprinkling with chocolate chips, pistachios and pomegranate seeds before serving. Leftovers should be kept refrigerated and eaten within 4 days of making, or within 2 days of defrosting if frozen.

NO-CHURN CHESTNUT ICE CREAM

Can be made ahead. Best if eaten within 1 week but can be kept up to 1 month in the freezer.

PASTA & LENTILS

Refrigerate leftovers as soon as possible. Will keep in the fridge for up to 3 days. Reheat gently in a saucepan, adding a little extra stock or water if liked, until piping hot.

INDEX